ADA CARTIANU

THE ETHICS OF ME

ETHICAL PRINCIPLES AND THE INDIVIDUALIST IDEAL

AN INVITATION TO A LIFELONG JOURNEY OF ETHICAL GROWTH AND DEVELOPMENT

THE ETHICS OF ME
ETHICAL PRINCIPLES AND THE INDIVIDUALIST IDEAL
AN INVITATION TO A LIFELONG JOURNEY OF ETHICAL GROWTH AND DEVELOPMENT

TABLE OF CONTENTS

13 Navigating Individualism in a Collective World
- THE FOUNDATIONS OF INDIVIDUALISM
  Defining Individualism
- Historical Perspectives on Individualism
- Ancient Foundations: Individualism in Early Civilizations
- The Renaissance: A Rebirth of Individual Thought
- Enlightenment Ideals: The Birth of Modern Individualism
- Romanticism: Individualism's Emotional Depth
- The 20th Century: Individualism in Crisis and Conformity
- The Contemporary Era: Individualism in a Globalized World
- Individualism in Eastern vs. Western Thought

37 Exploring Buddhism and Western Philosophy
- Core Principles of Buddhism
- Key Western Philosophers on Individualism
- Points of Convergence and Divergence
- The Role of Online Communities *in* Shaping Identity
- Challenges of Authenticity in Digital Spaces

53 The Guiding Lights Within:
- A Philosophical Exploration of Ethical Principles
- Ethical Principles and the Individualist Ideal

58 Stoicism and Its Relevance in Modern Life
- Principles of Stoicism
- Stoicism in the Face of Modern Challenges
- Integrating Stoic Practices into Daily Life

63 The Influence of Eastern Philosophies on Western Motivational Practices
- Overview of Eastern Philosophies

- Adoption of Eastern Concepts *in* Western Motivational Strategies

68 Ethics of Individualism in Contemporary Society
- Moral Implications of Individualistic Practices
  - Personal Responsibility
  - Community Engagement
  - Societal Cohesion
- Understanding Individualism

71 The Path Forward:
- A Balanced Ethical Individualism
- Balancing Personal Freedom *with* Social Responsibility
- Individual Rights vs. Collective Good
  Navigating Individualism in a Complex World

77 The Balance Between Community and Individuality in Modern Life
- The Role of Community in Shaping Identity
- Tensions Between Individual Desires and Community Needs
- FINDING HARMONY: Practical Strategies

81 Integrating Buddhist Principles into Everyday Decision-Making
- Mindfulness as a Decision-Making Tool
- Compassion and Ethical Considerations
- Practical Exercises for Everyday Living

86 Reflections on Personal Growth *and* Collective Well-Being
THE JOURNEY OF SELF-DISCOVERY
Navigating Individualism in a Complex World

89 A Call To Ethical Action:
Weaving Wisdom for a Harmonious Future

92 Unleash Your Potential
A Journey to Personal Growth and Confidence
THE AWAKENING OF POTENTIAL: *The Call to Change*

98   Personal Ethics and Morality:
       Navigating the Compass of One's Conscience

103   The Role of Philosophical Frameworks
- KANT'S DEONTOLOGICAL ETHICS:
     Duty Over Consequence
- MILL'S UTILITARIANISM:
     The Consequence of Actions and the Pursuit of Collective Happiness
- Balancing Personal Desires *and* Ethical Implications
- The Ethical Landscape of Choice
- Navigating Self, Duty, and Consequence
- The Journey Towards Ethical Maturity
- Embracing the Journey Ahead

116   The Power of Positive Affirmations
- Crafting Your Affirmations
- Integrating Affirmations into Daily Life
- Overcoming Doubts with Positive Self-Talk

120   Visualization: Creating Your Future
- The Science Behind Visualization
- Techniques for Effective Visualization
- Manifesting Your Dreams through Imagery

125   Cultivating a Growth Mindset
- The Difference Between Fixed *and* Growth Mindsets
- Strategies to Shift Your Mindset
- Embracing Challenges as Opportunities

131   Building Confidence from Within
- Identifying Your Strengths and Weaknesses
- Setting Achievable Goals
- Celebrating Small Wins

136   Overcoming Fear and Self-Doubt
- Understanding the Roots of Fear
- Techniques for Confronting Your Fears
- Developing Resilience through Adversity

143   The Journey Toward Personal Growth
- Defining Personal Growth
- Overcoming Obstacles to Growth:
- A Journey Towards Joy and Fulfillment
- Lifelong Learning and Happiness

151   The Role of Gratitude in Personal Growth
- The Benefits of a Gratitude Practice
- Creating a Daily Gratitude Ritual
- Shifting Perspectives *through* Thankfulness

146   Building Supportive Relationships
- The Importance of Community
- Identifying Toxic Relationships
- A Pathway to Personal Empowerment
- Cultivating Positive Connections:
- The Foundation of Growth and Confidence

162   Taking Action: The Key to Transformation
- Setting Intentions and Taking Steps
- The Importance of Consistency
- Measuring Your Progress

166   Sustaining Your Growth Journey
- Developing Lifelong Learning Habits
- Revisiting Your Goals and Aspirations
- Keeping the Momentum Going

172   The Pursuit of Joy: A Philosophical Journey to Happiness
- Defining Joy and Happiness
- A Deeper Exploration of Contentment and Flourishing
- Historical Perspectives on Joy
- Contemporary Understandings
- The Path to Joy:
  An Individual and Collective Responsibility

179   Understanding Happiness
- The Definition of Happiness

- Historical Perspectives on Happiness
- Modern Philosophical Approaches

189   The Role of Emotional Intelligence
- Defining Emotional Intelligence
- Emotional Intelligence and Personal Growth
- Cultivating Emotional Intelligence in Daily Life
- Understanding Emotional Intelligence
- The Importance of Self-Regulation *in* Finding Purpose
- Motivation: The Engine of Purpose
- Empathy: Bridging the Divide
- Social Skills: The Art of Connection
- Overcoming Adversity
- The Ripple Effect of Small Actions

205   The Power of Positive Thinking
- The Science Behind Positive Thinking
- Techniques for Cultivating Positivity
- The Impact of Positivity on Well-being

210   Exploring Existential Questions
- The Search for Meaning
- The Philosophical Perspective
- The Psychological Dimension
- The Spiritual Quest
- The Interplay of Emotional Intelligence *and* Meaning
- The Role of Self-Awareness *in* the Search for Meaning
- The Intersection of Happiness *and* Existentialism
- Understanding Existentialism
- The Quest for Authenticity
- The Role of Meaning
- Embracing Ambiguity and Suffering
- Redefining Happiness
- Embracing Uncertainty in Life

224   The Impact of Gratitude on Life Satisfaction

- Understanding Gratitude
- Practices to Foster Gratitude
- The Long-term Benefits of Gratitude

229 Philosophical Reflections on Love
- The Nature of Love
- The Ontological Dimension of Love
- Love as Ethical Imperative
- The Epistemological Quest of Love
- The Transformative Power of Love
- The Eternal Quest for Love
- Love as a Pathway to Happiness
- The Role of Relationships in Well-being

236 Building Meaningful Relationships
- The Importance of Connection
- Communication and Empathy
- Nurturing Healthy Relationships

242 Integrating Philosophy into Daily Life
- Practical Philosophical Exercises
- The Importance of Philosophy *in* Everyday Life
- PRACTICAL PHILOSOPHICAL EXERCISES
- Living with Intention
- A Journey Toward Purpose

257 The Ethics of Me:
- Navigating Individualism In A Collective World
  A Final Reflection
- Forging a Future of Ethical Individualism

INTRODUCTION

This book will explore the wisdom of both Western and Eastern philosophies, examining their strengths and limitations. From the rigorous logic of ancient Greek philosophy to the profound insights of Eastern spiritual practices, we will delve into diverse perspectives, seeking to synthesize a framework that is both intellectually sound and emotionally resonant. We will wrestle with timeless questions: What defines a virtuous life? What are our obligations to others? And how can we navigate the complexities of moral decision-making in our rapidly evolving world?

However, "The Ethics of Me" is more than just a theoretical exercise. It is a call to action: an appeal for each individual to become the architect of their own ethical framework. It acknowledges that the path to ethical individualism isn't paved with easy answers, but with difficult choices, uncomfortable truths, and a constant need for self-reflection. It recognizes that ethical living is not a destination, but a continuous process of striving, learning, and growth.

"The Ethics of Me" posits that the future we create will be shaped not by grand pronouncements or sweeping ideologies, but by the collective impact of countless individual choices, made in both moments of careful deliberation and spontaneous action. It is a belief in the power of the individual, not as an isolated entity, but as a vital component of the larger human organism. It is a belief that by embracing our unique potential, cultivating our capacity for compassion and reason, and striving to live in alignment with our highest ethical ideals, we can build a world that is more just, more sustainable, and more conducive to the flourishing of all. By striving to live in accordance with our highest ethical ideals, we can collectively build a world that is more just, more sustainable, and more conducive to the flourishing of all. Let us, therefore, embark on this journey together, becoming both the architects of our own ethical selves and the builders of a brighter future, one individual at a time.

But what does this journey truly entail? "The Ethics of Me" doesn't shy away from the practical realities of ethical living. It delves into the nitty-gritty of moral decision-making, offering tools and techniques to navigate the ethical dilemmas that confront us daily. How do we reconcile conflicting values? How do we make decisions when faced with imperfect information? How do we hold ourselves accountable for our actions? These are just some of the questions that will be explored with candor and pragmatism.

The book also recognizes the importance of context. Ethical principles are not abstract ideals to be applied rigidly, regardless of the situation. Rather, they are guides to be interpreted and applied with wisdom and discernment, taking into account the specific circumstances and the potential consequences of our actions. This requires a nuanced understanding of human psychology, social dynamics, and the complexities of the world around us. "The Ethics of Me" encourages us to develop our critical thinking skills, to question our assumptions, and to challenge the status quo. It urges us to be skeptical of simplistic solutions and to embrace the ambiguity that is inherent in ethical decision-making.

Furthermore, this journey of ethical self-discovery is not a solitary endeavor. We are all interconnected, and our actions have ripple effects that extend far beyond ourselves. "The Ethics of Me" emphasizes the importance of community, dialogue, and collaboration. It encourages us to engage in open and honest conversations with others about our values, our beliefs, and our ethical challenges. It recognizes that we can learn from each other's experiences, perspectives, and wisdom. It also highlights the importance of building strong and supportive relationships based on trust, respect, and empathy.

The book also addresses the challenges of living ethically in a world that often seems to reward selfishness, greed, and indifference. It acknowledges that it can be difficult to maintain our ethical compass in the face of societal pressures, economic inequalities, and political polarization. However, it argues that it is precisely during these times that ethical leadership is most needed. "The Ethics of Me" encourages us to be courageous in our convictions, to stand up for what we believe in, and to be a voice for the voiceless. It reminds us that even small acts of kindness, compassion, and justice can make a difference in the world.

Ultimately, "The Ethics of Me" is an invitation to a lifelong journey of ethical growth and development. It is a reminder that we are all capable of becoming more ethical individuals, and that by doing so, we can contribute to a more ethical world. It is a call to action, a plea for each of us to embrace our unique potential, to cultivate our capacity for compassion and reason, and to strive to live in accordance with our highest ethical ideals. It is a belief that by becoming the best versions of ourselves, we can collectively create a future that is more just, more sustainable, and more conducive to the flourishing of all. So let us begin this journey together, one step at a time, one decision at a time, one individual at a time. Let us become the architects of our own ethical selves and the builders of a brighter future, for ourselves, for our communities, and for generations to come.

This is the promise of "The Ethics of Me."

This is the power of ethical individualism.

This is the hope for a better world.

The Ethics of Me

NAVIGATING INDIVIDUALISM IN A COLLECTIVE WORLD

THE FOUNDATIONS OF INDIVIDUALISM

Defining Individualism

Defining individualism involves understanding it as a multifaceted philosophical, cultural, and ethical framework that emphasizes the inherent moral worth of the individual. It posits that individuals possess inalienable rights and responsibilities, championing personal autonomy, self-determination, and self-expression. This perspective stands in stark contrast to collectivist ideologies, which prioritize the interests and needs of the group, often at the expense of individual liberties. Individualism encourages people to pursue their own unique paths, make independent choices based on reason and conscience, and define their identities according to personal beliefs, values, and experiences, rather than blindly adhering to societal expectations or inherited norms. In the complex tapestry of contemporary society, individualism is particularly relevant as individuals navigate intricate social structures, evolving relationships, and the ever-present pressure to conform. It offers a framework for self-discovery, ethical decision-making, and the pursuit of a meaningful life, grounded in personal integrity and self-reliance.

However, the concept of individualism is not monolithic. It manifests differently across cultures and philosophical traditions, requiring a nuanced understanding to fully grasp its implications. In the context of Eastern philosophies, particularly Buddhism, individualism takes on uniquely complex dimensions. Buddhism teaches the crucial importance of self-awareness, introspection, and the profound understanding of one's own mind as a pathway to enlightenment. This focus on inner exploration can undoubtedly foster a strong sense of individual identity and personal agency. Yet, Buddhism simultaneously emphasizes interdependence and the interconnectedness of all beings, highlighting the fundamental truth that no individual exists in complete isolation from others. This inherent duality presents a rich ground for philosophical exploration, as it challenges the Western notion of individualism, often perceived as purely self-centered or egoistic, instead advocating for a balanced approach that recognizes both personal agency and communal responsibility, self-interest and altruism. The Buddhist perspective suggests that true individualism, or rather, a fulfilling individual existence, can only be achieved through understanding and embracing our interconnectedness with the world around us.

The relentless rise of social media platforms further complicates the already intricate discourse on individualism. On one hand, these platforms offer unprecedented opportunities for individuals to express their unique identities, showcase their talents and passions, and connect with like-minded individuals across geographical boundaries, fostering a potent sense of belonging and online community. Individuals can curate personalized profiles, share their thoughts and experiences, and engage in conversations that shape their perspectives and broaden their understanding of the world. On the other hand, the meticulously curated nature of online personas, often driven by the pursuit of validation and social acceptance, can lead to superficial and inauthentic expressions of individuality. The pressure to project a perfect image, to adhere to fleeting trends, and to garner likes and followers, can easily overshadow genuine self-discovery and self-acceptance. This paradox raises critical questions about the authenticity of individualism in an age where identity is often meticulously crafted for public consumption, challenging individuals to cultivate true self-awareness and self-expression amidst the relentless noise of the digital world. The constant exposure to idealized versions of reality can also fuel feelings of inadequacy and undermine self-esteem, hindering the very process of individual self-discovery that individualism aims to promote.

Stoicism, with its enduring emphasis on personal virtue, inner strength, and practical wisdom, offers invaluable insights into the ethics of individualism and provides a powerful antidote to the pitfalls of superficiality and external validation. Stoic philosophy advocates for self-control, rationality, and the unwavering pursuit of a life aligned with one's deeply held values and principles. It emphasizes the importance of focusing on what is within one's control — namely, one's thoughts, attitudes, and actions — and accepting with equanimity what is beyond one's influence. In a modern context, Stoicism provides a framework for individuals to navigate the pervasive pressures of societal expectations, consumerist culture, and social media influence, while remaining steadfastly true to themselves. It cultivates resilience in the face of adversity, fostering the ability to act with integrity and moral courage even when confronted with external challenges and temptations. This alignment of personal ethics with individualism, guided by Stoic principles, empowers individuals to make conscious choices that honor their authentic selves while remaining mindful of their impact on the community and contributing to the common good.

Ultimately, the delicate balance between individual autonomy and communal responsibility lies at the heart of defining modern individualism. While the freedom to pursue personal aspirations, express unique identities, and make independent choices is undeniably essential for human flourishing, it is equally important to acknowledge and appreciate that individuals exist within a wider social fabric, intricately woven with relationships, obligations, and shared experiences. The ethics of individualism must therefore necessarily incorporate a profound understanding of how personal choices, even those seemingly insignificant, inevitably affect others, directly or indirectly. This understanding fosters a sense of civic responsibility and promotes a culture of empathy, compassion, and mutual respect. By integrating valuable principles from both Western and Eastern philosophical traditions, we can cultivate a more holistic framework for individuals to navigate their complex identities, allowing for a harmonious coexistence of self and community in the relentless pursuit of ethical living and a more just and equitable world. This balanced approach to individualism, acknowledging both personal rights and social responsibilities, ultimately fosters a more enriching and sustainable path towards individual fulfillment and collective well-being.

Historical Perspectives on Individualism

The concept of individualism has evolved markedly throughout history, shaped by cultural, philosophical, and social factors. In ancient societies, collective identity often overshadowed personal autonomy.

Individualism, defined as the moral stance asserting the importance of the individual and his or her rights, has woven itself intricately into the fabric of human civilization. From the ancient civilizations to the modern technological era, individualism has seen various expressions, re-definitions, and challenges. We will explore the evolutionary historical perspectives on individualism, delving into the philosophical underpinnings and the cultural shifts that have shaped our understanding of the self in opposition to the collective.

Ancient Foundations:
Individualism in Early Civilizations

The pursuit of individual autonomy and self-definition is often considered a hallmark of modern Western thought. However, the seeds of individualism, and the inherent tensions between the individual and the collective, can be traced back to ancient civilizations, where these concepts were first articulated and debated. The societal landscapes of Ancient Greece and Rome, in particular, offer fertile ground for exploring the nascent stages of individualistic thought, revealing diverse perspectives on the self, its role in society, and the balance between personal liberty and communal obligation.

In Ancient Greece, a philosophical revolution unfolded, challenging traditional notions of authority and societal conformity. Thinkers such as Socrates, Plato, and Aristotle embarked on a profound exploration of the self, its nature, and its significance in the larger social fabric. Socrates, often hailed as the father of Western philosophy, famously emphasized the crucial importance of self-knowledge. His relentless questioning, epitomized by the Socratic method, urged individuals to critically examine their own beliefs, values, and assumptions. He posited that understanding oneself – one's virtues, limitations, and aspirations – was paramount to leading a virtuous and fulfilling life. This emphasis on personal introspection, on the relentless pursuit of self-awareness, laid the groundwork for a powerful current of individual thought that would later resurge during the Renaissance and continue to shape modern conceptions of the self. Socrates' conviction, even in the face of persecution and death, solidified the idea that individual conscience and moral integrity could supersede the demands of the state.

While Socrates focused on the individual's internal world, Plato, his student, grappled with the relationship between the individual and the ideal state. In his seminal work, *The Republic*, Plato envisioned a society structured to optimize collective harmony, with individuals assigned roles according to their natural aptitudes. However, even within this hierarchical structure, Plato recognized the importance of individual justice and the pursuit of knowledge. He believed that the ideal state could only be achieved through the cultivation of virtuous individuals, each contributing their unique talents to the common good. This nuanced perspective acknowledges the individual's inherent value, even within a tightly controlled social order. Furthermore, Plato's theory of Forms, which posits the existence of a higher realm of perfect ideals, implicitly encourages individuals to strive beyond the limitations of the material world and pursue their own personal understanding of truth and beauty.

Aristotle, Plato's student, further refined the understanding of individualism by connecting it to the concept of human flourishing, or *eudaimonia*. He argued that individuals achieved fulfillment not by conforming to a rigid societal mold, but by developing their unique potential and exercising their rational faculties. This emphasis on individual agency and self-actualization highlights the importance of personal choice and the pursuit of individual excellence. Aristotle's focus on empirical observation and logical reasoning also encouraged individuals to question established norms and formulate their own understanding of the world, fostering a spirit of intellectual independence.

In contrast to the Greek emphasis on philosophical introspection and individual virtue, the Romans brought forth a more civic-oriented approach to individualism, encapsulating the concept within their legal and political frameworks. The Roman idea of "civitas," or citizenship, highlighted the responsibilities and rights of individuals as integral components of a larger community. Roman law, with its emphasis on due process and individual rights, protected citizens from arbitrary power and ensured a degree of personal autonomy within the empire. The concept of *ius civile*, or civil law, established a framework for regulating interactions between individuals, recognizing their rights to property, contract, and fair treatment.

Herein lies an important dichotomy: while the Greeks prefigured modern individualism by focusing on self-knowledge and personal virtue, the Romans demonstrated that individual rights and freedoms can emerge and be protected within collective frameworks. The Roman emphasis on civic duty and participation in public life also reflects a different facet of individualism — not simply the pursuit of personal interests, but the responsible exercise of individual rights for the benefit of the community. Roman oratory, exemplified by figures like Cicero, celebrated individual eloquence and political engagement, highlighting the power of the individual to shape public opinion and influence the course of events. This civic individualism emphasized the importance of personal responsibility and participation in the political process, fostering a sense of collective ownership and shared destiny.

Furthermore, the Roman concept of *auctoritas*, often translated as "authority" or "influence," acknowledged the power of individuals to shape societal norms and values through their actions and reputation.

Individuals who possessed *auctoritas* commanded respect and wielded considerable influence, not through legal authority, but through their integrity, wisdom, and contributions to the community. This recognition of individual influence underscores the Roman understanding that individuals, through their character and actions, could significantly impact on the social fabric, fostering a dynamic interplay between individual agency and collective identity.

In conclusion, while the concept of individualism as understood today evolved significantly over centuries, its roots can be clearly traced to the intellectual and political landscapes of Ancient Greece and Rome. The Greeks, through their philosophical inquiries, emphasized the importance of self-knowledge, personal virtue, and the pursuit of individual excellence. The Romans, through their legal and political frameworks, highlighted the rights and responsibilities of individuals within a civic community. These contrasting yet complementary approaches to individualism laid the foundation for future developments in Western thought, shaping our understanding of the self, its relationship to society, and the ongoing tension between individual liberty and communal obligation. By examining these ancient foundations, we gain a deeper appreciation for the complex and enduring legacy of individualism in shaping the world we inhabit today.

The Renaissance:
A Rebirth of Individual Thought

The Renaissance, straddling the 14th and 16th centuries, stands as a pivotal epoch in human history, a period of profound transformation that irrevocably altered the course of Western civilization. More than just a stylistic rebirth of classical art and literature, it represents a monumental shift in the perspective on individualism, characterized by a resurgence of classical knowledge and a gradual, yet determined, departure from the rigid social, political, and religious constraints that defined the preceding Medieval period. This era witnessed the blossoming of individual potential, the challenging of established hierarchies, and the laying of intellectual foundations for the modern world, where individual rights and responsibilities are central to the societal discourse.

Fueling this paradigm shift was the rise of Humanism, a philosophical outlook that championed human potential and achievement as worthy pursuits in their own right, rather than solely as a means to divine grace. Drawing inspiration from the rediscovered texts of ancient Greece and Rome, Humanists emphasized reason, observation, and empirical evidence as pathways to understanding the world and shaping one's own destiny. Thinkers such as Petrarch, considered the "father of Humanism," actively sought out and translated classical manuscripts, bringing to light the wisdom and perspectives of the ancients, who placed a high value on individual excellence and civic engagement. This rediscovery provided a stark contrast to the prevailing Medieval focus on piety, obedience, and the collective submission to divine will.

Erasmus of Rotterdam, another towering figure of the Humanist movement, further contributed to the burgeoning emphasis on individualism through his advocacy for intellectual freedom and critical thinking. He challenged the unquestioning acceptance of dogma and encouraged individuals to engage directly with scripture, fostering a more personal and informed relationship with religion. His satirical writings, like "The Praise of Folly," cleverly exposed the hypocrisy and corruption prevalent within the Church and societal institutions, thereby encouraging individuals to question authority and form their own opinions. In doing so, Erasmus helped to pave the way for the Protestant Reformation, a monumental event that further fragmented religious authority and empowered individuals to choose their own spiritual path, thus solidifying the importance of individual conscience.

However, the impact of the Renaissance on the concept of individualism extended beyond the realms of theology and philosophy. It also profoundly influenced the sphere of politics, as exemplified by the groundbreaking work of Niccolò Machiavelli. His treatise, "The Prince," reflects a significant turning point where the role of the individual in the sphere of power became paramount. Departing from traditional moral frameworks that dictated princely behavior, Machiavelli argued that rulers should prioritize the stability and security of the state above all else, even if it meant employing morally questionable tactics. He suggested that individuals could, and often should, assert their will against traditional moral constraints in pursuit of personal and political achievement, even if it meant sacrificing personal virtue for the greater good of the state.

This assertion of individuality against collective norms became a hallmark of modern political theory, igniting discussions about personal rights and responsibilities that would resonate through subsequent centuries. Machiavelli's pragmatism, though often controversial, challenged the prevailing belief that rulers were divinely ordained and bound by absolute moral principles. Instead, he placed agency in the hands of the individual leader, empowering them to shape their own destiny and that of their state. This emphasis on individual action and strategic thinking, while arguably amoral, undeniably contributed to the development of modern political thought, emphasizing the importance of individual leadership and the ability to navigate complex political landscapes.

The Renaissance, therefore, represents far more than a simple revival of classical art and literature. It marks the dawn of a new era, one where individual thought, reason, and agency were increasingly valued. From the humanist scholars who championed human potential to the political theorists who redefined the role of the individual in the state, the Renaissance fostered a climate of intellectual inquiry and innovation that paved the way for the scientific revolution and the Enlightenment. The ideas that germinated during this transformative period continue to resonate today, shaping our understanding of individual rights, responsibilities, and the pursuit of personal and societal progress. The legacy of the Renaissance is not just the magnificent art and architecture it produced, but also the enduring emphasis it placed on the power and potential of the individual to shape the world around them.

Enlightenment Ideals:
The Birth of Modern Individualism

The Enlightenment stands as a pivotal era in human history, serving as the intellectual wellspring from which the modern concept of individualism emerged. Prior to this transformative period, societal structures often prioritized collective identities – family, clan, religious affiliation, or feudal obligation – over the rights and autonomy of the individual. The Enlightenment, however, catalyzed a profound re-evaluation, fundamentally altering the philosophical landscape and ushering in a new era where the individual stood as the foundational unit of moral and political thought. Thinkers such as John Locke and Jean-Jacques Rousseau, with their distinct yet interconnected perspectives, articulated a vision that continues to resonate in contemporary discussions of rights, freedoms, and the relationship between the individual and the state.

Locke's theory of the social contract, arguably the cornerstone of Enlightenment individualism, irrevocably shifted the paradigm of governance. No longer was authority considered divinely ordained or inherited through lineage. Instead, Locke posited that governmental authority was derived from the consent of the governed, a radical idea that placed sovereignty firmly in the hands of the people. Crucially, this consent was not unconditional; it was predicated on the government's ability to protect the inherent rights of individuals, most notably the rights to life, liberty, and property. Locke's emphasis on these "natural rights" served as a powerful indictment of absolute monarchies and paved the way for constitutionalism, where the power of the state was explicitly limited and the rights of individuals were enshrined in law. His writings provided the intellectual justification for revolutions aimed at overthrowing oppressive regimes and establishing governments based on the principles of individual liberty and self-governance. The American Revolution, in particular, drew heavily from Locke's philosophy, embedding his principles of individual rights into the Declaration of Independence and the Constitution.

Rousseau, while sharing Locke's commitment to individual freedom, offered a more nuanced and at times critical perspective on the potential pitfalls of unfettered individualism. While he recognized the importance of personal freedom and the individual's voice within the social framework, as evidenced in his concept of the "general will," he also cautioned against the dangers of egoism and the erosion of social solidarity. Rousseau argued that individuals, in entering into a social contract, must cede some degree of individual autonomy to the collective good. His vision emphasized the importance of civic virtue and the need for individuals to actively participate in the political process to ensure that the "general will" truly reflects the collective interests of society. This perspective provided a vital counterweight to the potential excesses of individualism, highlighting the importance of social responsibility and the interconnectedness of individuals within a community. His emphasis on the "noble savage," a hypothetical state of nature where individuals lived freely and harmoniously, served as a powerful critique of the corrupting influence of civilization and the need for societies to cultivate virtue and equality.

Beyond the realm of political philosophy, the Enlightenment also witnessed the rise of empiricism and rational thought, fundamentally transforming the way individuals understood the world around them. Thinkers like Isaac Newton, with his groundbreaking laws of physics, demonstrated the power of observation and reason to unlock the secrets of the universe. This intellectual movement encouraged individuals to seek knowledge through personal observation and reason rather than relying solely on tradition, dogma, or the pronouncements of authority figures. This emphasis on individual reason fostered a spirit of autonomy in thought, empowering individuals to question established norms and form their own independent judgments. The scientific revolution, closely interwoven with the Enlightenment, provided a powerful impetus for challenging traditional hierarchies and advocating for intellectual freedom. Individuals were encouraged to think for themselves, to conduct their own experiments, and to arrive at their own conclusions, free from the constraints of intellectual conformity.

This intellectual ferment, fueled by empiricism and rationalism, led to revolutionary changes in governance and society that would ultimately pave the way for democratic ideals. The resulting political revolutions in America and France, inspired by Enlightenment principles, violently challenged the legitimacy of absolute monarchies and aristocratic privilege. These revolutions emphasized the notion of individuals as free and equal, possessing inherent rights that no government could legitimately infringe upon. The Declaration of the Rights of Man and of the Citizen, adopted during the French Revolution, explicitly articulated these rights, including liberty, property, security, and resistance to oppression. These documents, along with the American Declaration of Independence, served as powerful beacons of hope for oppressed peoples around the world, setting a precedent for global human rights movements that continue to strive for the realization of Enlightenment ideals.

However, the legacy of Enlightenment individualism is not without its complexities and contradictions. Critics have argued that the emphasis on individual rights can lead to social fragmentation, inequality, and the neglect of collective needs. The rise of capitalism, often seen as a product of Enlightenment values, has also been criticized for exacerbating economic disparities and contributing to environmental degradation. Furthermore, the Enlightenment's emphasis on reason has been challenged by postmodern thinkers who question the possibility of objective truth and the universality of human experience. Despite these criticisms, the enduring impact of the Enlightenment on the development of modern individualism is undeniable. Its emphasis on individual rights, freedoms, and reason has shaped our legal systems, political institutions, and social norms. The ongoing debates surrounding the balance between individual liberty and social responsibility, the role of government in protecting individual rights, and the pursuit of knowledge through reason and observation all reflect the continuing relevance of Enlightenment ideals in the 21st century. The birth of modern individualism, therefore, was not a singular event but rather a protracted and complex process, one that continues to shape our world today.

Romanticism:
Individualism's Emotional Depth

As the Enlightenment, with its emphasis on reason and universal principles, gradually ceded ground to Romanticism in the late 18th and early 19th centuries, individualism underwent a significant transformation, shifting its axis from the purely rational towards the rich and often turbulent landscape of emotional depth. While the Enlightenment championed the individual as a rational actor within a structured society, Romantic thinkers, spearheaded by figures such as Jean-Jacques Rousseau, William Wordsworth, and later, Lord Byron and Mary Shelley, shifted the focus inward, prioritizing the exploration of the self and the authentic experience of emotion as the very wellspring of human understanding and value. This period celebrated not just individuality, but also the unbridled power of creativity, the sublime beauty of untamed nature, and the profound, often mystical connection between the natural world and the human spirit.

The Romantics mounted a passionate and often defiant counter-movement against the rising tide of industrialization and the burgeoning capitalist system. They perceived these forces as a profound threat to individual creativity, authentic human connection, and ultimately, the very essence of humanity. The burgeoning factories, the relentless pursuit of progress through mechanization, and the increasing urbanization were seen as crushing the individual spirit, forcing conformity and stifling the inherent creative potential within each person. In contrast to the Enlightenment's focus on universal truths discoverable through reason, the Romantics introduced the crucial importance of personal experience and emotional authenticity as foundational elements of individual identity. This shift framed the individual not merely as a rational actor, calculating advantages and disadvantages, but as a complex emotional being, driven by passion, intuition, and a deep yearning for connection and meaning. This emphasis on subjective experience allowed for a far broader and more nuanced understanding of the human condition, one that embraced the power of imagination, the inevitability of suffering, and the redemptive potential of love and compassion.

Furthermore, the Romantic emphasis on the individual extended beyond the purely personal realm to encompass a deep appreciation for the unique qualities of different cultures and heritages. The Enlightenment's focus on universal reason sometimes led to a dismissal or homogenization of cultural differences. The Romantics, however, sought to preserve and celebrate the distinct traditions, folklore, and artistic expressions of various cultures. This interest in the particular and the local contributed to a growing sense of national identity and a renewed appreciation for the richness and diversity of human experience. The rediscovery of folklore, the collection of ancient stories and myths, and the celebration of national languages were all integral parts of the Romantic project of defining and celebrating the unique character of individual nations and cultures.

This heightened awareness of individual and cultural uniqueness also fostered a deeper understanding of the darker aspects of human nature. Where the Enlightenment often focused on the potential for human progress and the perfectibility of society, the Romantics acknowledged the presence of irrationality, darkness, and even malevolence within the human soul. This acknowledgement is evident in the rise of the Gothic novel, which explored themes of horror, the supernatural, and the psychological depths of madness and obsession. By confronting these darker aspects of human existence, the Romantics sought to achieve a more complete and honest understanding of the human condition, recognizing that true individuality encompassed both light and shadow.

In conclusion, Romanticism profoundly reshaped the concept of individualism, moving beyond the Enlightenment's emphasis on rationality to embrace the complexities of emotion, intuition, and subjective experience. By championing creativity, celebrating the beauty and power of nature, and exploring the depths of the human spirit, the Romantics offered a compelling alternative to the dominant intellectual currents of their time. Their legacy continues to resonate today, reminding us of the importance of personal authenticity, artistic expression, and the profound connection between the individual and the world around them. The Romantic emphasis on emotional depth and the celebration of the individual's unique inner landscape remain powerful forces in shaping our understanding of ourselves and our place in the world.

The 20th Century: Individualism in Crisis and Conformity

The 20th century, a period marked by rapid technological advancement, global conflict, and profound social upheaval, presented unprecedented challenges to the understanding of individuality. While the century held the promise of liberation and progress, it also witnessed the rise of totalitarian regimes across Europe and elsewhere, regimes that actively sought to suppress the individual in favor of a monolithic collective identity. The stark contrast between the potential for individual flourishing and the brutal reality of enforced conformity led to a period of intense philosophical scrutiny and re-evaluation of the very meaning and implications of individualism.

The ideologies of both communism and fascism, despite their surface-level differences, shared a disturbing tendency to prioritize the needs of the state or the "collective" above the rights and freedoms of individual citizens. Under these systems, individual expression was often viewed with suspicion, dissent was met with swift and often violent repression, and personal autonomy was systematically eroded. The individual was reduced to a cog in the machine, a mere instrument serving the grand, overarching narrative of the state. This suppression of individuality manifested in various forms, from strict censorship and propaganda campaigns to forced collectivization and the eradication of dissenting voices through imprisonment, exile, or even death. The horrors of the Holocaust and the Gulags serve as stark reminders of the devastating consequences of prioritizing ideological purity over individual human dignity.

This assault on individuality sparked a fervent philosophical response, forcing thinkers to confront the fundamental questions of human autonomy and the relationship between the individual and society. One of the most radical voices to emerge during this period was Friedrich Nietzsche, whose philosophy served as a powerful critique of collectivist ideologies and traditional morality. Nietzsche questioned the very foundations upon which societal norms were built, arguing that they often served to stifle individual potential and reinforce a "slave morality" that valued conformity and obedience over self-affirmation and creative expression. His concept of the "Übermensch," often misunderstood and sometimes misused, was not intended as a blueprint for tyrannical rule, but rather as a metaphor for the individual who transcends conventional morality, embraces their own will to power, and creates their own values. The Übermensch, in Nietzsche's vision, is not bound by the constraints of tradition or the expectations of society, but rather strives to achieve self-mastery and realize their full potential. Nietzsche's emphasis on individual strength and self-creation provided a potent counterpoint to the dehumanizing forces of collectivism, encouraging individuals to challenge the status quo and forge their own paths in the world.

Simultaneously, the rise of existentialism, spearheaded by influential figures such as Jean-Paul Sartre and Simone de Beauvoir, offered a distinct yet complementary perspective on the nature of individuality in the 20th century. Existentialists vehemently rejected the notion of pre-determined human essence, proclaiming instead that "existence precedes essence." This assertion meant that individuals are not born with a fixed purpose or predetermined identity, but rather are thrown into a world devoid of inherent meaning, where they are free, and indeed condemned, to create their own essence through their choices and actions. This radical freedom, however, comes with a heavy burden of responsibility. Sartre argued that because individuals are ultimately responsible for defining themselves, they are also responsible for the world they create. This responsibility extends beyond the personal realm, encompassing a social and ethical dimension that demands individuals to actively engage with the world and strive to create a more just and meaningful existence for themselves and others.

The existentialist emphasis on individual freedom and responsibility resonated deeply with a generation grappling with the aftermath of war and the looming threat of totalitarianism. In a world where traditional values had been shattered and the individual seemed increasingly insignificant in the face of powerful social and political forces, existentialism offered a path toward authentic selfhood. It reinforced the idea that while society inevitably influences personal experience, the essence of the individual remains an unexplored territory, rife with potential and burdened with the weight of ultimate responsibility. This perspective not only empowered individuals to resist the forces of conformity and assert their own unique identities, but also challenged them to actively shape the world around them and create a more meaningful existence for all.

In conclusion, the 20th century presented a paradoxical landscape for the individual. While technological advancements and expanding social freedoms seemed to promise greater autonomy and self-expression, the rise of totalitarian ideologies threatened to erase individual identity altogether. In response to this crisis, philosophical movements like Nietzscheanism and existentialism emerged, offering powerful critiques of collectivism and reaffirming the importance of individual freedom, responsibility, and self-creation. These philosophies provided a crucial intellectual framework for navigating the complex ethical and political challenges of the 20th century, and their enduring relevance continues to inform our understanding of individuality in the 21st century, a century grappling with its own unique set of challenges to human autonomy and self-determination. From the pressures of social media to the increasing influence of artificial intelligence, the question of what it means to be an individual in the modern world remains a vital and ongoing debate.

The Contemporary Era:
Individualism in a Globalized World

In the contemporary context, individualism has taken on new dimensions alongside globalization, technological advances, and the rapid spread of information. Modern individualism tends to emphasize the importance of personal choice and self-expression through diverse mediums, including digital platforms. The emergence of social media has further complicated notions of individualism, as individuals curate their identities in public spheres while grappling with a paradoxical collective existence. As individuals gain more autonomy and independence in shaping their lives, they are increasingly confronted with a myriad of choices that can either empower or overwhelm them.

The concept of individualism has been a cornerstone of Western societies, emphasizing the value of personal freedom and self-reliance. In recent times, however, individualism has evolved beyond its traditional definition, taking on a more nuanced and complex form in the digital age. With the rise of social media and other online platforms, individuals are able to broadcast their thoughts, opinions, and experiences to a global audience. This newfound ability to reach out to others and share one's identity has led to a renewed emphasis on the self, as people strive to establish their unique presence in the online world.

The digital realm has opened up new avenues for self-expression and creativity, enabling individuals to explore their identities and connect with like-minded people from all corners of the globe. This has fostered a sense of belonging and solidarity among groups that were once marginalized or ostracized. At the same time, the online space has also become a platform for comparison, competition, and the commodification of personal identity. With the pressure to conform to certain standards of success and the constant bombardment of curated, idealized lives, individuals often find themselves questioning the authenticity of their self-expression.

The paradoxical nature of individualism in the digital age is further exemplified by the tension between personal freedom and collective responsibility. While social media allows individuals to express themselves freely and assert their unique perspectives, it also exposes them to a vast array of opposing viewpoints and diverse cultural backgrounds. This exposure can lead to both greater understanding and empathy, as well as increased polarization and conflict. As individuals engage in this digital melting pot of ideas and experiences, they must navigate the delicate balance between preserving their individuality and acknowledging the broader communal context in which they exist.

The challenges posed by contemporary individualism are not limited to the digital realm. In the physical world, the emphasis on personal freedom and self-expression has given rise to heated debates about the limits of individual rights and the role of government in protecting the common good. With the increasing focus on the self, some argue that there is a risk of losing sight of the importance of community, shared values, and collective action. The erosion of communal bonds and the rise of individualism have been linked to a range of social issues, including mental health problems, social isolation, and political polarization.

Despite these challenges, individualism in the contemporary era also offers numerous opportunities for growth and development. By empowering individuals to take control of their lives and make choices that align with their values and aspirations, modern individualism encourages personal growth, creativity, and innovation. Furthermore, the emphasis on self-expression and identity formation can foster a deeper understanding of one's place in the world and one's responsibility towards others.

To harness the positive aspects of individualism while mitigating its potential negative consequences, it is crucial to promote a balanced approach that acknowledges both the individual and the collective. This means fostering an environment that encourages personal freedom and self-expression while also nurturing a sense of community, shared responsibility, and empathy. By recognizing the interconnectedness of our lives and working together to build a more inclusive, compassionate society, we can ensure that individualism serves as a catalyst for positive change and progress.

Individualism in the contemporary era is an intricate and complex phenomenon, shaped by globalization, technological advances, and the rapid spread of information. While this newfound emphasis on personal choice and self-expression has empowered individuals and fostered creativity and innovation, it has also given rise to challenges related to the authenticity of self-expression, the commodification of personal identity, and the erosion of communal values. To navigate this ever-evolving landscape, it is essential to strike a balance between the individual and the collective, fostering an environment that encourages both personal freedom and social responsibility. By doing so, we can ensure that individualism serves as a force for positive change, empowering individuals to reach their full potential while also building stronger, more resilient communities.

For instance, in many Eastern traditions, particularly within Buddhism, the focus has traditionally been on the interconnectedness of all beings. This perspective emphasizes the importance of community and collective welfare over individual desires. As Buddhism spread and interacted with Western thought, elements of individualism began to emerge, particularly during the Renaissance, when humanism celebrated individual potential and personal achievement, setting the stage for modern interpretations of selfhood.

The Enlightenment marked a pivotal moment in the evolution of individualism, as philosophers like John Locke and Jean-Jacques Rousseau championed the rights of the individual, arguing that personal freedom and rational thought were central to human dignity. This period laid the groundwork for contemporary understandings of individual rights and personal agency. The emphasis on individualism during this time was rooted in the belief that each person possesses innate worth and the capacity for moral reasoning, which directly influenced Western legal and political systems. This shift toward valuing the individual paved the way for later philosophical debates about the balance between individual rights and social responsibilities.

As the Industrial Revolution transformed societies, the implications of individualism became more pronounced. The rise of capitalism and the emphasis on personal success encouraged a culture where individual achievement was celebrated. However, this newfound focus on self-reliance and personal ambition also led to concerns about alienation and disconnection from communal ties. The tension between individual aspirations and collective needs became a recurring theme in philosophical discourse. Thinkers like Karl Marx criticized the excesses of individualism, arguing that it could lead to social fragmentation and inequality, highlighting the need to reconcile personal freedoms with a sense of community.

In contemporary society, the advent of social media has further complicated the narrative of individualism. Platforms designed for self-expression often foster an environment where personal identity is constantly curated and performed. This phenomenon raises questions about authenticity and the impact of external validation on self-perception. The intersection of social media with individualism invites a reevaluation of how we define ourselves in relation to others. As individuals navigate the digital landscape, the challenge lies in balancing self-promotion with genuine self-reflection—an endeavor that resonates with both Stoic philosophy and Buddhist teachings on mindfulness and self-awareness.

The historical trajectory of individualism reveals a complex interplay between personal identity and communal responsibility. As individuals seek to carve out their own paths in an increasingly interconnected world, the ethical implications of individualism will continue to be relevant. Integrating insights from both Eastern and Western philosophies can provide valuable frameworks for understanding the nuances of personal agency within a collective context. By fostering a balance between the pursuit of individual goals and the recognition of shared humanity, individuals can navigate the challenges of modern life while remaining anchored in ethical considerations that prioritize both self and society.

Charting a Path Forward

The historical perspectives on individualism reveal a complex tapestry woven from threads of thought, culture, and society. Each era has contributed unique insights that challenge and enrich our understanding of what it means to be an individual within a collective. Today, as we stand at a crossroads, the lessons of history remind us of the delicate balance between individual rights and communal responsibilities.

In a world that increasingly embraces diversity yet often nudges towards conformity, it is essential to nurture an understanding of individualism that acknowledges our interdependence. Encouraging the exploration of personal values, fostering open dialogue, and promoting empathy can lead to a richer collective experience that honors the unique contributions of every individual. As history has shown, the evolution of individualism is not merely a philosophical inquiry; it is an ongoing journey that invites us to engage thoughtfully with the legacies of the past while actively shaping the future. In this ever-evolving narrative, each one of us holds the potential to redefine the essence of individuality in solidarity with the broader tapestry of humanity.

Individualism in Eastern vs. Western Thought

Individualism, a concept central to understanding human behavior and societal structures, manifests distinctly across Eastern and Western thought. These differing expressions reflect fundamental cultural, historical, and philosophical distinctions, shaping how individuals perceive themselves and their roles within the world. In the West, individualism is frequently celebrated as a cornerstone of personal freedom, autonomy, and self-expression. This perspective emphasizes the paramount importance of self-reliance, personal achievement, and the inviolable nature of individual rights. Philosophers like John Stuart Mill, with his advocacy for individual liberty and the harm principle, and Friedrich Nietzsche, who championed the will to power and the creation of one's own values, have profoundly influenced this understanding, advocating for personal expression and the pursuit of one's own happiness. This Western focus on the individual often fosters a strong sense of self-determination, encouraging people to carve their own paths, pursue their ambitions, and challenge societal norms, sometimes at the expense of communal values and social cohesion. The emphasis on competition and individual success, often seen in Western economic models, is a direct consequence of this individualistic ethos.

In stark contrast, Eastern philosophies, particularly those stemming from Buddhist, Confucian, and Daoist traditions, present a more interdependent view of the self. The concept of "anatta" or non-self in Buddhism challenges the very notion of a permanent, unchanging, and independent identity. Instead, it suggests that personal identity is fluid, constantly evolving, and inextricably shaped by relationships, experiences, and societal contexts. Confucianism, similarly, emphasizes the importance of social harmony and the individual's role within a hierarchical social structure, prioritizing filial piety, respect for elders, and adherence to social norms. Daoism, while promoting individual harmony with the natural world, also underscores the interconnectedness of all things. These perspectives encourage individuals to see themselves as integral parts of a larger whole, where one's actions and well-being are deeply intertwined with the welfare of the community. Such an understanding fosters compassion, empathy, and mindfulness, urging individuals to consider the consequences of their actions on others and to prioritize collective well-being over personal gain, a value system that can sometimes conflict with the Western emphasis on individual rights and freedoms. This emphasis on interconnectedness is often reflected in Eastern social structures, where family ties and community bonds are prioritized over individual ambition.

However, the dichotomy between Eastern collectivism and Western individualism is not as absolute as it may initially appear. Within Western thought, various philosophical traditions offer nuanced perspectives that challenge the simplistic notion of radical individualism. Stoicism, a philosophy that finds its roots in ancient Greece and Rome, provides valuable insights into the ethics of individualism in contemporary society. Stoicism emphasizes personal responsibility, resilience in the face of adversity, and the importance of cultivating virtue over seeking external validation or material possessions. While it advocates for individual strength and self-control, it also underscores the necessity of understanding one's role within the larger fabric of society and fulfilling one's duties as a citizen. This nuanced perspective, balancing personal development with community engagement, resonates with Eastern philosophies that promote harmony and social responsibility, suggesting that true individualism may not be about isolation or selfish pursuit but about navigating one's identity and purpose in relation to others. Furthermore, Western communitarianism, a philosophical movement that emphasizes the importance of community and social responsibility, also provides a counterpoint to the purely individualistic perspective.

The complex interaction between individualism and collectivism in both Eastern and Western thought raises critical questions about ethical decision-making in a rapidly changing and increasingly interconnected modern world. As individuals navigate their identities within a globalized context, constantly bombarded with diverse cultural values and perspectives, integrating insights from both perspectives can lead to a more nuanced and comprehensive understanding of self and society. By acknowledging the inherent value of personal autonomy and self-expression while simultaneously embracing the interconnectedness of all beings and the importance of social responsibility, individuals can cultivate a balanced approach to life. This balanced approach allows for the enrichment of their personal journeys while also contributing positively to the well-being of their communities and the wider world. The conscious integration of these seemingly disparate philosophies into everyday decision-making can foster a more harmonious and sustainable existence, where individual aspirations align with collective well-being, promoting a more just and equitable global society.

The ongoing dialogue between Eastern and Western perspectives on individualism highlights the limitations of viewing these concepts as mutually exclusive. Instead, it reveals the potential for a synthesis that incorporates the strengths of both approaches. A "balanced individualism," for example, could prioritize personal growth and self-discovery while remaining mindful of the impact of one's actions on others and the environment. This approach could foster innovation and creativity while simultaneously promoting social justice and environmental sustainability. Ultimately, the exploration of individualism in Eastern and Western thought offers valuable insights into the complexities of human nature and the ongoing quest for a more fulfilling and meaningful life, both individually and collectively. This ongoing dialogue can help us navigate the challenges of the 21st century and create a more harmonious and sustainable future for all.

EXPLORING BUDDHISM AND WESTERN PHILOSOPHY

Exploring Buddhism and Western Philosophy

For centuries, humanity has sought to understand the nature of reality, the meaning of existence, and the path to a fulfilling life. Two of the most profound and enduring traditions in this quest are Buddhism, originating in ancient India, and Western Philosophy, a lineage stretching from pre-Socratic Greece to the present day. While geographically and culturally distinct, both grapple with fundamental questions about consciousness, ethics, and the human condition. Exploring the convergences and divergences between Buddhism and Western Philosophy offers valuable insights into the complexities of these enduring inquiries and illuminates potential pathways for personal and societal flourishing.

One of the most striking points of intersection lies in their shared concern with the nature of suffering. Buddhism, at its core, identifies suffering (Dukkha) as a central reality of existence. The Four Noble Truths articulate this suffering, its causes (attachment and ignorance), its cessation (Nirvana), and the path to its cessation (the Eightfold Path). Western Philosophy, while not always framing it in precisely the same terms, has also grappled extensively with the problem of suffering. Thinkers like Arthur Schopenhauer, deeply influenced by Eastern thought, explicitly identified suffering as the driving force of human existence. Existentialists like Albert Camus and Jean-Paul Sartre explored the absurdity and anguish inherent in a seemingly meaningless universe. While the specific diagnoses and proposed solutions differ, both traditions acknowledge the pervasive presence of suffering and seek ways to alleviate it.

However, the approaches to understanding and overcoming suffering diverge significantly. Buddhism emphasizes the impermanence (Anicca) of all things, the lack of a permanent, independent self (Anatta), and the interconnectedness of all phenomena. Through practices like meditation and mindfulness, individuals can cultivate awareness of these truths, gradually detaching from clinging and aversion, thereby reducing suffering. Western Philosophy, particularly in its rationalist and empiricist traditions, often relies on reason, logic, and empirical observation to understand the world. While some philosophers, like the Stoics, advocated for acceptance of what we cannot control as a means of mitigating suffering, the emphasis is often on understanding the causes of suffering through intellectual analysis and developing rational strategies for coping.

The concept of the self presents another crucial point of comparison and contrast. As noted, Buddhism denies the existence of a fixed, independent self (Anatta). Instead, it proposes that the self is a constantly changing aggregation of physical and mental processes – the five skandhas (form, sensation, perception, mental formations, and consciousness). This understanding challenges the Western philosophical tradition's long-held assumption of a stable, enduring self, often associated with concepts like the soul or the Cartesian "I think, therefore I am." However, some Western philosophers, like David Hume, also questioned the existence of a unified self, arguing that it is merely a bundle of perceptions. More recently, philosophers influenced by neuroscience and cognitive science have explored the idea of the self as a constructed narrative, aligning in some ways with the Buddhist perspective.

Ethics is another fertile ground for comparison. Buddhist ethics, grounded in the principle of non-harming (Ahimsa) and the cultivation of compassion (Karuna) and loving-kindness (Metta), emphasizes the importance of intention and the interconnectedness of actions and consequences (Karma). The Eightfold Path provides a framework for ethical conduct, encompassing right understanding, thought, speech, action, livelihood, effort, mindfulness, and concentration. Western ethical theories are diverse, ranging from consequentialism (utilitarianism), which focuses on maximizing overall happiness, to deontology (Kantian ethics), which emphasizes adherence to universal moral principles, and virtue ethics, which emphasizes the cultivation of virtuous character traits. While there are overlaps — for example, the Golden Rule resonates with Buddhist principles of compassion — the underlying frameworks and justifications for ethical behavior differ significantly. Kantian ethics, with its emphasis on duty and reason, contrasts with the Buddhist emphasis on compassion and mindful awareness. Utilitarianism, with its focus on aggregate happiness, can sometimes clash with the Buddhist emphasis on individual liberation and the avoidance of harm to all sentient beings.

Furthermore, the role of spiritual practice differs between the two traditions. In Buddhism, meditation is a central practice for cultivating mindfulness, insight, and compassion. Through sustained meditation, practitioners aim to directly experience the nature of reality and transform their minds. While some forms of Western Philosophy, particularly in the contemplative traditions of ancient Greece (e.g., Stoicism and Epicureanism), involved practices aimed at cultivating inner peace and wisdom, the emphasis is generally on intellectual understanding rather than direct experiential transformation. However, contemporary philosophers are increasingly exploring the potential benefits of mindfulness and meditation practices for enhancing cognitive function, emotional regulation, and overall well-being, leading to a growing dialogue between Buddhist practice and Western psychology and neuroscience.

The ultimate goals of Buddhism and Western Philosophy, while both concerned with human flourishing, are often framed differently. Buddhism aims for Nirvana, a state of liberation from suffering and the cycle of rebirth, achieved through the extinction of craving and ignorance. Western Philosophy, depending on the particular school of thought, may aim for happiness (eudaimonia), wisdom, self-knowledge, or a just and equitable society. While Nirvana may seem radically different from these Western ideals, some philosophers have argued that it can be interpreted as a state of profound peace, freedom from attachment, and complete fulfillment, aligning in some ways with Western conceptions of ultimate well-being.

In conclusion, exploring the relationship between Buddhism and Western Philosophy reveals both fascinating parallels and significant divergences. Both traditions offer valuable insights into the nature of suffering, the self, ethics, and the path to a fulfilling life. By engaging in a critical and open-minded dialogue between these two profound traditions, we can deepen our understanding of the human condition and cultivate a more compassionate, wise, and meaningful existence. Further research could explore specific areas in more detail, such as the implications of the Buddhist concept of emptiness (Sunyata) for Western metaphysics, the role of emotions in ethical decision-making from both Buddhist and Western perspectives, or the potential for integrating Buddhist mindfulness practices into Western therapeutic approaches. The ongoing conversation between Buddhism and Western Philosophy promises to be a rich and fruitful endeavor for years to come.

Buddhism, Western Philosophy, *and the* Philosophy of Individualism

Buddhism, originating in ancient India, and Western Philosophy, a diverse collection of thought traditions arising primarily in Greece and Europe, offer distinct yet sometimes overlapping perspectives on the nature of reality, the human condition, and the path to a meaningful life. Juxtaposing these with the philosophy of Individualism, a prominent ideology, particularly in Western societies, reveals complex and fascinating points of convergence and divergence. While seemingly disparate, a closer examination reveals how these three systems of thought can illuminate each other, challenging our assumptions and expanding our understanding of ourselves and the world.

Buddhism, at its core, centers on the Four Noble Truths, which diagnose the problem of suffering (Dukkha), identify its cause (attachment and craving), offer a solution (the cessation of craving), and prescribe a path to liberation (the Eightfold Path). This path emphasizes wisdom, ethical conduct, and mental discipline, all aimed at achieving Nirvana, a state of profound peace and freedom from suffering. Key Buddhist concepts such as impermanence (Anicca), non-self (Anatta), and interdependence highlight the interconnectedness of all things and the illusory nature of a fixed, independent self.

Western Philosophy, on the other hand, encompasses a vast range of schools and thinkers. From the rationalism of Plato and Descartes, emphasizing reason and innate ideas, to the empiricism of Locke and Hume, prioritizing sensory experience, Western thought has grappled with fundamental questions about knowledge, reality, and morality. Existentialism, with figures like Sartre and Camus, focuses on individual existence, freedom, and responsibility in a seemingly absurd world. Unlike Buddhism's emphasis on escaping suffering, Western philosophy often seeks to understand and engage with the world, even in its imperfections.

The philosophy of Individualism, with its emphasis on individual rights, autonomy, and self-reliance, has profoundly shaped Western culture and political systems. Rooted in Enlightenment ideals, Individualism champions the importance of personal freedom, self-expression, and the pursuit of individual goals. It often emphasizes competition and achievement, viewing individual success as a sign of merit and a driver of societal progress. However, this emphasis on the individual can also lead to a sense of isolation, alienation, and a neglect of collective responsibility.

Points of Contrast

One of the most significant contrasts between Buddhism and Individualism lies in their understanding of the "self." Buddhism, through the concept of Anatta, deconstructs the notion of a permanent, independent self, arguing that what we perceive as "I" is merely a collection of constantly changing physical and mental processes. Individualism, conversely, typically assumes the existence of a bounded, autonomous self, responsible for its own actions and entitled to certain rights and freedoms. This fundamental difference has profound implications for how we understand our relationship to others and the world. While Individualism might encourage self-assertion and the pursuit of personal gain, Buddhism promotes compassion, empathy, and the recognition of our interconnectedness with all beings.

Another key difference lies in their approaches to suffering. Buddhism sees suffering as an inherent part of the human condition, arising from attachment and ignorance. The goal is to overcome suffering through detachment and the cultivation of wisdom. Individualism, while acknowledging the existence of suffering, often frames it as a problem to be solved through individual effort, technological advancement, or social reform. There's a tendency to focus on external solutions to alleviate suffering, rather than addressing its root causes within the individual mind, as Buddhism suggests.

Furthermore, Western Philosophy, especially in its modern and postmodern forms, often grapples with skepticism and uncertainty, questioning the possibility of objective truth and universal values. Buddhism, while acknowledging the limitations of language and conceptual thought, offers a path to experiential knowledge and a direct realization of reality through meditation and mindfulness. This emphasis on direct experience provides a sense of certainty and grounding that may be lacking in some strands of Western Philosophy.

Points *of* Convergence

Despite these contrasts, there are also areas of potential convergence between Buddhism, Western Philosophy, and even aspects of Individualism. For example, some existentialist philosophers, like Sartre, emphasize the importance of individual responsibility and the freedom to create one's own meaning in a meaningless world. This resonates with Buddhism's emphasis on self-reliance and the need to take responsibility for one's own liberation. Although the concept of "no-self" might seem paradoxical, it can be interpreted as liberating, freeing us from the constraints of a fixed identity and allowing us to embrace change and growth.

Moreover, the emphasis on ethics and compassion found in Buddhism aligns with certain ethical frameworks in Western Philosophy, such as utilitarianism (which seeks to maximize happiness for the greatest number) and deontology (which emphasizes moral duties and principles). While the motivations may differ – Buddhist ethics are rooted in the desire to alleviate suffering, while Western ethics may be based on reason or social contract – both strive to promote moral behavior and a more just society.

Furthermore, a healthy form of Individualism can be compatible with Buddhist principles. Self-reliance, when tempered with compassion and wisdom, can empower individuals to take responsibility for their own well-being and contribute positively to society. The pursuit of personal growth and self-improvement, when guided by ethical considerations, can be a valuable endeavor. However, it's crucial to avoid the pitfalls of excessive self-centeredness and the neglect of our interconnectedness with others.

The Challenge *of* Integration

The challenge lies in integrating these different perspectives in a way that fosters both individual well-being and collective flourishing. A purely individualistic approach, devoid of compassion and ethical considerations, can lead to selfishness, exploitation, and social inequality. A purely Buddhist approach, focused solely on detachment and the cessation of suffering, may neglect the importance of social engagement and the need to address systemic injustices. And a purely Western philosophical approach may get lost in abstract thought and not translate into meaningful change in the world.

A balanced approach requires a critical examination of our own assumptions and biases, a willingness to learn from different traditions, and a commitment to cultivating both individual wisdom and social responsibility. We can draw on the strengths of each perspective to create a more holistic and meaningful way of life. This might involve embracing individual freedom and creativity while also recognizing our interconnectedness with all beings and working to alleviate suffering in the world. It might involve using reason and critical thinking to understand the complexities of the world while also cultivating mindfulness and compassion to connect with our inner selves and others.

Exploring the intersection of Buddhism, Western Philosophy, and Individualism reveals a rich tapestry of ideas and values. While these three systems of thought may appear contradictory at times, they also offer valuable insights into the human condition and the path to a more fulfilling life. By engaging in critical dialogue and seeking common ground, we can harness the wisdom of each tradition to create a more just, compassionate, and sustainable world. Ultimately, the goal is not to choose one perspective over another, but to integrate them in a way that promotes both individual well-being and the flourishing of all. The journey of understanding these interconnected yet distinct perspectives is a continuous process of self-discovery and engagement with the world around us, leading to a more nuanced and comprehensive understanding of ourselves and our place in the universe.

Core Principles *of* Buddhism

Buddhism is grounded in a set of core principles that guide its philosophy and practices, offering profound insights into the nature of existence, suffering, and the path to enlightenment. At the heart of Buddhism are the Four Noble Truths, which articulate the reality of suffering (dukkha), its origin in attachment and desire (tanha), the possibility of cessation (nirodha), and the path leading to liberation (magga). This framework serves as a foundation for understanding not only the self but also the interconnectedness of individuals within a community. Each truth encourages self-reflection and acknowledgment of one's experiences, providing a pathway to transcend individual suffering and create a more compassionate society.

The Eightfold Path, another fundamental aspect of Buddhist teachings, outlines practical steps for ethical living and mental cultivation. It encompasses principles such as the right understanding, right intention, right speech, right action, right livelihood, right effort, right mindfulness, and right concentration. These guidelines emphasize the importance of intentionality and mindfulness in both personal and communal contexts. In today's world, where social media often distorts self-perception and identity, the Eightfold Path can empower individuals to engage in more authentic self-reflection and foster healthier relationships with themselves and others.

Buddhism's emphasis on impermanence (anicca) and non-self (anatta) challenges the Western notion of a fixed, independent self. This shift in perspective encourages individuals to recognize the fluidity of identity and the influence of social contexts. By understanding that the self is not a static entity but rather a dynamic interplay of experiences and relationships, individuals can cultivate resilience in the face of change. This understanding aligns with contemporary discussions around the ethics of individualism, as it promotes a balance between self-identity and community engagement, advocating for a more harmonious coexistence of personal and collective interests.

The principles of compassion (karuna) and loving-kindness (metta) are also central to Buddhist ethics, urging practitioners to extend empathy beyond individual concerns. In a society increasingly driven by individualistic pursuits, these values highlight the ethical responsibility of individuals to contribute positively to their communities. By integrating compassion into everyday decision-making, individuals can navigate the complexities of modern life while fostering an environment that prioritizes collective well-being. This ethical framework resonates with the core tenets of Stoicism, which also emphasizes virtue and duty to others, demonstrating the relevance of Eastern philosophies in contemporary ethical discussions.

Ultimately, the core principles of Buddhism invite a deeper examination of the relationship between individuality and community. By embracing the teachings of Buddhism, individuals can cultivate a more nuanced understanding of their identity, enhancing their capacity for self-reflection and ethical decision-making. Such integration not only enriches personal growth but also contributes to a more compassionate society, where the values of interconnectedness and mindfulness guide interactions. In navigating the challenges of modern life, these principles serve as a beacon, illuminating pathways to a balanced existence that honors both the self and the collective.

Key Western Philosophers *on* Individualism

Key Western philosophers have long grappled with the concept of individualism, providing a rich discourse that informs contemporary ethical considerations. At the forefront of this exploration is René Descartes, whose assertion "Cogito, ergo sum"—I think, therefore I am— highlights the primacy of individual consciousness. Descartes posits that self-awareness and rational thought are central to human existence, laying the groundwork for a philosophy that prioritizes the individual's capacity for self-reflection. His emphasis on doubt and inquiry encourages individuals to seek knowledge from within, fostering a sense of autonomy that resonates with modern pursuits of identity in an increasingly interconnected world.

John Stuart Mill further expands on individualism through his advocacy for personal freedom and autonomy in "On Liberty." Mill argues that individuals should have the liberty to pursue their own paths, provided they do not harm others. His utilitarian approach suggests that personal development and self-actualization contribute to the greater good of society. In contemporary contexts, particularly in the realm of social media, Mill's ideas prompt reflection on how digital platforms can both enhance and undermine individual expression. The challenge lies in navigating these spaces while maintaining personal integrity and ethical standards, a dilemma that echoes Mill's concerns about the balance between individual liberty and social responsibility.

Friedrich Nietzsche introduces a more radical interpretation of individualism, celebrating the concept of the "Übermensch" or "Overman." He critiques societal norms and moral codes that suppress individuality, urging individuals to transcend conventional morality and create their own values. Nietzsche's philosophy encourages a profound self-examination and re-evaluation of one's beliefs, fostering a sense of empowerment that resonates with those seeking to carve out their unique identities. This call to self-creation aligns with the growing interest in personal branding and self-expression prevalent in today's social media landscape, where individuals are tasked with constructing and curating their identities.

Simone de Beauvoir's existentialist framework also contributes to the discourse on individualism, particularly in her exploration of freedom and choice in "The Second Sex." She argues that individuals must confront the societal constructs that limit their autonomy, particularly concerning gender roles. De Beauvoir's insistence on the importance of personal choice in defining one's identity speaks to modern discussions surrounding empowerment and the ethical implications of individualism. Her work invites introspection on how societal expectations shape self-perception, urging individuals to reclaim their narratives and assert their presence in both personal and collective spheres.

The interplay between these philosophical perspectives offers a nuanced understanding of individualism in contemporary society. As individuals navigate the complexities of modern life, including the influence of social media, the insights of these key Western thinkers serve as a guiding light. Their explorations of autonomy, freedom, and self-reflection encourage a balance between personal identity and social interconnectedness, ultimately enriching the ethical considerations surrounding individualism. By integrating these philosophical principles, individuals can better navigate the challenges of self-discovery and ethical decision-making in a collective world, fostering a deeper understanding of their role within the tapestry of society.

Points *of* Convergence *and* Divergence

In examining the points of convergence and divergence between Buddhism and Western philosophy, one can observe a rich tapestry of ideas that both complement and challenge one another. Both traditions grapple with the nature of self and identity, yet their approaches reveal distinct cultural underpinnings. Buddhism emphasizes the transient nature of the self and advocates for detachment from personal identity as a route to enlightenment. In contrast, many Western philosophies, particularly those stemming from existentialism, celebrate individual agency and the importance of personal identity. This divergence highlights a fundamental difference in how each tradition navigates the complexities of selfhood within a broader societal context.

The impact of social media on self-reflection and identity further complicates the dialogue between individualism and collectivism. Social media platforms often promote a curated self, encouraging users to present idealized versions of their lives. This phenomenon can create an illusion of individuality while simultaneously fostering a sense of belonging to a larger community. The Buddhist principle of non-attachment serves as a counterpoint to this trend, inviting individuals to reflect on the impermanence of online personas and the desire for validation. Thus, the convergence of these ideas offers a framework for understanding how modern technology influences self-perception and social dynamics.

Stoicism, with its emphasis on virtue and resilience, presents another intersection with Eastern philosophies. Both traditions espouse the importance of inner peace and self-control, albeit through different lenses. Stoicism encourages individuals to focus on what they can control while accepting the external circumstances beyond their influence. Similarly, Buddhism teaches the importance of mindfulness and acceptance of the present moment. The convergence of these philosophies provides valuable insights for modern individuals seeking to navigate life's challenges while remaining grounded in their values and ethics.

The influence of Eastern philosophies on Western motivational practices is increasingly evident in contemporary self-help movements. Concepts such as mindfulness, meditation, and the pursuit of balance resonate with individuals striving for personal growth. These practices encourage a holistic approach to success, emphasizing well-being alongside achievement. However, this integration often raises ethical questions about the commodification of spiritual practices in a consumer-driven society. The divergence in intentions—spiritual enlightenment versus personal gain—invites deeper reflection on the underlying motivations for adopting these philosophies in everyday life.

The balance between community and individuality in modern life continues to be a pressing concern. While individualism champions personal freedom and self-expression, it can sometimes lead to isolation and disconnection from the communal fabric. In contrast, the communal aspects of Buddhism advocate for interconnectedness and compassion, urging individuals to consider the collective well-being. Finding harmony between these opposing forces is essential for fostering a society that values both personal growth and social responsibility. Integrating Buddhist principles into everyday decision-making can serve as a guide for maintaining this balance, encouraging individuals to reflect on their actions' impact on themselves and the community at large.

The Role *of* Online Communities *in* Shaping Identity

Online communities have become a significant factor in shaping personal identity in contemporary society. These platforms provide individuals with a space to express their beliefs, values, and experiences while also engaging with diverse perspectives. As people navigate their identities, they often seek validation and connection with others who share similar interests or backgrounds. This dynamic creates a complex interplay between individual expression and communal influence, highlighting the ethical considerations of individualism in a collective environment.

In the context of exploring the intersection of Buddhism and Western philosophy, online communities serve as a modern-day forum for discussing philosophical ideas and principles. Individuals drawn to these discussions may find that their identities are shaped by the synthesis of Eastern and Western thought. For example, the Buddhist emphasis on interconnectedness may resonate with those who engage in online dialogues about community, fostering a sense of belonging while simultaneously prompting self-reflection on one's values. This blending of ideas encourages individuals to reconsider their identities in light of broader philosophical frameworks, leading to a more nuanced understanding of self.

The influence of Eastern philosophies on Western motivational practices is also evident in online communities, where concepts like mindfulness and self-compassion are increasingly integrated into discussions of personal development. These principles encourage individuals to engage in a reflective process that can reshape their identities. By participating in communities that prioritize these values, individuals may find themselves adopting a more holistic approach to growth, one that values collective well-being alongside personal achievement. This shift can cultivate a sense of responsibility toward both self and community, challenging the often rigid boundaries of individualism.

The balance between community and individuality in modern life is heavily influenced by online interactions. As adults traverse the complexities of identity formation, they must navigate the ethical implications of their online presence. The integration of Buddhist principles into everyday decision-making can offer valuable insights into how one might approach this balance. By fostering a sense of interconnectedness while remaining grounded in personal values, individuals can create identities that honor both their unique experiences and their roles within the larger community, thereby contributing to a more ethical understanding of individualism in a collective world.

Challenges *of* Authenticity *in* Digital Spaces

In the digital age, the concept of authenticity faces significant challenges, particularly as individuals navigate the complexities of online identities. Social media platforms, while providing opportunities for self-expression, often encourage the curation of idealized versions of oneself. This phenomenon leads to a disconnect between individuals' true selves and their online personas, raising ethical questions about the nature of authenticity. The desire for validation and acceptance can push individuals to present a façade that aligns more with societal expectations than with their genuine identities, undermining the principles of honesty and self-awareness central to both Buddhism and Stoicism.

As individuals engage with digital spaces, the impact of social media on self-reflection and identity becomes increasingly pronounced. Users frequently compare themselves to others, fostering a culture where self-worth is tied to likes and followers. This comparison can distort self-perception and hinder authentic self-exploration. Instead of encouraging meaningful connections, social media often amplifies feelings of inadequacy and isolation, complicating the pursuit of an authentic self. The challenge lies in resisting the urge to conform to external standards while simultaneously seeking validation in a community that thrives on superficial metrics.

The intersection of individualism and community in digital spaces poses additional ethical dilemmas. While online platforms offer a sense of belonging, they can simultaneously promote isolation through the proliferation of echo chambers. Individuals may find themselves surrounded by like-minded voices, leading to a reinforcement of narrow perspectives rather than fostering genuine dialogue and understanding. This dynamic complicates the balance between individual expression and communal engagement, raising questions about the value of authenticity when collective identities often overshadow personal truths.

Eastern philosophies, particularly Buddhism, advocate for mindfulness and self-awareness, which can serve as essential tools in navigating these challenges. Integrating Buddhist principles into everyday decision-making encourages individuals to reflect on their motivations and the impact of their online interactions. By cultivating a sense of presence and awareness, individuals can better discern their true selves from the personas they project in digital spaces. This practice fosters an authentic engagement with both oneself and the broader community, allowing for a more balanced approach to individuality and collective identity.

The challenges of authenticity in digital spaces highlight the need for a thoughtful approach to self-presentation and community interaction. As individuals grapple with the ethical implications of their online lives, it becomes crucial to cultivate genuine connections that transcend superficial engagement. Embracing the insights of both Eastern and Western philosophies can guide individuals in navigating these complexities, fostering a deeper understanding of authenticity that honors both individual identity and communal belonging. By prioritizing authenticity, individuals can contribute to a digital landscape that values meaningful interactions and encourages the flourishing of both self and community.

THE GUIDING LIGHTS WITHIN

A Philosophical Exploration *of* Ethical Principles

Ethical principles, the bedrock upon which moral judgements are built, are far more than just societal guidelines; they are the very frameworks through which we navigate the complex terrain of human interaction, striving to discern right from wrong, just from unjust, and good from harmful. To delve into the philosophy of ethical principles is to confront fundamental questions about human nature, the nature of good, and the ultimate meaning of a life lived well. This essay will explore the landscape of ethical principles, examining various philosophical perspectives and highlighting the inherent tensions and challenges that arise when attempting to apply these principles in a complex and ever-changing world.

One of the most enduring approaches to ethical thought is deontology, championed by Immanuel Kant. Deontological ethics emphasizes duty and adherence to universal moral laws, regardless of consequences. Kant's Categorical Imperative, a cornerstone of this philosophy, proposes that actions are moral only if they can be universalized without contradiction. For example, lying can never be morally justifiable because a world where everyone lies would be inherently self-defeating. The strength of deontology lies in its emphasis on rationality and objectivity, providing a seemingly unwavering guide in ethical dilemmas. However, critics argue that its rigid adherence to rules can be inflexible and lead to morally questionable outcomes in certain situations. Imagine lying to protect someone from a murderer; a strict deontologist might argue that lying is always wrong, even if it saves a life.

In contrast to deontology, consequentialism focuses on the outcomes of actions. Utilitarianism, a prominent consequentialist theory, argues that the best action is the one that maximizes overall happiness or well-being for the greatest number of people. Promulgated by thinkers like John Stuart Mill, utilitarianism offers a practical approach to ethical decision-making, prioritizing the common good. However, it faces challenges in accurately predicting consequences and can potentially justify actions that harm individuals or minorities for the sake of the majority. For example, a utilitarian argument could potentially justify sacrificing one innocent person to save the lives of many others, a conclusion that many find morally repugnant.

Another influential perspective is virtue ethics, championed by Aristotle. Unlike deontology and consequentialism, virtue ethics focuses on character rather than rules or consequences. It emphasizes the cultivation of virtuous traits, such as honesty, courage, compassion, and justice, which are seen as essential for living a flourishing life. According to Aristotle, ethical behavior stems from habituating oneself to act in accordance with these virtues, finding the "golden mean" between extremes. While virtue ethics offers a holistic and nuanced approach to morality, it can be criticized for being subjective and lacking clear guidelines for specific situations. What constitutes courage in one context may be recklessness in another, highlighting the challenges of applying virtue ethics in a complex and uncertain world..

These different ethical frameworks are not mutually exclusive, and often, a combination of principles is necessary to navigate complex ethical dilemmas. Consider the issue of global climate change. A deontological approach might emphasize our duty to future generations and the intrinsic value of the environment, requiring us to take action to mitigate climate change regardless of immediate costs. A consequentialist perspective might weigh the potential harms of climate change against the economic costs of transitioning to renewable energy, seeking to maximize overall well-being. Virtue ethics would encourage us to cultivate virtues like environmental stewardship and responsibility, promoting sustainable practices.

The pursuit of ethical principles is an ongoing and challenging endeavor. There is no single, universally agreed-upon ethical system, and different cultures and individuals may hold conflicting values. Furthermore, the application of ethical principles in the real world is often complicated by factors such as self-interest, power dynamics, and incomplete information. However, the very act of engaging in ethical reflection — of questioning our assumptions, considering different perspectives, and striving to act in accordance with our values — is crucial for building a more just and compassionate world.

Ethical principles, whether rooted in duty, consequences, or virtue, serve as guiding lights in the moral landscape. While each framework has its strengths and limitations, they all contribute to our understanding of what it means to live a good and meaningful life. By grappling with these philosophical perspectives and engaging in continuous ethical reflection, we can strive to create a world where ethical principles are not merely abstract ideals, but rather, the lived reality of a just and compassionate society.

Ethical Principles and the Individualist Ideal

The relationship between ethical principles and individualism is a complex and often fraught one, akin to a tightrope walk between personal freedom and social responsibility. On one side lies the allure of individual autonomy, the self-governing spirit that champions personal goals and self-determination. On the other, looms the imperative of ethical conduct, the adherence to principles that guide our actions towards the greater good and ensure a harmonious society. This essay will explore the inherent tension between these two forces, arguing that while individualism is a valuable and necessary component of a thriving society, it must be tempered by a commitment to ethical principles to avoid descending into self-serving isolation and moral decay.

Individualism, at its heart, emphasizes the worth and autonomy of the individual. It encourages critical thought, independent judgment, and the pursuit of personal aspirations. Philosophically, it draws inspiration from thinkers like John Stuart Mill, who championed the principle of individual liberty, arguing that society benefits from the diverse perspectives and innovative endeavors that arise when individuals are free to think and act autonomously. A society that fosters individualism can be a hotbed of creativity, innovation, and progress, as individuals are empowered to challenge the status quo and strive for personal excellence. This freedom allows individuals to define their own values, pursue their passions, and ultimately, contribute to the overall richness and dynamism of society.

However, unbridled individualism, unchecked by ethical considerations, can degenerate into a destructive force. When personal ambition trumps all else, the potential for exploitation, disregard for the well-being of others, and ultimately, societal fragmentation increases dramatically. Ayn Rand's philosophy of objectivism, while advocating for individual achievement and rational self-interest, often faces criticism for its potential to justify selfishness and a lack of concern for the vulnerable. A purely egoistic pursuit of individual goals can lead to a world where the ends justify the means, fostering a culture of competition and disregard for ethical constraints. The unraveling of social bonds, the erosion of trust, and the widening of social inequalities can all be attributed to a lack of ethical grounding in an overly individualistic society.

Ethical principles, on the other hand, provide a framework for navigating the complexities of social interaction. They offer guidelines for distinguishing right from wrong, promoting fairness, and fostering compassion. Whether rooted in deontological ethics, emphasizing duty and adherence to universal rules, or consequentialist ethics, prioritizing the outcomes of actions, ethical frameworks serve as a compass, guiding individuals towards actions that benefit not just themselves, but also the wider community. Principles like justice, fairness, and respect for human dignity are essential for maintaining social cohesion and ensuring the protection of vulnerable populations.

The crucial challenge lies in striking a balance between these two seemingly opposing forces. A society that completely suppresses individual expression in the name of ethical conformity risks stagnation and the stifling of innovation. Conversely, a society that elevates individual ambition above all else risks moral decay and the erosion of social solidarity. The ideal, therefore, lies in fostering a culture of **ethical individualism.** This entails cultivating individuals who are both empowered to pursue their own goals and committed to acting in accordance with principles of fairness, compassion, and respect for others.

Achieving this ethical individualism requires a concerted effort on multiple fronts. Education plays a vital role in instilling ethical values and promoting critical thinking skills, enabling individuals to discern the potential consequences of their actions and make informed decisions. Social institutions, from families and communities to legal systems and governments, must also reinforce ethical norms and provide mechanisms for accountability. Furthermore, fostering a culture of empathy and understanding, where individuals are encouraged to consider the perspectives and needs of others, is crucial for mitigating the potential for self-centeredness and fostering a sense of shared responsibility.

The relationship between ethical principles and individualism is a dynamic and essential aspect of a healthy society. Individualism provides the engine for progress and innovation, while ethical principles provide the guiding framework for ensuring that this progress benefits all members of society. The tightrope walk between these two forces requires constant vigilance, critical reflection, and a commitment to cultivating ethical individuals who are both empowered to pursue their own goals and dedicated to contributing to the common good. Only by striking this delicate balance can we hope to create a society that is both vibrant and just, prosperous and compassionate, and truly worthy of the individuals who call it home.

STOICISM AND ITS RELEVANCE IN MODERN LIFE

Principles *of* Stoicism

Stoicism, an ancient Greek philosophy founded in the early 3rd century BCE, offers profound insights into the nature of human existence and the pursuit of virtue. Central to Stoic thought is the belief that individuals can cultivate a resilient mindset through the practice of self-discipline, rationality, and emotional regulation. This philosophy emphasizes the importance of distinguishing between what is within our control and what is not, allowing practitioners to focus their energies on their own actions and responses rather than external circumstances. In a contemporary context, where external influences—such as social media and societal expectations—can lead to anxiety and confusion regarding identity, the principles of Stoicism provide valuable tools for maintaining clarity and purpose.

One of the core tenets of Stoicism is the idea that virtue is the highest good. For Stoics, living in accordance with reason and virtue leads to true happiness, which is not contingent on external factors but is rooted in one's character and choices. This perspective resonates with modern individuals grappling with the pressures of individualism in a collective world. As people navigate their identities, often influenced by social media portrayals, the Stoic focus on internal values encourages a shift away from superficial comparisons and toward a deeper understanding of oneself. By prioritizing personal ethics and virtues, individuals can develop a stronger sense of self that remains intact despite external judgments.

Another essential principle of Stoicism is the acceptance of fate, encapsulated in the concept of "amor fati" or love of fate. This principle teaches that individuals should embrace their circumstances, recognizing that many aspects of life are beyond their control. In a world where uncertainty is prevalent, particularly in the age of rapid technological advancements and shifting social dynamics, Stoicism offers a reassuring framework. By accepting the unpredictable nature of life and focusing on how one responds to challenges, individuals can cultivate resilience. This acceptance does not equate to passivity; rather, it empowers individuals to take proactive steps in shaping their responses and actions, fostering a sense of agency amid chaos.

The Stoic practice of mindfulness, particularly through techniques such as negative visualization, further enhances self-reflection and identity. By contemplating potential challenges and losses, individuals prepare themselves for adversity and cultivate gratitude for what they currently possess. This practice aligns closely with certain Buddhist principles, where mindfulness and awareness of the present moment play significant roles. Integrating these Stoic techniques into daily life can help individuals manage stress and enhance their well-being, as they learn to approach life's uncertainties with equanimity and clarity.

Stoicism encourages individuals to engage with their communities while maintaining a strong sense of individuality. The Stoic belief in cosmopolitanism asserts that all human beings are part of a larger whole, promoting the idea that one's actions should contribute positively to society. This balance between community and individuality is particularly relevant in contemporary discussions about ethics and social responsibility. By applying Stoic principles, individuals can navigate the complexities of their relationships and societal roles, fostering a sense of belonging while honoring their unique identities. In this way, Stoicism not only enriches personal growth but also enhances collective well-being, creating a harmonious interplay between the self and the community.

Stoicism *in the* Face *of* Modern Challenges

Stoicism, an ancient Greek philosophy, offers profound insights that remain relevant in addressing the complexities of modern life. As individuals navigate a landscape dominated by rapid technological advancements and pervasive social media, Stoic principles provide a framework for maintaining resilience and clarity. The core tenets of Stoicism emphasize the importance of focusing on what is within our control while accepting what lies beyond it. This approach can help individuals cultivate a sense of inner peace amid external chaos, allowing for more thoughtful engagement with the world.

In the face of the overwhelming influence of social media, many individuals find themselves grappling with issues of self-identity and validation. Stoicism encourages self-reflection and the development of personal virtues over the pursuit of external approval. By prioritizing internal values and cultivating a sense of self that is not contingent upon online personas or the fleeting nature of likes and shares, individuals can strengthen their sense of identity. This shift in focus allows for a more authentic existence, fostering connections that are grounded in genuine understanding rather than superficial interactions.

The blend of Stoicism and Eastern philosophies, such as Buddhism, can enhance one's ability to cope with modern challenges. Both traditions emphasize mindfulness and the importance of the present moment. By integrating these teachings, individuals can learn to observe their thoughts and emotions without being overwhelmed by them. This practice not only aids in emotional regulation but also promotes a balanced perspective on life's ups and downs, encouraging a sense of gratitude and acceptance that is often overlooked in a fast-paced society.

The ethical implications of individualism in a collective world also resonate with Stoic thought. In an era where personal achievement is often celebrated, Stoicism reminds us of the interconnectedness of all individuals. The philosophy advocates for a sense of duty towards the community, emphasizing that our actions should contribute positively to the collective well-being. By fostering a balance between personal aspirations and community responsibilities, individuals can navigate the ethical dilemmas of modern life while remaining true to their values.

Embracing Stoicism in today's world equips individuals with the tools necessary for navigating the complexities of life with grace and integrity. By cultivating resilience, focusing on personal virtues, and fostering a sense of community, one can achieve a harmonious balance between individuality and collective responsibility. This holistic approach not only enriches personal growth but also contributes to a more compassionate and understanding society, aligning individual actions with the greater good.

Integrating Stoic Practices *into* Daily Life

Integrating Stoic practices into daily life can serve as a powerful approach to enhance personal resilience and ethical decision-making. At its core, Stoicism emphasizes the importance of virtue, wisdom, and self-control, encouraging individuals to focus on what they can control while accepting what they cannot. This mindset is particularly relevant in a contemporary landscape often dominated by external pressures, such as social media and societal expectations, which can distort self-perception and identity. By adopting Stoic principles, individuals can cultivate a sense of inner peace and clarity, allowing for more intentional living that aligns with their values.

One effective way to incorporate Stoic practices is through daily reflection. Setting aside time each day to contemplate one's thoughts and actions can foster greater self-awareness. Journaling, as suggested by many Stoic philosophers, provides a structured method to assess one's responses to various situations. This practice encourages individuals to evaluate their reactions, identify patterns, and consider alternative, more rational responses. Over time, this can lead to a more deliberate and thoughtful approach to challenges, aligning closely with the ethical considerations of individualism in a collective society.

Mindfulness is another key aspect of Stoicism that can be seamlessly integrated into daily routines. By remaining present and fully engaged in the moment, individuals can better understand their emotions and reactions. This practice helps to mitigate the noise created by social media, which often promotes comparison and distraction. Instead of being swept away by external influences, one can cultivate a Stoic detachment, allowing for clearer judgment and a stronger sense of personal identity. This balance between mindfulness and Stoicism can significantly enhance one's ability to navigate the complexities of modern life.

The Stoic practice of negative visualization can provide a profound perspective shift. By contemplating potential losses and challenges, individuals can foster gratitude for what they currently possess while preparing themselves mentally for adversity. This technique not only reinforces resilience but also aligns with the ethical implications of individualism, as it encourages individuals to acknowledge their interconnectedness with others while maintaining a strong sense of self. Embracing this practice can enhance one's ability to engage with the community while remaining grounded in personal values.

Cultivating virtues such as courage, justice, and temperance is fundamental to Stoic philosophy and can be practiced daily through intentional actions. Whether through simple acts of kindness, standing firm in one's beliefs, or practicing moderation in consumption, these virtues can guide behavior and decisions. By integrating these principles into everyday life, individuals strengthen their capacity for ethical decision-making and contribute positively to their communities. This commitment to virtue not only enriches personal identity but also fosters a sense of belonging and responsibility in a collective world, harmonizing individualism with community engagement.

THE INFLUENCE OF EASTERN PHILOSOPHIES ON WESTERN MOTIVATIONAL PRACTICES

Overview *of* Eastern Philosophies

Eastern philosophies encompass a broad spectrum of thought that has shaped cultural, spiritual, and ethical frameworks across Asia and increasingly, the world. At their core, these philosophies often emphasize interconnectedness, balance, and the pursuit of inner peace. Unlike many Western philosophies that prioritize individualism and rational thought, Eastern traditions such as Buddhism, Confucianism, and Taoism advocate for harmony within oneself and with the surrounding community. This perspective encourages individuals to reflect on their place within a larger context, fostering a sense of responsibility towards others while simultaneously nurturing personal growth.

Buddhism, in particular, offers profound insights into the nature of self and identity. Central to Buddhist teachings is the concept of anatta, or non-self, which challenges the notion of a fixed, unchanging identity. This idea has significant implications for self-reflection and the way individuals perceive their identities, particularly in the age of social media where curated personas often clash with authentic self-expression. By embracing the fluidity of identity, individuals can navigate the pressures of societal expectations and cultivate a deeper understanding of their true selves, allowing for more meaningful connections with others.

Stoicism, though rooted in Western thought, finds relevance in many Eastern philosophies, particularly in its emphasis on mindfulness and emotional resilience. Both Stoicism and Eastern traditions advocate for the practice of self-control and the acceptance of circumstances beyond one's control. This alignment offers valuable tools for contemporary individuals who seek to balance personal aspirations with communal responsibilities. By incorporating these teachings into daily life, individuals can develop a robust ethical framework that honors both personal agency and the interconnectedness of human experience.

The influence of Eastern philosophies extends into modern motivational practices as well. Concepts such as mindfulness and meditation have gained popularity in the West, often reinterpreted to fit a more individualistic framework. However, the essence of these practices lies in their ability to foster awareness and compassion, not only for oneself but also for others. By integrating these principles, individuals can cultivate a more balanced approach to personal ambition and social responsibility, reinforcing the idea that personal success should not come at the expense of community welfare.

Navigating the ethics of individualism in contemporary society requires a delicate balance between self-interest and collective well-being. Eastern philosophies provide a rich tapestry of thought that encourages individuals to reflect on their actions and their impact on others. As modern life becomes increasingly complex, drawing from these philosophical traditions can help individuals forge a path that honors both their unique identity and their interconnectedness with the world around them. This holistic approach not only enriches personal lives but also contributes to a more compassionate and cohesive society.

Adoption *of* Eastern Concepts *in* Western Motivational Strategies

The adoption of Eastern concepts in Western motivational strategies signifies a profound shift in how individuals approach personal development and fulfillment. As Western societies increasingly grapple with issues of individualism and community, the integration of principles from Buddhism and other Eastern philosophies has emerged as a valuable resource. These philosophies emphasize interconnectedness, mindfulness, and the pursuit of inner peace, providing a counterbalance to the often competitive and materialistic motivations prevalent in Western culture.

One of the most notable influences is the incorporation of mindfulness practices into motivational frameworks. Mindfulness, rooted in Buddhist traditions, encourages individuals to engage fully with the present moment, fostering self-awareness and emotional regulation. In the context of personal motivation, this practice allows individuals to cultivate a deeper understanding of their desires and goals, leading to more authentic and meaningful pursuits. By shifting the focus from external validation to intrinsic motivation, mindfulness helps individuals align their actions with their values, promoting a more sustainable and ethical approach to personal growth.

The principles of compassion and non-attachment found in Eastern philosophies are increasingly recognized as essential elements of effective motivation. In Western contexts, where success is often measured by individual achievement, the integration of compassion encourages individuals to consider the impact of their actions on others. This shift not only enhances interpersonal relationships but also fosters a sense of community and belonging, counteracting the isolating effects of extreme individualism. Non-attachment, on the other hand, teaches individuals to pursue goals without being overly attached to specific outcomes, reducing anxiety and fear of failure while encouraging resilience.

The influence of Eastern thought on Western motivational practices can also be seen in the rise of holistic approaches to well-being. These approaches advocate for a balance between mental, emotional, and physical health, recognizing that true motivation stems from a comprehensive understanding of oneself. Programs incorporating yoga, meditation, and other Eastern practices are increasingly utilized in corporate environments and personal development workshops, illustrating a growing acknowledgment of the importance of well-rounded personal growth. This holistic perspective not only enhances individual motivation but also aligns with ethical considerations of individualism, emphasizing the responsibility one has toward the collective.

The adoption of Eastern concepts in Western motivational strategies offers a rich framework for navigating the complexities of individualism and community in contemporary society. By integrating mindfulness, compassion, non-attachment, and holistic well-being into personal development practices, individuals can cultivate a more balanced, ethical approach to motivation. This synthesis not only reflects a deeper understanding of the self but also fosters a sense of connection with others, ultimately leading to a more harmonious coexistence in a rapidly changing world.

CASE STUDIES:

Eastern Influence in Popular Culture

Eastern philosophies, particularly Buddhism, have significantly influenced various aspects of popular culture, manifesting in art, film, literature, and even social media. This influence can be observed in the themes and narratives that emphasize mindfulness, interconnectedness, and the balance between individual desires and community well-being. For instance, films like "The Matrix" illustrate concepts of reality and illusion that resonate with Buddhist teachings on perception and enlightenment. Such representations invite audiences to reflect on their own lives, challenging them to consider the nature of existence and the pursuit of happiness.

In literature, authors like Haruki Murakami have brought elements of Eastern thought to Western readers, weaving philosophical inquiries into engaging narratives. His works often explore existential questions, the search for identity, and the notion of self within the larger fabric of society. These themes resonate with Stoic principles, highlighting the importance of accepting circumstances beyond one's control while remaining true to oneself. As readers engage with these texts, they are encouraged to reflect on their own beliefs and values, fostering a deeper understanding of the interplay between individualism and collective consciousness.

Social media platforms have further facilitated the spread of Eastern philosophies, allowing for a dynamic exchange of ideas across cultural boundaries. Influencers and thought leaders often share insights rooted in mindfulness and compassion, encouraging followers to adopt practices that promote self-reflection and personal growth. This digital space serves as a modern agora, where discussions about the ethics of individualism and community engagement thrive. Users are prompted to consider how their online identities align with their real-world values, often leading to a re-evaluation of their roles within both their immediate circles and the global community.

Many contemporary motivational practices draw heavily from Eastern philosophies, emphasizing holistic well-being over material success. Mindfulness meditation and yoga, for example, have gained immense popularity in the West, encouraging individuals to cultivate awareness and presence in their daily lives. These practices not only promote personal health but also foster a sense of connection with others, bridging the gap between individual aspirations and communal responsibilities. By integrating these principles into their routines, individuals often find a greater sense of balance, navigating the complexities of modern life with a renewed perspective.

The integration of Buddhist ethics into decision-making processes has profound implications for how individuals approach challenges and relationships. By prioritizing compassion and understanding, individuals can make choices that reflect both personal values and the well-being of their communities. This ethical framework encourages a shift away from rigid individualism towards a more nuanced understanding of self in relation to others. As popular culture continues to reflect and shape these ideas, it becomes essential for individuals to consciously engage with the teachings of Eastern philosophies, fostering a more harmonious existence within the collective human experience.

ETHICS OF INDIVIDUALISM IN CONTEMPORARY SOCIETY

Moral Implications of Individualistic Practices

The moral implications of individualistic practices are versatile, especially when viewed through the lens of different philosophical traditions. Individualism, often celebrated in Western cultures as a hallmark of personal freedom and self-expression, raises significant ethical questions. It can foster a sense of autonomy and self-determination, but it can also lead to isolation, neglect of communal responsibilities, and an erosion of social bonds. When individuals prioritize their personal desires over the collective good, the ethical fabric of society risks fraying, creating a tension between personal integrity and social obligation.

In our contemporary society, individualism stands as a cornerstone of our cultural consciousness, shaping our beliefs, behaviors, and aspirations. While its advocacy for personal freedom, autonomy, and self-expression has forged a path towards innovation and social progress, it also raises profound ethical questions that require our scrutiny. The balance between the rights of the individual and the welfare of the collective challenges our moral framework. This essay explores the ethical dimensions of individualism, dissecting its implications for personal responsibility, community engagement, and societal cohesion, ultimately arguing that a reflective and responsible approach to individualistic practices can foster both personal fulfillment and greater social harmony.

Understanding Individualism

Individualism, while often celebrated as the essence of freedom, calls for a nuanced understanding. At its core, individualism emphasizes the significance of the self—its rights, values, and unique identity. Rooted in Enlightenment thought, it champions the belief that each person possesses intrinsic worth and agency. This ideology has paved the way for democratic principles, human rights movements, and a culture of innovation. However, individualism is not without its drawbacks. An overemphasis on the self can lead to egotism, a detachment from communal bonds, and a disregard for collective well-being.

To appreciate the impact of individualism fully, one must recognize its dual nature. It can be empowering, driving individuals to seek their true potential and challenge societal norms. Yet, it may also engender an environment where relational ties become secondary, giving rise to alienation and societal fragmentation. The challenge lies in finding a moral equilibrium that acknowledges the importance of the self while fostering compassion, solidarity, and shared responsibility.

THE MORAL IMPLICATIONS OF INDIVIDUALISTIC PRACTICES

Personal Responsibility

One of the primary ethical considerations arising from individualistic practices is the concept of personal responsibility. Individualism champions the idea that one must carve out their path and take ownership of their choices. This notion promotes accountability, encouraging individuals to strive towards self-improvement and ethical decision-making. In a society that values personal agency, the expectation is that individuals should not only seek their own success but also recognize the moral weight of their actions upon others.

However, this focus on personal responsibility can, at times, devolve into a blame culture, where societal challenges are solely attributed to individual failings. Such a perspective can lead to the devaluation of systemic factors that contribute to inequality, injustice, and marginalization. A richer understanding of moral responsibility recognizes the interplay between individual actions and collective conditions. As ethically aware individuals, we must advocate for systems that promote fairness and justice, ensuring that our pursuit of self-interest does not undermine the rights and dignities of others.

Community Engagement

While individualism celebrates the self, it is vital to acknowledge the communal context in which we exist. Human beings are inherently social creatures, and our individual identities are often shaped and enriched by our relationships with others. An ethical approach to individualism recognizes the necessity of community engagement and cooperative dynamics. It posits that our aspirations cannot be fully realized in isolation; instead, they thrive in synergy with others.

Community engagement fosters empathy and social responsibility. When individuals actively contribute to their communities, they cultivate a sense of belonging and purpose. They also combat the isolation that can arise from hyper-individualistic practices. Participating in collective efforts encourages a shared vision of progress, empowering individuals to contribute to the greater good. Ultimately, the ethical import of individualism is not solely about self-actualization but rather harmonizing individual aspirations with communal welfare.

Societal Cohesion

The tension between individualism and communal harmony is further reflected in societal cohesion. A society dominated by extreme individualistic practices may grapple with social fragmentation, diminished trust, and weakened social bonds. Such disintegration endangers the fabric of democracy, as civic engagement declines and shared values erode. Hence, to cultivate a morally responsible individualism, we must actively engage in practices that promote inclusivity and solidarity.

Ethically, it is essential to recalibrate our understanding of success. A narrow definition of achievement—rooted in personal gain, wealth, or status—neglects the importance of contributing to a cohesive and supportive society. Shifting our values toward a more holistic vision of success entails recognizing the interconnectedness of our pursuits. It involves celebrating not just personal accomplishments but also collective endeavors, with an emphasis on shared responsibility and collaborative growth.

The Path Forward: A Balanced Ethical Individualism

As we navigate the complexities of contemporary society, the question arises: how can we reconcile individualism with the moral imperatives of community and social justice? The answer rests in cultivating a balanced ethical individualism—an approach that promotes personal empowerment while emphasizing relational and civic responsibilities.

1. Reflective Self-Consciousness

A critical first step towards balanced individualism is cultivating reflective self-consciousness. This involves a deeper understanding of one's identity, motivations, and the impact of one's choices on others. By fostering self-awareness, individuals can navigate their aspirations with sensitivity to the ethical dimensions of their actions. Engaging in practices such as introspection, dialogue, and reflection encourages a sense of moral agency that transcends self-interest.

2. Encouraging Cooperative Action

Next, individuals ought to engage in cooperative actions that resonate with communal goals. Simple acts of kindness, community service, and advocacy for social causes foster a sense of belonging and mutual support. By participating in collective endeavors, individuals reaffirm their interconnectedness and contribute to the welfare of society. Emphasizing shared objectives can serve to harmonize individual aspirations with collective well-being.

3. Promoting Education and Dialogue

Institute educational programs that highlight the importance of ethical individualism. These programs should teach critical thinking, ethical reasoning, and the impact of individual choices on society. Encouraging open dialogues about individual rights and communal responsibilities fosters a more profound understanding of ethical practices, enabling individuals to navigate the paradoxes of individualism responsibly.

As we reflect on the ethical dimensions of individualism in contemporary society, we are reminded that individual rights and communal responsibilities are not mutually exclusive. The moral implications of individualistic practices extend far beyond self-fulfillment; they encompass a broader understanding of our roles within the social fabric. By embracing a balanced ethical individualism—rooted in self-awareness, cooperation, and community engagement—we not only enrich our lives but also foster a more just, cohesive, and empathetic society.

The path forward requires us to confront the challenges inherent in an increasingly individualistic world. It beckons us to champion our personal freedoms while steadfastly honoring the bonds that unite us as human beings. Only then can we transcend the limits of individualism and contribute meaningfully to a future that recognizes the dignity and worth of all individuals within a thriving community.

In the context of Buddhism, individualistic practices challenge the core tenets of interdependence and compassion. While Buddhism acknowledges the importance of personal insight and enlightenment, it simultaneously emphasizes the interconnectedness of all beings. Thus, a purely individualistic approach may conflict with the Buddhist principle of recognizing the suffering of others and the moral responsibility to alleviate it. This dichotomy highlights the need for individuals to reflect on how their pursuits may impact the broader community, encouraging a balance between self-realization and social responsibility.

Stoicism provides a philosophical framework that can mediate the tension between individualism and communal ethics. By advocating for self-control, virtue, and rationality, Stoicism encourages individuals to focus on what they can control while acknowledging their responsibilities to others. This perspective fosters resilience in the face of adversity and promotes a sense of duty towards the community. In modern life, Stoicism serves as a reminder that individual achievements are often interwoven with the contributions and sacrifices of others, urging a more ethical approach to personal success that does not disregard the collective.

Integrating Buddhist principles into decision-making can offer practical guidance for navigating the moral implications of individualistic practices. By cultivating mindfulness and compassion, individuals can better assess the impact of their actions on themselves and their communities. This integration not only enriches personal growth but also fosters a sense of shared humanity, prompting individuals to consider how their individual pursuits align with the welfare of others. Ultimately, the challenge lies in finding a harmonious balance between celebrating individual autonomy and recognizing the ethical importance of community, allowing for a more holistic approach to living in a collective world.

Balancing Personal Freedom *with* Social Responsibility

Balancing personal freedom with social responsibility is a complex endeavor that requires individuals to navigate their desires and aspirations within the context of their communities. In an increasingly interconnected world, the choices we make as individuals do not exist in a vacuum; they ripple outward, influencing others and shaping societal norms. This dynamic interplay can be examined through various philosophical lenses, including Buddhism and Western thought, which provide valuable insights into the importance of finding equilibrium between self-expression and communal well-being.

Buddhism emphasizes interdependence and the notion that individual actions have far-reaching consequences. This perspective encourages individuals to consider how their freedoms impact others, fostering a sense of responsibility that extends beyond mere compliance with social norms. In contrast, Western philosophy often champions individualism, celebrating personal autonomy and self-determination. However, the challenge lies in reconciling these often opposing views, recognizing that while personal freedom is essential, it must be exercised with an awareness of its implications for the wider community.

Social media serves as a contemporary arena where the struggle between individual expression and collective responsibility is particularly pronounced. Platforms that allow for self-reflection and identity exploration can also lead to negative repercussions, such as cyberbullying or the spread of misinformation. As adults engage with these platforms, they are faced with the ethical dilemma of prioritizing their right to self-expression while being mindful of the potential harm their words and actions may inflict on others. Striking a balance in this digital landscape requires a commitment to ethical engagement, where the values of respect and empathy guide interactions.

Stoicism, a school of thought rooted in the importance of virtue and wisdom, offers practical tools for navigating this balance. By practicing self-control and focusing on what is within their power, individuals can cultivate a sense of agency that aligns personal goals with social obligations. Stoicism teaches that true freedom is found not in unchecked self-indulgence but in the ability to act in accordance with reason and ethical principles. This perspective encourages adults to reflect on their responsibilities to others while pursuing their own paths, fostering a harmonious relationship between personal ambitions and social duties.

The integration of Eastern philosophies, such as Buddhism, with Western motivational practices can help create a more balanced approach to individualism in contemporary society. By embracing the interconnectedness of all beings and recognizing the impact of one's actions, individuals can cultivate a sense of responsibility that complements their desire for personal freedom. This synthesis not only enhances self-awareness but also promotes a more compassionate and engaged society, where the pursuit of personal goals occurs hand-in-hand with a commitment to the collective good. In navigating the ethics of individualism, it becomes clear that personal freedom and social responsibility are not mutually exclusive but rather two essential components of a well-rounded and ethical life.

Individual Rights vs. Collective Good

In the discourse surrounding individual rights versus the collective good, a nuanced understanding emerges, particularly when viewed through the lens of both Eastern and Western philosophies. Individual rights, often championed in Western thought, emphasize personal autonomy, freedom of expression, and self-determination. This tradition is deeply rooted in Enlightenment ideals that valorize the individual as the fundamental unit of society. In contrast, Eastern philosophies, particularly Buddhism, advocate for interdependence and the interconnectedness of all beings, suggesting that personal well-being is intrinsically tied to the health of the community. This divergence invites a critical examination of how these philosophies inform our understanding of ethics and morality in modern life.

The tension between individualism and collectivism is particularly pronounced in contemporary society, where social media has transformed the way identities are constructed and perceived. Platforms that encourage self-expression can simultaneously foster a sense of isolation, as individuals curate their lives for public consumption. This dynamic raises important ethical questions about the nature of identity and its relation to community. Are we sacrificing genuine connections for the sake of individual recognition? The Buddhist principle of 'anatta,' or non-self, encourages us to reflect on the illusion of a fixed identity, highlighting the importance of community and shared experiences in shaping who we are.

Incorporating Stoic philosophy into this discussion offers a practical framework for navigating the balance between individual rights and collective responsibility. Stoicism teaches the importance of virtue and ethical conduct as a means of contributing to the greater good while maintaining personal integrity. Stoics emphasize the need to focus on what is within our control, encouraging individuals to act with wisdom and compassion. This approach aligns with Buddhist teachings, which advocate for mindful decision-making that considers the consequences of our actions on others, thus fostering a more harmonious coexistence.

The influence of Eastern philosophies on Western motivational practices further complicates the individual-collective dichotomy. Many contemporary self-help movements draw heavily from Buddhist concepts, emphasizing mindfulness, compassion, and the understanding of suffering. These principles not only enhance individual well-being but also promote a sense of social responsibility. By integrating these philosophies into everyday decision-making, individuals can cultivate a mindset that prioritizes both personal growth and the welfare of the community, thereby reinforcing the idea that true fulfillment arises from a balance of self-interest and altruism.

The challenge lies in finding a harmonious integration of individual rights and the collective good in our daily lives. As adults navigating the complexities of modern society, it is essential to reflect on our values and the broader implications of our choices. By fostering an ethic of interdependence, where individual aspirations are aligned with communal well-being, we can work toward a society that honors both the self and the collective. This balance not only enriches our personal experiences but also cultivates a sense of belonging and purpose, essential in a world increasingly marked by division and isolation.

THE BALANCE BETWEEN COMMUNITY AND INDIVIDUALITY IN MODERN LIFE

The Role *of* Community *in* Shaping Identity

The role of community in shaping identity is a multifaceted concept that draws from various philosophical traditions and modern social dynamics. At the heart of community lies the network of relationships that individuals engage in, which profoundly influence their perceptions of self. From a Buddhist perspective, the interconnectedness of all beings emphasizes that one's identity is not isolated but rather a product of interactions with others. This view aligns with Western philosophical thoughts that recognize the social nature of human beings, where identity is often formed in relation to societal norms, values, and expectations.

Stoicism, with its emphasis on personal virtue and wisdom, offers a framework for understanding the balance between community and individuality. Stoics argue that while individuals are responsible for their own actions and thoughts, they are also part of a larger whole. This philosophy encourages individuals to cultivate resilience and inner strength, allowing them to engage with their communities meaningfully without losing sight of their personal values. In this way, Stoicism can serve as a guide for navigating the complexities of identity in a collective world, promoting a sense of belonging while fostering personal integrity.

Eastern philosophies, particularly Buddhism, provide additional insights into how community influences identity. The teachings of interdependence highlight that one's sense of self is deeply rooted in relationships and social contexts. This perspective encourages individuals to cultivate compassion and mindfulness within their communities, leading to a more profound understanding of both self and others. By integrating these principles into everyday decision-making, individuals can create a more harmonious balance between their personal identities and their roles within their communities, ultimately fostering a sense of collective well-being.

The relationship between community and individuality in modern life raises important ethical considerations. As individuals seek to assert their identities, they must also navigate the responsibilities and expectations that come with being part of a community. The ethics of individualism must be balanced with a commitment to the collective good, prompting reflections on how personal choices impact others. Embracing this duality can lead to a richer understanding of identity that honors both personal aspirations and communal connections, ensuring that individuals do not merely exist in isolation but thrive within a supportive network of relationships.

Tensions Between Individual Desires *and* Community Needs

Tensions between individual desires and community needs have long been a focal point of philosophical discourse, particularly in the intersection of Eastern and Western thought. In many Eastern philosophies, including Buddhism, there is a strong emphasis on the interconnectedness of all beings. This perspective encourages individuals to consider the impact of their actions on the community, promoting a sense of collective responsibility. Conversely, Western philosophical traditions often celebrate individualism, positing that personal freedom and self-expression are paramount. This divergence creates a complex landscape where personal ambitions can sometimes clash with communal requirements, leading to ethical dilemmas that are particularly relevant in modern society.

Incorporating principles from Stoicism can provide a framework for addressing this conflict. Stoicism teaches that individuals should strive for virtue and wisdom, recognizing that their actions impact both themselves and the community at large. By fostering self-control and resilience, Stoicism encourages individuals to evaluate their desires critically. This reflective practice can help individuals align their personal goals with the greater good, cultivating a sense of duty to the community. The Stoic approach emphasizes that true fulfillment comes not from the pursuit of personal desires alone, but from contributing to the welfare of others, thus bridging the gap between individuality and collectivity.

Eastern philosophies offer complementary insights into this balance. The Buddhist principle of interdependence highlights that individual happiness is intricately linked to the well-being of others. This understanding fosters compassion and encourages individuals to act in ways that promote harmony within the community. By integrating Buddhist mindfulness practices into decision-making, individuals can cultivate awareness of their impact on others, which can lead to more ethical choices. This approach not only benefits the community but also enhances personal fulfillment, as individuals find deeper meaning in their contributions to the collective.

Navigating the tensions between individual desires and community needs requires a nuanced understanding of both personal and collective ethics. Adults today must grapple with the implications of their choices in an increasingly interconnected world. By drawing from both Eastern and Western philosophies, individuals can cultivate a more balanced perspective that honors personal aspirations while acknowledging the importance of community. This ethical integration can lead to a more harmonious existence, where individual fulfillment is achieved alongside the nurturing of communal bonds, thus creating a more resilient society that values both the self and the collective.

FINDING HARMONY:
Practical Strategies

Finding harmony in a world that often emphasizes individualism over collectivism requires practical strategies that draw from both Eastern and Western philosophies. One effective approach is to cultivate mindfulness, a principle rooted deeply in Buddhist practice. Mindfulness encourages individuals to remain present and fully engaged in the moment, which can help mitigate the distractions often posed by social media. By practicing mindfulness, one can develop a greater awareness of their thoughts and feelings, allowing for more intentional self-reflection and a clearer understanding of personal identity. This clarity can foster a sense of balance between individual aspirations and communal responsibilities.

Another strategy to find harmony involves the application of Stoic principles. Stoicism teaches the importance of distinguishing between what we can control and what we cannot. In the context of social media, individuals are often bombarded with external opinions and influences that can skew self-perception. By focusing on internal values and accepting the limitations of external validation, individuals can cultivate resilience and a stronger sense of self. This Stoic perspective allows for a healthier engagement with social media, promoting self-reflection based on personal standards rather than societal pressures.

Integrating Eastern philosophies can also provide valuable insights for decision-making in everyday life. The Buddhist concept of interdependence emphasizes the interconnectedness of all beings. By recognizing that personal choices impact the community, individuals can develop a more ethical framework for their actions. This awareness encourages decisions that not only serve personal goals but also contribute positively to the collective well-being. Such an approach fosters harmony by aligning individual desires with the greater good, creating a more cohesive social fabric.

Additionally, embracing the idea of community can play a crucial role in balancing individuality with collective identity. Engaging in community activities or volunteer work can reinforce the notion that personal fulfillment is often linked to the welfare of others. This collective engagement cultivates a sense of belonging, which is vital in a hyper-individualistic society. By participating in shared experiences, individuals can enrich their understanding of themselves while also recognizing the value of collaboration and mutual support, ultimately leading to a more harmonious existence.

The practice of gratitude can serve as a practical strategy to enhance harmony in daily life. Regularly acknowledging and appreciating both personal achievements and community contributions fosters a mindset that values interconnectedness. Gratitude can shift focus from individual success to a more collective perspective on growth and fulfillment. This shift is particularly relevant in modern society, where competition can overshadow collaboration. By fostering an attitude of gratitude, individuals can cultivate deeper connections with others, enhancing both personal identity and community ties, leading to a more harmonious balance between the self and society.

INTEGRATING BUDDHIST PRINCIPLES INTO EVERYDAY DECISION MAKING

Mindfulness *as a* Decision-Making Tool

Mindfulness serves as a powerful decision-making tool, particularly in our fast-paced and often chaotic modern world. By cultivating a mindful approach, individuals can enhance their awareness of thoughts, emotions, and external influences that shape their decisions. This heightened awareness allows for a more deliberate consideration of options, enabling individuals to align their choices with their values and long-term goals. In the context of the intersection of Buddhism and Western philosophy, mindfulness becomes a bridge that connects ancient wisdom with contemporary ethical considerations, fostering a deeper understanding of individualism within a collective framework.

Incorporating mindfulness into decision-making processes encourages individuals to pause and reflect before acting. This practice is especially relevant in today's society, where social media often pressures individuals to respond impulsively to stimuli. By taking a moment to breathe and observe one's thoughts, individuals can step back from the noise and distractions of external opinions. This practice not only promotes clarity but also helps to mitigate the influence of fleeting emotions, allowing for decisions grounded in reason rather than reaction. As adults navigate the complexities of identity shaped by online interactions, mindfulness can serve as a stabilizing force, encouraging authenticity and self-reflection.

The principles of Stoicism resonate with the practice of mindfulness, as both emphasize the importance of self-control and rational thought. Mindfulness encourages individuals to recognize their emotional responses while simultaneously fostering a sense of detachment from those emotions. This aligns with Stoic teachings that advocate for the examination of one's thoughts and feelings without becoming overwhelmed by them. Consequently, integrating mindfulness into decision-making can lead to a more balanced approach, where individuals weigh their choices against their ethical beliefs and the potential impact on their community.

Buddhism contributes valuable insights into the nature of decision-making. The Buddhist concept of interdependence highlights the interconnectedness of all beings, prompting individuals to consider how their decisions affect not only themselves but also the broader community. This perspective encourages a sense of responsibility and ethical consideration, fostering a mindset that values collective well-being alongside personal aspirations. By integrating these principles, individuals can cultivate a decision-making process that respects both individual desires and the needs of the community, creating a harmonious balance between self and society.

Ultimately, mindfulness as a decision-making tool promotes a more thoughtful and ethical approach to navigating the challenges of modern life. It empowers individuals to engage in self-reflection, fostering a deeper understanding of their motivations and values. As adults strive to balance individuality with communal responsibilities, mindfulness offers a framework for making choices that are not only personally fulfilling but also contribute positively to the collective. By embracing this practice, individuals can navigate the complexities of contemporary society with greater clarity, compassion, and ethical integrity.

Compassion *and* Ethical Considerations

Compassion serves as a fundamental pillar within both Buddhist philosophy and various Western ethical frameworks, creating a bridge between individual well-being and collective responsibility. In navigating the complexities of modern life, where individualism often clashes with communal values, understanding the role of compassion can enhance our ethical decision-making. Both Buddhism and Western philosophies emphasize the importance of compassion—not only as a moral imperative but also as a practical tool for fostering deeper connections within our communities. By cultivating compassion, individuals can mitigate the inherent tensions between personal desires and the needs of the group, ultimately enriching both their own lives and those of others.

The ethical considerations surrounding compassion require us to examine the implications of our actions on a broader scale. In the digital age, social media platforms can amplify both individual expression and collective discourse, often blurring the lines between personal identity and societal influence. The quest for self-reflection is complicated by the curated identities presented online, which may lead to a detachment from authentic experiences. By embracing compassion, individuals can critically assess their online interactions, prioritizing empathy over judgment. This shift not only aids personal growth but also fosters a more supportive and understanding online community, countering the divisive nature of much contemporary discourse.

In the context of Stoicism, compassion aligns with the Stoic emphasis on rationality and the interconnectedness of humanity. Stoics advocate for recognizing shared human experiences, which can enhance our capacity for compassion. This understanding fosters resilience and encourages individuals to respond to adversity with empathy rather than apathy. By integrating Stoic principles with compassionate action, individuals can navigate challenges with a balanced perspective, ensuring that their responses contribute positively to both their own well-being and that of others. Thus, the intersection of Stoicism and compassion presents a viable path for ethical living in a self-focused society.

Eastern philosophies, particularly Buddhism, highlight the significance of compassion as a means of alleviating suffering. Integrating these principles into everyday decision-making can be transformative. When individuals consciously apply compassion in their interactions— whether in personal relationships, workplace environments, or community engagement—they create a ripple effect that extends beyond their immediate circles. This practice not only enhances personal fulfillment but also contributes to a more compassionate society, where the well-being of the individual is intrinsically linked to the health of the community. The ethical imperative of compassion becomes a guiding principle for individuals striving to balance their own needs with those of others.

Ultimately, the exploration of compassion and ethical considerations underscores the importance of maintaining a balance between individualism and collectivism in contemporary society. As individuals navigate the complexities of modern life, they must grapple with the ethical implications of their choices. Embracing compassion facilitates a deeper understanding of the interconnectedness of human experiences, promoting a more harmonious coexistence. By fostering a compassionate mindset, individuals can effectively navigate the challenges of individualism, contributing to a collective ethos that values both personal growth and communal well-being.

Practical Exercises *for* Everyday Living

Practical exercises for everyday living serve as vital tools for individuals seeking to navigate the complexities of individualism in a collective society. By integrating principles from both Buddhism and Western philosophy, these exercises encourage self-reflection and foster a deeper understanding of one's identity. Engaging with these practices can lead to enhanced emotional intelligence and more meaningful connections with others, ultimately helping individuals balance their personal aspirations with the needs of their community.

One effective practice is mindfulness meditation, which aligns well with both Buddhist teachings and modern psychological approaches. Setting aside a few minutes each day to focus on the present moment can significantly enhance self-awareness. This practice involves observing thoughts and emotions without judgment, allowing individuals to gain insight into their habitual responses and biases. By cultivating mindfulness, one can develop a clearer sense of self that is less influenced by external validation, particularly from social media, thus fostering a more authentic identity.

Another practical exercise is the **daily reflection on ethical dilemmas encountered in everyday life**. This can be done through journaling or discussions with peers. By evaluating decisions through the lenses of various ethical frameworks, such as virtue ethics from Western philosophy or the Four Noble Truths from Buddhism, individuals can explore the implications of their choices. This practice helps clarify personal values and guides individuals in making decisions that honor both their individuality and their responsibilities to others, reinforcing the balance between self and community.

Contributing to the community not only strengthens social bonds but also cultivates a sense of purpose and belonging. Whether through volunteering or simply helping a neighbor, these actions can shift the focus from individual desires to collective well-being. This shift is particularly important in an age dominated by social media, where the emphasis on personal branding can overshadow the value of community engagement.

Practice of gratitude can transform one's perspective on individualism and collective identity. By regularly acknowledging the contributions of others and expressing appreciation for the interconnectedness of life, individuals can foster a mindset that values both personal achievement and community support. This practice can include writing thank-you notes or maintaining a gratitude journal, which serves as a reminder that personal successes often arise within a network of support and shared experiences. Embracing gratitude not only enhances individual well-being but also nurtures healthier relationships, reinforcing the ethical principles of coexistence and mutual respect in a complex world.

Reflections *on* Personal Growth *and* Collective Well-Being

THE JOURNEY OF SELF-DISCOVERY

Navigating Individualism in a Complex World

The journey of self-discovery is a profound and multifaceted exploration, often marked by a series of pivotal moments that challenge our pre-conceived notions and compel us to delve into the depths of our identity. It's a process of peeling back layers of learned behavior, societal conditioning, and external expectations to unearth the authentic self that lies beneath. In the context of individualism, prevalent in many Western societies, this journey becomes even more significant and complex, as it navigates the delicate and often tension-filled balance between personal beliefs, desires, and freedoms, and the pervasive expectations of the wider community. The intersection of Eastern philosophies like Buddhism and established Western philosophical traditions provides a rich and insightful framework for understanding this intricate process of self-discovery. Both traditions, despite their diverse origins and approaches, emphasize the importance of introspection, mindfulness, and the enduring quest for authenticity. By critically examining and integrating the wisdom offered by these philosophies, individuals can hope to cultivate a deeper, more nuanced awareness of themselves, their values, and their place within the intricate tapestry of collective existence.

The rise of platforms designed to encourage constant sharing and connectivity has created a powerful, albeit often ambiguous, force in shaping our understanding of ourselves. While social media can undoubtedly serve as a mirror, reflecting our thoughts, experiences, and aspirations back to us, it can also create an artificial environment that pressures individuals to conform to curated identities, designed to garner approval and validation. This inherent duality necessitates a critical and discerning approach to self-discovery in the digital age, prompting individuals to engage in mindful reflection about the often stark contrast between their carefully constructed digital personas and their more vulnerable, authentic selves. The challenge lies in consciously leveraging social media as a tool for genuine self-exploration, a platform for connecting with like-minded individuals and sharing meaningful experiences, while simultaneously remaining vigilant against its potential to distort self-perception, foster unrealistic expectations, and ultimately hinder the organic process of self-discovery. The constant comparison with others, the pressure to project an idealized image, and the addictive nature of online validation can all contribute to a fragmented and distorted sense of self, making the journey to authenticity even more challenging.

Stoicism, with its enduring emphasis on personal virtue, resilience in the face of adversity, and acceptance of what lies beyond our control, offers particularly valuable and practical insights into the process of self-discovery. This ancient philosophy encourages individuals to focus their energies on what is truly within their control — their thoughts, actions, and reactions — and to cultivate an inner life grounded in reason, virtue, and a deep understanding of their own values. By diligently applying Stoic principles to the challenges and complexities of modern life, individuals can foster a profound sense of agency over their own lives, regardless of external circumstances. The daily practice of reflecting on one's thoughts, motivations, and actions through a Stoic lens can significantly enhance self-awareness and promote a more profound understanding of one's core values and enduring motivations. This introspective approach, coupled with the Stoic emphasis on living in accordance with nature and accepting the impermanence of all things, can ultimately guide individuals on their journey toward authentic self-discovery, providing them with the tools to navigate life's inevitable challenges with grace, wisdom, and unwavering self-reliance.

Eastern philosophies, particularly those rooted in Buddhism and its emphasis on mindfulness, meditation, and the interconnectedness of all things, have increasingly influenced Western motivational practices and approaches to personal growth. Concepts such as mindfulness, the impermanence of self, and the practice of non-attachment challenge the rigid notions of identity often prevalent in individualistic cultures. By integrating these principles into everyday decision-making, individuals can cultivate a more fluid and adaptable understanding of the self, viewing identity not as a fixed and immutable state, but rather as a continuous journey of learning, growth, and self-transformation. This perspective encourages openness to change, adaptability in the face of adversity, and a greater willingness to embrace new experiences and perspectives, allowing individuals to navigate their chosen paths with greater ease and acceptance, even amidst the often overwhelming pressures of societal expectations and the inherent uncertainties of life. Embracing the Buddhist notion of impermanence can be particularly liberating, freeing individuals from the need to cling to rigid self-definitions and allowing them to embrace the ever-changing nature of reality.

The ethics of individualism in contemporary society necessitate a thoughtful and ongoing examination of the intricate interplay between community and individuality. As individuals embark on their personal journeys of self-discovery, they must consciously consider how their personal identities both contribute to and are shaped by the communities in which they reside. Striking a harmonious balance between personal authenticity and social responsibility is absolutely crucial for creating a society that fosters both individual flourishing and collective well-being. By recognizing that individual growth can readily coexist with communal well-being, and that active participation in the community can itself be a powerful catalyst for self-discovery, adults can foster a more integrated and holistic approach to identity that honors both the unique needs and aspirations of the self and the shared values and responsibilities of the collective. This nuanced understanding ultimately enriches their journeys of self-discovery, transforming them into more compassionate, engaged, and contributing members of society, capable of navigating the complexities of the modern world with wisdom, empathy, and a deep sense of purpose. The journey of self-discovery is not a solitary endeavor, but rather a collaborative process that unfolds in the context of our relationships with others and our participation in the wider world.

A CALL TO ETHICAL ACTION:

Weaving Wisdom *for a* Harmonious Future

Moving forward in an increasingly complex and interconnected world demands a profound commitment to ethical action, one that skillfully balances individual needs with a deep sense of collective responsibility. The rich tapestry woven from the threads of Buddhism and Western philosophy offers invaluable insights into how we might effectively navigate this often-delicate balance. By embracing foundational principles such as mindfulness, compassion, and the inherent interconnectedness of all things, we can cultivate a deeper understanding of our roles within our communities, both local and global. This call to ethical action strongly encourages adults to embark on a journey of self-reflection, critically examining their personal values and meticulously considering the broader implications of their choices, particularly in an era increasingly dominated by the pervasive influence of social media and the relentless march of rapid technological advancements.

Stoicism, with its unwavering emphasis on personal virtue, inner resilience, and the acceptance of what lies beyond our control, remains remarkably relevant and profoundly useful in today's relentlessly fast-paced and often chaotic world. At its core, Stoicism teaches us to diligently focus our energies on what we can directly influence – our thoughts, actions, and reactions – and to respond to external challenges and unforeseen adversities with equanimity, a state of mental calmness and composure. By consciously integrating Stoic principles into the very fabric of our daily lives, we can develop a stronger and more robust ethical framework, one that consistently emphasizes personal responsibility and accountability while simultaneously acknowledging our profound and unbreakable interconnectedness with others within the vast human family. This powerful approach not only empowers individuals to act with integrity, guided by a strong moral compass, but also fosters a palpable sense of community, born from the recognition that our seemingly small actions have significant and far-reaching consequences, rippling outwards to affect the lives of those around us, both near and far. The potential synergy between Stoicism and Eastern philosophies, such as Buddhism and Confucianism, can effectively guide us toward a more meaningful and impactful ethical action, one that honors both the inherent value of individuality and the vital importance of collective welfare.

The growing influence of Eastern philosophies on Western motivational practices and self-help methodologies highlights the crucial need for a more holistic, integrated, and balanced approach to personal development and fulfillment. Core concepts such as compassion for self and others, the recognition of interdependence as a fundamental truth, and the relentless pursuit of wisdom as a lifelong endeavor can significantly enhance our understanding of what truly constitutes success and lasting fulfillment in life. By thoughtfully applying these principles, we can redefine our motivations, consciously shifting away from a purely individualistic, ego-driven perspective to one that genuinely values community well-being and the common good. This fundamental reorientation invites us to engage in ethical actions that actively contribute to the betterment of society, enriching not only our own lives but also the lives of those around us, fostering a sense of shared purpose and collective upliftment. Embracing this balanced and compassionate approach enables us to cultivate a more just, equitable, and compassionate society, characterized by empathy, understanding, and a commitment to the well-being of all.

To foster such a society, ethical action must extend beyond the individual and become embedded within institutions and organizations. Corporations, governments, and educational systems must prioritize ethical considerations in their decision-making processes. This requires transparency, accountability, and a willingness to challenge unethical practices. Furthermore, education plays a vital role in cultivating ethical awareness and critical thinking skills. By incorporating ethical frameworks into curricula, we can equip future generations with the tools they need to navigate complex moral dilemmas. This also involves promoting interdisciplinary approaches that integrate philosophical insights with practical applications in various fields such as business, technology, and healthcare.

Ultimately, the greatest challenge lies in skillfully integrating these diverse and often complementary philosophical insights into our everyday decision-making processes, at every level of society. As we strive to move forward on our personal and collective journeys, navigating the complexities and challenges of the 21st century, we must remain perpetually vigilant in our ethical commitments, constantly questioning our motivations and biases, seeking alignment between our deeply held values and our concrete actions. This requires a persistent and unwavering dedication to self-reflection, striving to understand the underlying assumptions that shape our perspectives and influence our choices. We must also remain open to the profound wisdom offered by both Eastern and Western traditions, allowing ourselves to learn from the diverse perspectives and experiences that shape the human story. By embracing this ongoing process of learning and self-discovery, we can navigate the complexities of modern life with a greater sense of purpose, direction, and ethical clarity, fostering a culture that champions both individual expression and collective responsibility, recognizing that true progress lies in the harmonious integration of these seemingly opposing forces. The call to ethical action is not merely an abstract philosophical invitation; it is a concrete and necessary step toward a more harmonious, sustainable, and fulfilling existence in an increasingly interconnected world. It's a call to build a future where individual aspirations are aligned with the collective good, and where compassion and wisdom guide our path forward. It's a call we must all answer.

UNLEASH YOUR POTENTIAL
A JOURNEY TO PERSONAL GROWTH AND CONFIDENCE

THE AWAKENING OF POTENTIAL

The Call *to* Change

Change is an inevitable part of life, yet it often comes with a mix of fear and excitement. The call to change is not merely an external signal; it resonates deeply within us, urging us to break free from the chains of complacency. It is a moment when we recognize the need for growth, a whisper that suggests we can be more than we currently are. This call can manifest as a feeling of restlessness, a dissatisfaction with the status quo, or even a moment of clarity that illuminates the path forward. Embracing this call is the first step toward unleashing your true potential.

When we heed this call, we open ourselves to new possibilities. It is essential to understand that change does not happen overnight; it is a gradual process that requires patience and dedication. Each step taken, no matter how small, contributes to the larger journey of personal growth. This is where positive affirmations come into play. By affirming our ability to change and grow, we cultivate a mindset that embraces challenges rather than shying away from them. These affirmations serve as reminders of our strength and resilience, urging us to take that leap of faith into the unknown.

In the quiet moments of existence, when the din of modern life subsides, one may hear the subtle whispers of potential beckoning us forward. It is a call that transcends the mundane routines of daily life, urging us to explore the depth of our capabilities. The awakening of this potential is not merely an exercise in self-betterment; it is a profound journey that transforms our very understanding of who we are and what we can achieve. The path to personal growth and confidence requires introspection, resilience, and the willingness to embrace change.

The Nature *of* Potential

Potential is often described as the innate qualities and abilities that lie dormant within us, waiting to be discovered and cultivated. Philosophers throughout history have pondered the essence of human potential. Aristotle believed that every individual has a unique purpose or "telos," and that our ultimate fulfillment lies in realizing this purpose. In this light, our potential is not a fixed trait; it is a dynamic attribute inherent in our very humanity. The awakening of potential, therefore, requires an understanding that it can be nurtured and expanded through experience, knowledge, and self-reflection.

The Impediments *to* Growth

In our quest for self-actualization, we often encounter internal and external obstacles that inhibit our potential. Fear is perhaps the most formidable barrier; it whispers insidiously in our minds, convincing us that we are unworthy or incapable. Societal expectations can further stifle our aspirations, as we often measure our worth against the standards set by others. In confronting these barriers, we must learn to reframe our perception of failure and embrace vulnerability as a natural part of the growth process.

Failure is not a final destination but rather a steppingstone on the path to success. It is through our failures that we gain invaluable insights about ourselves and our capabilities. The philosopher Friedrich Nietzsche famously asserted, "What does not kill me makes me stronger." This perspective urges us to seek growth in adversity, recognizing that each setback offers a new opportunity for reflection, learning, and, ultimately, resurgence.

The Journey *of* Self-Discovery

The journey toward unlocking our potential begins with introspection—a deep dive into the innermost recesses of our psyche. Self-discovery requires a willingness to confront our fears, biases, and limitations. Journaling is one effective tool in this process, allowing us to articulate our thoughts and uncover patterns that may hold us back. It is within these pages that we can begin to confront the narratives we have internalized about ourselves. As we explore our beliefs, passions, and values, we uncover the threads that will weave the fabric of our authentic selves.

Mindfulness practices can enhance self-discovery by anchoring us in the present moment. By practicing mindfulness, we cultivate the ability to observe our thoughts without judgment, allowing us to gain clarity and wisdom about our desires and motivations. In this state of heightened awareness, we can tap into our creative capacities and envision the future we wish to create.

Courageous Steps Toward Confidence

As we embark on this journey, the paradox of confidence emerges. Confidence is not the absence of fear but the courage to face it head-on. Each step taken outside of our comfort zone builds a foundation of self-assurance. Engaging in new experiences, whether through travel, education, or social interactions, allows us to expand our horizons and challenge our pre-existing beliefs.

Setting goals is a pivotal aspect of nurturing confidence. Goals provide direction and purpose, serving as milestones in our journey. However, it is crucial that these objectives are rooted in our values and aspirations rather than external validation. The philosopher Søren Kierkegaard once said, "Life can only be understood backwards; but it must be lived forwards." Thus, reflecting on our experiences while moving forward with intention allows us to align our actions with our true selves.

The Power *of* Community

While the journey to personal growth is deeply individual, it is equally enriched by the communities and relationships we cultivate. Surrounding ourselves with like-minded individuals who encourage our aspirations fosters an atmosphere of support and accountability. In community, we find the strength to bear our vulnerabilities and share our triumphs.

Historically, philosophers such as Martin Buber have emphasized the importance of relationships in shaping our identity. Buber's concept of "I-Thou" relationships highlights the transformative power of genuine connection. Engaging authentically with others not only affirms our potential but also accelerates our growth by exposing us to different perspectives and ideas.

The Ongoing Journey *of* Growth

Personal growth is not a linear trajectory but rather a cyclical process characterized by continuous learning and evolution. The path is dotted with moments of clarity and confusion alike, but in recognizing that each stage is a necessary part of the journey, we become more resilient. The poet Rainer Maria Rilke beautifully articulated this sentiment: "Be patient toward all that is unsolved in your heart and try to love the questions themselves."

Embracing the unknown fosters a spirit of exploration and innovation, allowing our potential to flourish. Our lives unfold like a complex tapestry, and it is in our willingness to embrace all of its threads—both vibrant and muted—that we create a masterpiece uniquely our own.

A Call to Action

The awakening of our potential is a journey that invites us to transcend societal limitations and internal doubts. It calls us to venture beyond our comfort zones and embrace the uncertainty of growth with courage and tenacity. It is about recognizing the richness of our inner landscape and forging connections that affirm our capabilities. Each of us is imbued with a uniqueness that, when unleashed, has the power to inspire not only ourselves but also the world around us.

As we embark on this transformative journey of personal growth and confidence, let us carry the torch of potential within us. May we walk boldly into the unknown, armed with the wisdom of our experiences and the strength of our communities. Let us awaken the dormant possibilities within and unleash a force that ignites not only our passions but also the collective potential of humanity. The journey begins now—let us embrace it fully.

Developing a growth mindset is crucial in responding to the call to change. This mindset shifts our perspective from viewing challenges as obstacles to seeing them as opportunities for growth. Embracing this approach allows us to approach difficulties with curiosity and a willingness to learn. We become more resilient, understanding that setbacks are merely part of the journey. By fostering a growth mindset, we empower ourselves to take risks, explore new avenues, and ultimately evolve into the best version of ourselves.

Building confidence and self-esteem is a natural byproduct of answering the call to change. As we embark on new experiences and confront our fears, we discover our strengths and capabilities. Each success, no matter how minor, reinforces our belief in ourselves. This newfound confidence propels us forward, encouraging us to embrace change with open arms rather than resistance. The journey of personal growth is not solely about the destination; it is about the transformation we undergo along the way. In answering the call to change, we not only unleash our potential but also inspire others to embark on their own journeys of growth and self-discovery.

Understanding Your Current Self

Understanding your current self is the first step on the incredible journey of personal growth. It is essential to take a moment to pause, reflect, and truly assess where you stand in life. This self-exploration requires you to peel back the layers of your experiences, beliefs, and emotions. By doing so, you begin to uncover patterns that have shaped your identity, helping you recognize both your strengths and areas for improvement. The journey of self-discovery is not just about identifying what you want to change; it's also about celebrating who you are right now.

To engage in this self-understanding, start by embracing mindfulness. This practice allows you to connect with your thoughts and feelings without judgment. By observing your inner dialogue, you can identify limiting beliefs that may hold you back. Challenge these thoughts by asking yourself if they are genuinely true or simply reflections of past experiences. As you navigate this process, remember that acknowledging your flaws does not diminish your worth. Instead, it offers you the opportunity to transform those flaws into steppingstones toward growth and self-improvement.

Visualization plays a pivotal role in understanding yourself. Picture your ideal self—the person you aspire to be. What qualities does this person possess? How do they carry themselves? By creating a vivid mental image of your goals, you cultivate a powerful motivation that can propel you forward. This exercise not only helps you clarify your aspirations but also aligns your current self with your desired self. As you visualize your journey, allow positivity and affirmation to fill your mind. Affirmations can serve as daily reminders of your potential, reinforcing the belief that you can achieve the transformation you seek.

Another crucial aspect of understanding your current self is developing a growth mindset. Embrace the belief that your abilities and intelligence can be developed through dedication and hard work. This perspective fosters resilience and a love for learning, essential components of personal growth. By viewing challenges as opportunities rather than obstacles, you empower yourself to take risks and step outside of your comfort zone. Recognize that every setback is a lesson, and each lesson brings you closer to the person you aim to become.

Building confidence and self-esteem is an ongoing process rooted in self-acceptance and understanding. Celebrate your achievements, no matter how small, and acknowledge the effort you put into every endeavor. Surround yourself with supportive individuals who uplift and inspire you. Engage in activities that ignite your passion and allow you to express your authentic self. As you cultivate a deeper understanding of who you are, you will find that confidence naturally flourishes. Remember, the journey of personal growth is not a race; it is a beautiful exploration of your potential, and the first step begins with understanding your current self.

PERSONAL ETHICS AND MORALITY
Navigating the Compass
of One's Conscience

In an increasingly complex world where moral dilemmas are rife, it becomes imperative for each individual to engage deeply with the nature of ethics and morality. The cornerstone of ethical deliberation lies within the concept of personal ethics—an internal compass shaped by principles, experiences, culture, and, significantly, philosophy. At the heart of this exploration is an essential question: what guides our decisions, and how do we balance our personal desires with the ethical implications of our choices? Through the lenses of prominent philosophical perspectives such as those advanced by Immanuel Kant and John Stuart Mill, we shall navigate this intricate terrain of personal ethics and morality as a means to explore our individual moral compasses.

Understanding Personal Ethics

Personal ethics encompasses the moral principles that guide an individual's decisions and behaviors. It is an introspective lens through which one views the world, often informed by a myriad of experiences, teachings, and reflections. The formation of personal ethics begins in childhood, influenced by family values, social environments, and educational exposure. As we grow, we face dilemmas that challenge our initial moral frameworks, prompting us to critically assess and often recalibrate our beliefs.

This introspective journey requires grappling with fundamental questions: What is right? What is wrong? What values do I hold dear? The answers to these questions can be nuanced and may evolve over time, shaped by both reason and emotion. Each encounter with moral choices serves to refine our ethical beliefs, deepening our understanding of ourselves and others.

A Journey into the Soul of Individuality

In the contemporary world, where chaos often reigns and cultural narratives constantly clash, personal ethics serve as a guiding light, illuminating the paths we choose in our daily lives. While society often imposes a collective ethical framework—stemming from legal systems, cultural norms, and societal expectations—personal ethics represent the intricate web of beliefs, values, and principles that shape our individual consciences. Understanding and cultivating personal ethics is not merely an intellectual exercise; it is a profound journey into the depths of our own humanity, fostering an enriched sense of self and creating a more compassionate and just society.

The Nature of Personal Ethics

To understand personal ethics, it is essential first to dissect its core components. At its essence, personal ethics encompasses the principles that govern an individual's behavior in their interactions with others, themselves, and the wider world. These principles are often rooted in complex origins, including family teachings, religious beliefs, cultural contexts, and personal experiences. Unlike societal laws that are often rigid and prescriptive, personal ethics are fluid, shaped by introspective reflection and the lessons learned throughout life.

Ethics, in general, can be classified into various theories: consequentialism, deontology, virtue ethics, and others. However, personal ethics lies at the intersection of these broader theories and the unique life story of each individual. It is the personal narrative, the lived experience that informs ethical reasoning, prompting the lifelong quest to define what is right in a world strung with moral ambiguity.

The Role of Self-Reflection

Self-reflection is a pivotal component in constructing one's personal ethical framework. As Socrates famously stated, "The unexamined life is not worth living." To embrace personal ethics, one must venture into self-inquiry: Who am I? What do I value? What principles will guide my actions? This journey often requires confronting uncomfortable truths about oneself, acknowledging shortcomings, biases, and the influences that mold our beliefs.

Moreover, self-reflection promotes empathy—a crucial element of personal ethics. By examining our motivations and engaging with diverse perspectives, we cultivate a deeper understanding of others' experiences. This understanding not only fosters connections with those around us but also encourages ethical principles that prioritize compassion and justice. In essence, personal ethics thrive in the fertile ground of self-awareness.

The Intersection of Personal Ethics and Society

While personal ethics are inherently individualistic, they do not exist in isolation. The relationship between personal ethics and societal norms often yields a rich landscape of moral discourse. Individuals must grapple with how their personal ethics align or diverge from prevailing societal expectations. A noteworthy illustration of this tension can be seen in movements for social justice, where personal ethical convictions compel individuals to challenge unjust systems and advocate for equity.

Consider the civil rights movement in the United States. Individuals such as Martin Luther King Jr. and Rosa Parks drew upon their personal ethical beliefs—rooted in a sense of justice, equality, and moral duty—to confront systemic oppression. Their examples illustrate how personal ethics can transform into collective action, forging paths for social progress. In this way, personal ethics not only enrich individual lives but can also inspire systemic change.

The Challenges of Personal Ethics

Despite the empowering nature of personal ethics, the journey toward ethical clarity is fraught with challenges. In a world increasingly marked by moral relativism, the assertion of personal ethics can lead to conflict. Navigating differing cultural perspectives, moral dilemmas, and the complexities of human behavior often tests even the most steadfast ethical principles.

The practice of personal ethics requires courage—the courage to stand firm in one's convictions despite societal pressure and the fear of alienation. The conviction that produces ethical resilience can also lead to moments of isolation, as individuals wrestle with feelings of loneliness when their beliefs diverge from those of their communities. However, these moments of solitude can ultimately lead to personal growth and the forging of authentic connections with likeminded individuals.

Personal Ethics as a Lifelong Practice

Understanding personal ethics is not a destination but a lifelong journey. It requires perpetual engagement, adaptation, and evolution in response to new experiences and insights. Like a compass that occasionally needs recalibration, one's ethical framework must remain open to revision, allowing for the integration of new knowledge, changing circumstances, and emotional growth. This adaptability can often foster resilience in one's ethical beliefs. The willingness to learn—about oneself, about others, and about the world—strengthens the moral foundation upon which individuals build their lives.

The ongoing practice of personal ethics demands accountability. Individuals must hold themselves responsible for their actions and choices, ensuring that they align with their articulated values. This relentless pursuit of alignment engenders authenticity and promotes a consistent and meaningful existence. In this way, personal ethics serve not only as guidelines but as active principles—lighthouses guiding individuals safely through life's turbulent moral waters.

Understanding personal ethics is an intricate dance between introspection, societal engagement, and ethical practice. As we navigate the complexities of our own conviction, we must remember that ethics is not a static concept but a dynamic and evolving tapestry woven through the strands of our experiences. The quest for personal ethics equips us not only with the ability to navigate our lives with integrity, but it also empowers us to contribute positively to the world.

In striving to understand our moral landscapes, we cultivate a deeper connection to the diverse fabric of humanity, fostering a spirit of empathy that transcends individualism. As we acknowledge the power of personal ethics, we step into a role not simply as passive observers but as active participants in shaping a more compassionate and just world. The journey into personal ethics is ultimately a journey into love—love for ourselves, love for others, and love for the principles that unify us in our shared human experience.

THE ROLE OF PHILOSOPHICAL FRAMEWORKS

The need for philosophical frameworks becomes evident when navigating the complexities of morality. Two prominent figures, Immanuel Kant and John Stuart Mill, offer contrasting but enriching insights that aid individuals in constructing their moral compasses.

KANT'S DEONTOLOGICAL ETHICS: Duty Over Consequence

Immanuel Kant's deontological ethics offers a powerful and often challenging framework for understanding morality. In contrast to consequentialist approaches that judge the moral worth of an action based on its outcomes, Kantian ethics prioritizes duty and adherence to universal moral laws. According to Kant, the moral value of an action resides not in its consequences, however beneficial they might be, but in its conformity to a universal moral principle that one could consistently and rationally will to be adopted by all rational beings. This foundational principle is encapsulated in his celebrated categorical imperative, which commands individuals to "Act only according to that maxim whereby you can at the same time will that it should become a universal law." Morality, in the Kantian view, is thus conceived as an obligation, a binding imperative emanating from reason itself, independent of personal inclinations, desires, or the anticipated results of our actions.

The emphasis on universalizability is crucial to understanding Kant's system. He argues that a moral principle must be applicable to all rational agents in similar circumstances. If a maxim cannot be universalized without logical contradiction or undermining the very possibility of rational agency, then it is deemed morally impermissible. For example, the maxim "It is permissible to lie whenever it is convenient" cannot be universalized because if everyone lied whenever they found it convenient, trust would collapse, rendering communication and social interaction impossible. The very act of lying relies on an underlying assumption of truthfulness. Therefore, a universal law permitting lying undermines the conditions necessary for the act itself, creating a logical contradiction. This demonstrates Kant's rigorous demand for consistency and universality in moral reasoning.

The implications of Kantian ethics for personal decision-making are profound and often demanding. Individuals are constantly faced with choices that involve navigating competing interests, desires, and potential outcomes. Integrating Kantian ethics into this complex landscape requires a commitment to identifying and adhering to moral duties, even when doing so is personally inconvenient or leads to undesirable consequences. A classic example illustrating this tension can be found in situations involving honesty versus kindness. Consider a scenario where a friend has worked diligently on a creative project, such as a painting or a piece of writing, and presents it to you for feedback. You find the work to be, frankly, not very good. Telling a harsh truth about its shortcomings might spare your friend from repeating the same mistakes in future endeavors, potentially leading to their artistic growth. However, it would also likely cause immediate pain, disappointment, and perhaps even damage your friendship.

In this ethical dilemma, a consequentialist approach might weigh the potential benefits of honesty (future improvement) against the potential harms (immediate hurt feelings and strained relationship). A decision might then be made to soften the truth, or even offer a white lie, in the interest of minimizing pain and preserving harmony. Kant, however, would argue that the morally right action is to be truthful, regardless of the emotional fallout. The duty to be honest, he would assert, is a universal moral obligation that cannot be overridden by considerations of personal comfort or the desire to avoid negative consequences. To lie, even with the intention of kindness, violates the categorical imperative by treating the recipient of the lie as a means to an end (your own desire for a comfortable interaction) rather than as an end in themselves. Every rational being deserves to be treated with respect and honesty, and lying undermines their autonomy and their ability to make informed decisions based on truthful information.

Balancing personal desires for harmony and pleasant interactions against the unwavering duty to be honest represents a commonly faced ethical clash. Kantian ethics resists the temptation to sacrifice moral duty for the sake of convenience, personal gain, or even the desire to alleviate suffering. It urges individuals to remain steadfast and principled, even in adversity, to recognize that the true moral worth of an action lies not in its outcomes but in its adherence to the universal moral law. This commitment to duty can be particularly challenging in situations where the consequences of acting morally are personally painful or socially unpopular.

Furthermore, Kantian ethics emphasizes the importance of acting from a sense of duty, not merely in accordance with it. He distinguishes between acting "in conformity with duty" and acting "from duty." The former describes actions that happen to align with moral principles but are motivated by other factors, such as self-interest or fear of punishment. The latter, however, refers to actions that are motivated solely by a recognition of and respect for the moral law. Only actions performed from duty, according to Kant, possess true moral worth. For instance, a shopkeeper who is honest with customers simply because it is good for business is acting in conformity with duty. However, a shopkeeper who remains honest even when they could easily cheat a customer without being caught, and who does so solely because they believe it is morally wrong to deceive, is acting from duty.

In conclusion, Kant's deontological ethics provides a rigorous and demanding framework for moral decision-making. It emphasizes the primacy of duty, the importance of universalizable principles, and the inherent worth of every rational being. While the application of Kantian principles can often lead to challenging choices and require a willingness to prioritize duty over personal inclination, it offers a powerful foundation for a consistent and principled moral life. By focusing on the rightness of the action itself, rather than its potential consequences, Kantian ethics provides a bulwark against the temptation to justify immoral behavior based on situational factors or desired outcomes, ultimately promoting a society founded on respect, honesty, and unwavering commitment to the moral law.

MILL'S UTILITARIANISM:
The Consequence of Actions
and the Pursuit of Collective Happiness

In the realm of ethical philosophy, various schools of thought offer frameworks for navigating the complexities of moral decision-making. In contrast to approaches based on duty, virtue, or divine command, John Stuart Mill presents a compelling consequentialist approach in his doctrine of utilitarianism. Mill posits that the moral rightness of actions is fundamentally determined by their consequences, specifically in terms of the overall happiness or utility produced. An action, according to Mill, is considered morally right if it leads to the greatest happiness for the greatest number of people affected. This perspective demands that individuals actively assess their choices based on the potential outcomes they will generate, rather than blindly adhering to rigid, pre-determined moral laws or personal sentiments.

Utilitarianism, at its core, is a philosophy of maximizing well-being. It moves beyond the individualistic focus often found in other ethical theories and encourages a broader contemplation of ethical decisions, prompting individuals to consider the wider societal impact of their actions. This focus on the collective good necessitates a careful evaluation of the potential consequences of one's choices, forcing a consideration of the needs and desires of all those who might be impacted. For instance, when faced with the decision of whether to support a new policy that promises to benefit the majority of the population but potentially infringes upon the rights of a minority group, a utilitarian framework requires a rigorous examination of the overall welfare created by the proposed policy. The potential gains in happiness for the majority must be weighed against the potential suffering inflicted upon the minority, leading to a complex ethical calculation.

This approach often brings moral dilemmas into stark focus, presenting a challenging tug-of-war between personal desires for fairness or justice versus the utilitarian pursuit of collective happiness. Consider a situation where a doctor has the opportunity to save five lives by sacrificing one healthy individual for organ donation. While the utilitarian calculus might suggest sacrificing the one to save the five, our intuitions regarding individual rights and the sanctity of life rebel against such a decision. This conflict highlights the inherent tension within utilitarianism and prompts us to question the feasibility of consistently applying a purely consequentialist approach in all moral situations.

Furthermore, utilitarianism is not without its complexities regarding the definition and measurement of happiness. Mill himself addressed concerns that utilitarianism prioritized base pleasures, arguing for a distinction between higher and lower pleasures. He believed that intellectual and moral pleasures were inherently superior to purely sensual ones, even if the latter might be experienced with greater intensity. This distinction attempts to address criticisms that utilitarianism could justify actions that, while maximizing overall pleasure, are morally repugnant, such as the use of slaves for the benefit of a privileged few. However, the subjectivity involved in defining and ranking pleasures remains a challenge for the practical application of utilitarian principles.

Despite these inherent challenges, utilitarianism remains a powerful and influential ethical framework. It forces us to consider the real-world impact of our actions and to strive for outcomes that promote the greatest good for the greatest number. By demanding a rigorous assessment of consequences, utilitarianism can guide us towards more responsible and ethical decision-making, even when those decisions are difficult and require careful consideration of competing values. It encourages empathy and a broader understanding of the interconnectedness of individuals within society, prompting us to move beyond self-interest and embrace a commitment to collective well-being. While the pursuit of universal happiness may remain an elusive goal, the striving for it, guided by the principles of utilitarianism, can lead to a more just and equitable world for all.

Balancing Personal Desires *and* Ethical Implications

Navigating the interplay between personal desires and ethical implications raises essential discourse on moral integrity. It is a balancing act requiring an individual to acknowledge their selfish inclinations while also considering the ethical landscape that extends beyond their immediate sphere. This tension, present in both grand societal decisions and everyday personal choices, demands a critical examination of our motivations, values, and the potential impact of our actions on ourselves, others, and the world around us. To achieve a truly ethical life, we must constantly strive to reconcile the pull of individual ambition with the broader responsibility we have to uphold principles of fairness, compassion, and justice.

The very concept of personal desire is multifaceted, encompassing everything from fundamental needs like food and shelter to more complex aspirations such as professional success, romantic fulfillment, and creative expression. These desires are often deeply ingrained, fueled by biological imperatives, societal conditioning, and individual experiences. The pursuit of these desires is, in many ways, what drives progress and innovation. Individuals strive to improve their lives, contributing to advancements in technology, art, and social structures. However, unbridled pursuit of personal desires, without regard for ethical consequences, can lead to exploitation, injustice, and even destruction.

The "ethical implications" referred to extend far beyond simply obeying the law. Ethics encompasses a broader framework of moral principles that guide our behavior and shape our interactions with the world. These principles often involve considering the impact of our actions on various stakeholders, including individuals, communities, and the environment. This requires a level of empathy and foresight, demanding that we step outside of our own immediate perspective and consider the potential consequences of our choices on others. It also necessitates a critical examination of the underlying power dynamics at play, recognizing how our actions can perpetuate inequalities and harm vulnerable populations.

One of the primary challenges in balancing personal desires and ethical implications lies in the inherent subjectivity of morality. What one individual considers ethical, another may view as morally reprehensible. Cultural norms, religious beliefs, and personal experiences all contribute to shaping our individual moral compasses. This inherent subjectivity can lead to conflicting interpretations of ethical principles and make it difficult to establish a universal standard of ethical conduct. For example, the pursuit of profit maximization, a common personal desire in the business world, can often clash with ethical considerations such as fair labor practices, environmental responsibility, and consumer safety. Striking a balance between these competing interests requires a constant process of negotiation, compromise, and ethical reasoning.

The complexities of modern society often obscure the ethical implications of our actions. We live in a world of interconnected systems, where our choices have far-reaching and often unforeseen consequences. The food we eat, the clothes we wear, and the technology we use are all products of complex global supply chains that can involve exploitation and environmental degradation. To make ethically sound decisions, we must actively seek to understand these complex systems and hold ourselves accountable for the consequences of our consumption. This requires a commitment to critical thinking, research, and a willingness to challenge the status quo.

Navigating the tension between personal desires and ethical implications requires a commitment to cultivating moral intelligence and fostering a sense of social responsibility. This involves developing the ability to recognize ethical dilemmas, analyze the potential consequences of different courses of action, and make decisions that align with our values and principles. It also requires a willingness to engage in difficult conversations, challenge our own biases, and learn from our mistakes. By fostering a culture of ethical awareness and accountability, we can create a society that prioritizes not only individual success but also the well-being of all its members and the health of the planet. In conclusion, the ongoing quest to balance personal desires with ethical imperatives remains a critical undertaking, essential for creating a more just, equitable, and sustainable future for all. It is a journey that demands constant self-reflection, critical engagement, and a unwavering commitment to the pursuit of moral integrity.

The Ethical Landscape of Choice

Navigating Self, Duty, and Consequence

The act of choosing is the cornerstone of human existence. From the mundane decisions that shape our daily routines to the pivotal moments that define our life's trajectory, we are constantly confronted with the necessity of selecting from a myriad of possibilities. Yet, underlying this seemingly simple act lies a complex and often challenging ethical landscape. Every choice, no matter how insignificant it may appear, carries with it the potential to impact not only our own lives, but the lives of those around us. To effectively navigate this intricate terrain requires a conscious effort to cultivate self-awareness, embrace critical thinking, and foster a deep understanding of the ethical frameworks that guide our moral compass.

To effectively navigate this landscape, individuals must cultivate self-awareness and critical thinking. This involves engaging in a process of rigorous introspection, questioning the motivations behind our desires and critically evaluating the potential consequences of our actions. We must learn to dissect the seemingly straightforward decisions that confront us, recognizing the subtle ethical dimensions often hidden beneath the surface. This begins with asking oneself vital questions: What impact might my choices have on those around me? This query forces us to expand our perspective beyond the immediate gratification of our own needs and consider the ripple effect our actions might create. Am I prioritizing my desires at the expense of another's well-being? This challenging question demands honesty and a willingness to acknowledge the potential for selfishness in our decision-making. It necessitates a critical assessment of whether our personal ambition or comfort is being pursued at the cost of another's opportunity, happiness, or even safety. Are my actions justifiable within a universal ethical framework? This final, crucial question encourages us to transcend personal biases and consider whether our choices align with broader principles of fairness, justice, and respect for human dignity. It prompts us to examine whether our actions could be defended if applied universally, avoiding the trap of situational ethics that often leads to moral compromise.

The duality of Kantian and Millian ethics underscores the spectrum of moral reasoning, encouraging individuals to consider both duties and consequential impacts. Immanuel Kant's emphasis on duty suggests that certain actions are inherently right or wrong, regardless of their outcomes. This deontological perspective compels us to adhere to moral principles, such as honesty and respect for autonomy, even when doing so might lead to less desirable immediate consequences. Conversely, John Stuart Mill's utilitarianism focuses on the consequences of our actions, arguing that the best choice is the one that maximizes overall happiness and minimizes suffering. This consequentialist approach encourages us to weigh the potential benefits and harms of our choices, striving to create the greatest good for the greatest number. Understanding both Kantian and Millian ethics allows for a more nuanced approach to ethical decision-making. We can strive to uphold our moral duties while simultaneously considering the potential impact of our actions on the well-being of others. This synthesis enables us to navigate complex ethical dilemmas with a greater degree of moral sensitivity and intellectual rigor.

Furthermore, the practice of empathetic engagement becomes a transformative tool in developing personal ethics. Empathy, the ability to understand and share the feelings of another, allows us to step outside of our own limited perspective and experience the world through the eyes of others. By understanding the experiences and feelings of others, individuals can better assess the ethical ramifications of their actions. This relational approach, grounded in both ethical philosophies, underscores the importance of considering the human cost of our choices. It prompts us to ask not just what we want, but how our actions will affect the lives and livelihoods of those around us. Empathy allows us to move beyond abstract ethical principles and connect with the concrete realities of human experience, fostering a deeper sense of responsibility and compassion.

Analyzing the ethical landscape of choice requires a commitment to a collective moral framework that recognizes the human interconnectedness that transcends individuality. We are not isolated agents operating in a vacuum, but rather members of a complex and interdependent social web. Our choices, therefore, have the power to either strengthen or weaken the bonds that connect us. By embracing self-awareness, engaging in critical thinking, and cultivating empathy, we can strive to make choices that not only benefit ourselves, but also contribute to the well-being of the larger community. This requires a constant willingness to learn, to adapt, and to challenge our own assumptions, always striving to make ethical choices that reflect our shared humanity. It is through this collective effort that we can create a more just, equitable, and compassionate world, one choice at a time. The journey towards ethical awareness and action is ongoing, a lifelong pursuit that demands humility, courage, and a unwavering commitment to the pursuit of moral excellence.

The Journey Towards Ethical Maturity

Personal ethics and morality are far from static; they are dynamic entities, constantly evolving through continuous reflection, immersive experiences, and critical self-assessment. Our moral compass is not pre-set; rather, it is shaped and refined by the challenges we face, the relationships we cultivate, and the wisdom we glean from diverse sources. Engaging with philosophical perspectives, such as the deontological framework of Immanuel Kant and the utilitarian principles of John Stuart Mill, can profoundly deepen our understanding of the ethical implications of our actions and the foundational principles guiding our decisions. These frameworks offer lenses through which we can examine the consequences of our choices, the inherent duties we owe to others, and the complex interplay between individual rights and the common good. As individuals strive to align their actions with their deeply held moral values, they embark on a lifelong journey toward ethical maturity—a transformative process that integrates duty, compassion, and a profound awareness of the wider impact of their choices.

The journey towards ethical maturity is not a linear progression, but rather a complex and often circuitous path marked by moments of clarity, periods of confusion, and the inevitable confrontation with moral ambiguity. It requires a willingness to confront uncomfortable truths, to question ingrained beliefs, and to embrace the inherent messiness of the human condition. For instance, Kantian ethics, with its emphasis on universal moral laws and the inherent dignity of each individual, challenges us to consider whether our actions can be universally applied without contradiction and whether we are treating others as ends in themselves, rather than merely as means to our own ends. This requires a deep level of self-reflection and a commitment to acting according to principles that respect the autonomy and inherent worth of all rational beings.

Conversely, Mill's utilitarianism, which prioritizes the greatest good for the greatest number, compels us to weigh the consequences of our actions and to consider the potential impact on the overall well-being of society. This approach necessitates a nuanced understanding of the potential benefits and harms associated with different courses of action, as well as a willingness to make difficult choices that may prioritize the collective good over individual desires. However, it also raises questions about the potential for the marginalization of minority interests and the challenge of accurately predicting the long-term consequences of our decisions.

The integration of these philosophical perspectives, and others, is crucial for developing a robust and nuanced ethical framework. It allows us to move beyond simplistic notions of right and wrong and to engage with the complexities of moral decision-making in a more informed and considered manner. This process of ethical reflection is not merely an intellectual exercise; it is a deeply personal journey that shapes our character, influences our relationships, and ultimately defines who we are as individuals.

Thus, as we forge our paths in the multifaceted tapestry of life, the compass of our personal ethics serves as both a guide and a challenge. It beckons us to examine the tensions between duty and desirability, inviting us to embrace the complexities of our decisions as opportunities for growth and moral reflection. The allure of personal gain or immediate gratification often clashes with the call of duty and the recognition of our responsibilities to others. Navigating these tensions requires a constant process of self-assessment, empathy, and a willingness to prioritize ethical considerations over personal convenience.

In navigating this ethical terrain, we not only define who we are but also contribute meaningfully to the world around us. Our actions, both large and small, have a ripple effect, shaping the lives of those around us and contributing to the overall moral climate of our communities. By striving to live ethically, we inspire others to do the same, creating a virtuous cycle of moral progress. The quest for ethical understanding is, ultimately, the pursuit of a more humane existence for ourselves and for future generations. It is a commitment to building a world where compassion, justice, and respect for human dignity are not merely ideals but are guiding principles that shape our individual actions and our collective aspirations. It is a journey that demands continuous learning, critical self-reflection, and a unwavering commitment to living a life of purpose and integrity. And in that journey, we find not only our own ethical maturity but also the potential to contribute to a more just and compassionate world for all.

Embracing the Journey Ahead

Embracing the journey ahead is a powerful declaration of your commitment to personal growth. It is an invitation to step into the unknown with courage, knowing that every step you take, no matter how small, is a part of your evolution. Life is not merely a series of events; it is a magnificent tapestry woven from the threads of your experiences, choices, and dreams. By embracing the journey, you open yourself to infinite possibilities, allowing your true potential to unfold in ways you may have never imagined.

As you embark on this path, it is essential to cultivate a growth mindset. This mindset empowers you to view challenges not as obstacles, but as opportunities for learning and development. Each setback is a lesson, each failure is a steppingstone toward success. By shifting your perspective, you begin to see that your abilities and intelligence can be developed through dedication and hard work. Embrace this mindset, and you will find that resilience and adaptability become your greatest allies on this journey.

Picture yourself achieving your goals and living the life you desire. Create a vivid mental image of your future self, filled with confidence, joy, and fulfillment. This practice not only helps clarify your aspirations but also ignites the passion within you to pursue them relentlessly. As you visualize your success, your mind starts to align with your goals, making it easier to take actionable steps towards realizing them.

Positive affirmations play a crucial role in reinforcing your commitment to this journey. By regularly affirming your worth, capabilities, and potential, you dismantle the limiting beliefs that may have held you back for far too long. Each affirmation acts as a declaration of your intentions, paving the way for self-discovery and empowerment. Speak kindly to yourself, and the world will respond in kind. The more you nurture your self-esteem, the more confidence you will exude as you face the challenges that lie ahead.

Embracing the journey ahead is about celebrating your progress, no matter how incremental it may seem. Each day presents new opportunities for growth, and every experience contributes to your story. Acknowledge your achievements, honor your struggles, and remain steadfast in your pursuit of self-improvement. By doing so, you not only unleash your potential but also inspire those around you to embark on their unique journeys of growth and transformation. As you step boldly into the future, remember that the journey is just as important as the destination, and every moment is a chance to embrace the incredible adventure that is your life.

THE POWER OF POSITIVE AFFIRMATIONS

Crafting Your Affirmations

Crafting your affirmations is a transformative process that invites you to engage deeply with your inner self. It begins with reflection—understanding your desires, aspirations, and the challenges that hold you back. Take a moment to explore what you genuinely want to manifest in your life. Your affirmations should resonate with your true self, serving as a bridge between where you are and where you wish to be. This is the heart of personal growth; it's about recognizing your potential and daring to dream beyond your current circumstances.

Once you have a clear vision of your goals, the next step is to articulate them in a positive, present-tense format. Instead of saying, "I want to be confident," rephrase it to "I am confident and capable." This shift in language not only empowers your mindset but also aligns your subconscious with your affirmations. Each phrase should embody positivity, acting as a catalyst for change. Remember, the words you choose are not just affirmations; they are declarations of your reality, shaping your beliefs and actions in profound ways.

Incorporate emotional resonance into your affirmations to elevate their impact. Visualize yourself embodying these statements in your daily life. As you recite your affirmations, feel the emotions associated with achieving your goals. This practice enhances the effectiveness of your affirmations, embedding them deeper into your psyche. The combination of positive language and vivid visualization creates an energetic shift that can propel you toward your aspirations. Embrace the feelings of joy, pride, and fulfillment that arise from these affirmations; they are your guiding light.

Consistency is vital in the practice of affirmations. Establish a daily routine where you can dedicate time to recite your affirmations, ideally in the morning or before bed when your mind is most receptive. This ritual not only reinforces your intentions but also creates a sacred space for personal growth. Over time, as you integrate affirmations into your life, you'll notice a gradual transformation in your mindset and self-perception. You begin to cultivate a growth mindset, one that welcomes challenges and views setbacks as opportunities for learning and growth.

Lastly, be patient and compassionate with yourself throughout this journey. Change takes time, and the path to building confidence and self-esteem is often nonlinear. Celebrate the small victories and remain open to adjusting your affirmations as you evolve. Your journey is uniquely yours, and the affirmations you craft will evolve alongside you. Embrace this dynamic process, knowing that each affirmation is a step toward unleashing your full potential and creating a life filled with purpose and confidence.

Integrating Affirmations into Daily Life

Integrating affirmations into daily life is not merely a practice; it is an empowering journey that can transform your mindset and elevate your sense of self-worth. Imagine waking up each morning, facing the day with a renewed sense of purpose, armed with words that resonate deeply within you. Affirmations serve as a foundation for building a positive inner dialogue and can be seamlessly woven into the fabric of your daily routine. By committing to this practice, you are taking significant steps toward nurturing a growth mindset that fosters resilience, confidence, and personal development.

To begin this integration, choose a few affirmations that resonate with your goals and aspirations. These could be simple statements like, "I am capable of achieving my dreams," or "I radiate confidence and positivity." Write them down where you can see them frequently—on your bathroom mirror, in your planner, or as reminders on your phone. The act of reading these affirmations aloud, especially in front of a mirror, can create a powerful connection between your words and your self-perception. This daily ritual not only reinforces your intentions but also serves as a reminder of your inherent worth and potential.

Another effective strategy is to incorporate affirmations into moments of transition throughout your day. Whether you are commuting to work, preparing for a meeting, or winding down in the evening, use these moments to recite your affirmations. This practice can reframe your thoughts and attitudes, helping you to approach challenges with a positive mindset. Visualize the success you desire as you repeat your affirmations, allowing the feelings of achievement and confidence to wash over you. This visualization technique amplifies the impact of your words, aligning your mindset with your aspirations.

Additionally, consider the environment around you when integrating affirmations into your life. Surround yourself with positive influences, including books, podcasts, and people who uplift and inspire you. Create a space that encourages growth and reflection, where your affirmations can thrive. You might even choose to share your affirmations with friends or family members, inviting them to join you in this transformative practice. By fostering a supportive community, you not only enrich your own journey but also inspire others to embrace their potential.

Remember that consistency is key. Just as any habit takes time to form, the integration of affirmations into your daily life requires dedication and patience. Celebrate your progress, no matter how small, and be gentle with yourself on days when affirmations may feel challenging to embrace. Over time, you will notice a shift in your mindset, an increase in your confidence, and a profound sense of empowerment as you unleash your potential. Embrace this journey with an open heart, and watch how affirmations can help you sculpt a reality filled with possibility and self-assurance.

Overcoming Doubts with Positive Self-Talk

Doubt can be a formidable barrier on the path to personal growth and self-improvement. It creeps in quietly, often disguised as rational thoughts, but its effects can be paralyzing. To counteract these doubts, we must harness the power of positive self-talk. This practice is not merely about repeating affirmations; it is about transforming our inner dialogue into a source of strength and encouragement. By consciously choosing words that uplift rather than diminish, we can begin to reshape our perception of ourselves and our capabilities.

Positive self-talk serves as a powerful tool for redefining our self-image. When faced with challenges, it is easy to succumb to negative thoughts that highlight our weaknesses or past failures. Instead, we can replace these limiting beliefs with affirmations that celebrate our strengths and potential. For instance, instead of thinking, "I can't do this," we can affirm, "I am capable of overcoming any challenge." This shift in language creates a new narrative, one that empowers us to embrace our abilities and face obstacles with confidence.

Visualization practices complement positive self-talk beautifully. By picturing ourselves succeeding, we create a mental blueprint for achievement. When we combine this visualization with affirmations, we reinforce our belief in our capabilities. Imagine standing before an audience, feeling the warmth of their attention, and confidently delivering a presentation. As you repeat affirmations such as, "I am a skilled communicator," the mental image aligns with the words, forging a powerful connection that enhances your self-assuredness.

Building confidence and self-esteem is a gradual process that requires patience and persistence. Each time we engage in positive self-talk, we lay another brick in the foundation of our self-belief. It is essential to remember that setbacks are part of this journey. Instead of allowing failure to spiral into self-doubt, we can use positive self-talk to reframe our experiences. By saying to ourselves, "Every setback is an opportunity to learn and grow," we cultivate resilience and maintain a growth mindset, essential components for long-term success.

In conclusion, overcoming doubts through positive self-talk is not just an exercise in optimism; it is a critical strategy for personal transformation. As we practice this skill, we unlock the door to our potential, allowing confidence and self-esteem to flourish. Embrace the power of your words, visualize your success, and let your inner voice become your greatest ally. As you embark on this journey, remember that the most significant changes often begin with the simplest of thoughts.

VISUALIZATION CREATING YOUR FUTURE

The Science Behind Visualization

Visualization is not merely a fanciful exercise; it is grounded in science and psychological principles that enhance its effectiveness. At its core, visualization involves creating vivid mental images of desired outcomes or goals. Research shows that when individuals visualize success, their brains respond similarly to when they physically engage in the activity. This phenomenon is rooted in the concept of neuroplasticity, which suggests that our brains can reorganize themselves based on experiences and thoughts. By consistently practicing visualization, we can train our minds to approach challenges with greater confidence and resilience.

Neuroscientific studies reveal that visualization activates the same neural pathways as actual performance. When you see yourself achieving a goal—whether it's delivering a successful presentation, running a marathon, or mastering a skill—your brain engages in processes that prepare your body for those actions. This mental rehearsal strengthens the connections between neurons, making it easier for you to perform in real life. The more vividly you can imagine your success, the more equipped you become to turn those images into reality. This connection between thought and action highlights the power of our minds in shaping our experiences.

Moreover, visualization can significantly reduce anxiety and stress, which often hinder personal growth. When faced with daunting tasks or challenges, the mind tends to spiral into negative thought patterns. By actively visualizing a positive outcome, you can counteract these anxieties. This technique allows you to create a mental buffer, where you envision yourself navigating obstacles smoothly and confidently. As you practice this, you cultivate a sense of calm and assurance that can be transformative in high-pressure situations. The ability to visualize success empowers you to face challenges head-on, reinforcing your belief in your capabilities.

In addition to reducing anxiety, visualization enhances motivation and goal-setting. When you picture your goals clearly, it becomes easier to map out the steps necessary to achieve them. This clarity fosters a sense of purpose and direction, essential elements in any journey of personal growth. By regularly revisiting your visualized goals, you ignite the passion and commitment needed to pursue them relentlessly. The imagery you create serves as a powerful reminder of what you are working towards, keeping your motivation high even when the journey becomes difficult.

Integrating visualization into your daily routine can be a game-changer in your journey toward personal growth and confidence. Whether you take a few moments each day to visualize your success or incorporate it into your meditation practice, the benefits are profound.

By harnessing the scientific principles behind visualization, you not only enhance your self-esteem but also cultivate a resilient mindset. As you embrace this practice, you open the door to endless possibilities, transforming your dreams into attainable realities and unleashing your true potential.

Techniques for Effective Visualization

Visualization is a powerful technique that can significantly enhance personal growth and confidence. By imagining your goals vividly, you create a mental blueprint that guides your actions and decisions. This process involves more than just daydreaming; it requires intentionality and clarity.

- Start by identifying what you truly desire in your life, whether it's a career achievement, improved relationships, or enhanced self-esteem. Once you have a clear vision, dedicate time each day to immerse yourself in that mental image, allowing it to resonate deeply within you. This practice not only motivates you but also aligns your subconscious mind with your aspirations.

- One effective technique for visualization is to engage all your senses. Instead of merely picturing your goal, try to feel, hear, and even smell the environment you envision. For instance, if your goal is to deliver a successful presentation, imagine the room, the audience's reactions, and the sound of your voice as you speak with confidence. This multisensory approach creates a more vivid experience, making it easier for your mind to believe in the possibility of achieving that vision. When you can feel the emotions associated with your success, you strengthen your commitment to making it a reality.

- Another powerful method is to create a vision board. This tangible representation of your goals can serve as a daily reminder of what you aspire to achieve. Gather images, quotes, and symbols that resonate with your desired outcomes and arrange them in a way that inspires you. Place your vision board in a prominent location where you will see it regularly. As you visualize the images, allow yourself to connect with the emotions they evoke. This practice not only reinforces your goals but also cultivates a positive mindset that nurtures your self-esteem.

- Incorporating affirmations into your visualization practice can amplify its effectiveness. Positive affirmations are statements that reinforce your belief in your abilities and potential. As you visualize your goals, repeat affirmations that align with your vision. For example, if you aspire to be more confident in social situations, affirmations like "I am confident and capable" can transform your mindset. The combination of visualization and affirmations creates a powerful synergy that builds your self-belief and encourages you to take action towards your goals.

Consistency is key to mastering visualization techniques. Set aside dedicated time each day to practice visualization, making it an integral part of your routine. As you cultivate this habit, you will notice a shift in your mindset and behavior. Embrace setbacks as learning opportunities and remain committed to your vision. Over time, the continuous practice of visualization will not only enhance your personal growth but also empower you to unleash your full potential, paving the way for a life filled with confidence and fulfillment.

Manifesting Your Dreams through Imagery

Imagery is a powerful tool that can help you manifest your dreams and transform your life. When you visualize your goals, you create a mental picture that serves as a guide to what you want to achieve. This process is not just about daydreaming; it involves engaging your emotions and senses to bring your aspirations to life. By seeing yourself in the situations you desire, you begin to align your thoughts and actions with those visions, paving the way for success. The act of visualization can be a catalyst for change, allowing you to break free from limiting beliefs and unlock your true potential.

As you embark on this journey of manifesting your dreams through imagery, it's essential to set aside time for focused visualization. Find a quiet space where you can relax and concentrate fully on your desires. Close your eyes and immerse yourself in the details of your vision. What do you see? What do you hear? How do you feel? Engaging all your senses will not only make the experience more vivid but will also strengthen your emotional connection to your dreams. This practice can ignite a sense of motivation within you, encouraging you to take actionable steps toward realizing your aspirations.

Incorporating positive affirmations into your visualization practice enhances its power. Affirmations are statements that reflect your goals and the person you want to become. As you visualize, repeat these affirmations silently or aloud, reinforcing your belief in your ability to achieve your dreams. For instance, if you aspire to be more confident in public speaking, affirmations like "I am a captivating speaker" or "I engage my audience effortlessly" can shift your mindset. This combination of imagery and affirmations can create a fertile environment for growth, enabling you to cultivate a positive self-image and a resilient mindset.

The journey of manifesting your dreams through imagery also involves letting go of fear and self-doubt. Often, the biggest barriers to success lie within us. When you visualize, it is natural for negative thoughts to surface, questioning your capabilities and worthiness. Acknowledge these thoughts but don't let them dictate your narrative. Instead, counter them with the empowering imagery you have created. Envision yourself overcoming challenges and celebrating your achievements. This practice helps build resilience, fostering a growth mindset that embraces challenges as opportunities for learning and growth.

As you continue to practice visualization and affirmations, you will notice a gradual shift in your confidence and self-esteem. Each time you envision your dreams and affirm your beliefs, you reinforce a positive self-image that propels you forward. The more you engage in this practice, the more aligned your actions will become with your aspirations. Over time, you will not only begin to see changes in your external circumstances but will also experience a profound transformation within. By manifesting your dreams through imagery, you are taking a significant step toward unleashing your potential and living a life filled with purpose and fulfillment.

CULTIVATING A GROWTH MINDSET

The Difference Between Fixed *and* Growth Mindsets

In the realm of personal growth, understanding the distinction between fixed and growth mindsets serves as a crucial turning point on your journey to self-improvement. A fixed mindset is characterized by the belief that your abilities, intelligence, and talents are static traits. When you embrace this mindset, challenges can feel overwhelming, and failure becomes a reflection of your inherent limitations. Such a perspective can stifle your potential, leaving you feeling trapped within the confines of your perceived abilities. It's essential to recognize how this mindset can hinder your progress and prevent you from pursuing your goals with vigor and enthusiasm.

Conversely, a growth mindset opens the door to endless possibilities. This mindset is rooted in the belief that your skills and intelligence can be developed through dedication, effort, and resilience. Embracing a growth mindset means viewing challenges as opportunities for growth rather than as insurmountable obstacles. With this perspective, failures are not final verdicts but rather valuable lessons that propel you forward. Adopting this mindset can ignite a passion for learning and exploration, allowing you to push beyond your limits and unlock your true potential.

The impact of these mindsets extends beyond individual performance; they also influence how we perceive ourselves and our relationships with others. A fixed mindset can lead to a fear of judgment and a reluctance to seek feedback, as criticism may be construed as an attack on one's character. In contrast, a growth mindset encourages open communication and collaboration, fostering an environment where everyone feels empowered to share ideas and learn from one another. This shift in perspective not only enhances personal development but also strengthens connections with those around you, creating a supportive network that champions growth and innovation.

Cultivating a growth mindset requires conscious effort and practice. Begin by recognizing and challenging negative self-talk and limiting beliefs that may be rooted in a fixed mindset. Replace those thoughts with positive affirmations that reinforce your ability to learn and adapt. Visualization practices can also play a significant role in developing a growth mindset. By envisioning yourself overcoming obstacles and achieving your goals, you create a mental framework that aligns with your aspirations. Each small step you take toward embracing this mindset contributes to a more confident and resilient version of yourself.

The difference between fixed and growth mindsets shapes your journey toward personal growth and self-esteem. By choosing to embrace a growth mindset, you empower yourself to take risks, learn from experiences, and celebrate progress, no matter how small. This transformative shift in thinking not only enhances your capabilities but also enriches your life with a sense of purpose and fulfillment. As you embark on this journey, remember that the power to unleash your potential lies within your mindset—choose wisely, and watch as your life flourishes in ways you never imagined possible.

Strategies to Shift Your Mindset

To shift your mindset, the first step is to cultivate awareness of your current thought patterns. This requires a conscious effort to observe the internal landscape of your mind, noticing the narratives that play out throughout the day. Acknowledge the limiting beliefs that may have clouded your perception of yourself and your potential. These beliefs often stem from past experiences, societal pressures, or negative self-talk, and they can manifest as feelings of inadequacy, fear of failure, or a general sense of being stuck. By identifying these thoughts, you empower yourself to challenge and change them. You are, in essence, shining a light on the hidden corners of your mind, bringing these limiting beliefs into the open where they can be examined and dismantled. Start by journaling your thoughts, focusing on any recurring negative narratives. Don't censor yourself; simply write down what comes to mind, even if it seems trivial or illogical. This practice not only clarifies your mindset by revealing the patterns that govern your thinking, but also serves as a foundation for transformation, providing concrete examples of the beliefs you need to address. Consider the context in which these thoughts arise — are they triggered by specific situations or certain people? Understanding the triggers can help you anticipate and manage these thoughts more effectively. The goal is to become a detached observer of your own mind, recognizing that your thoughts are not necessarily facts, but rather interpretations of reality.

Once you have a clear understanding of your limiting beliefs, introduce positive affirmations into your daily routine. Affirmations are powerful tools that can rewire your brain and foster a more positive self-image. They work by repeatedly exposing your subconscious mind to desired realities, gradually replacing negative thought patterns with more empowering ones. Choose statements that resonate with your aspirations and repeat them regularly. For example, saying, "I am capable of achieving my goals" can instill a sense of belief in your abilities. It's important to craft affirmations that feel authentic and believable to you. Avoid overly grandiose or unrealistic statements that might trigger resistance from your subconscious. Instead, focus on small, incremental improvements that you can genuinely believe in. Over time, these affirmations can help replace negative thoughts with empowering ones, reinforcing a mindset that supports growth and resilience. Consistency is key; make affirmations a daily habit, ideally performed at the start of the day to set a positive tone and before bed to reinforce the message during sleep. You can say them aloud, write them down, or even create a visual reminder to keep them top of mind. Consider tailoring your affirmations to specific areas of your life where you want to see improvement, such as career, relationships, or health. The more specific and personalized your affirmations are, the more effective they will be in shaping your mindset.

Visualization is another effective strategy in shifting your mindset. By vividly imagining yourself achieving your goals, you create a mental blueprint that guides your actions. This process activates the same neural pathways in your brain as actually experiencing the success, strengthening the connection between your aspirations and your ability to achieve them. Spend a few minutes each day in a quiet space, picturing yourself succeeding in your endeavors. Engage all your senses in this practice, envisioning not just the outcome, but also the journey and the feelings associated with it. What does it look like, sound like, smell like, feel like to achieve your goal? The more detailed and immersive the visualization, the more powerful its impact. This technique not only boosts motivation by creating a tangible sense of possibility, but also prepares your mind to recognize opportunities aligned with your aspirations. When you consistently visualize success, you become more attuned to noticing situations and resources that can help you achieve your goals. Consider creating a vision board to further enhance your visualization practice. A vision board is a collage of images, words, and symbols that represent your desired future. By visually immersing yourself in your aspirations on a regular basis, you reinforce your commitment to achieving them.

Building a growth mindset involves embracing challenges and viewing failures as opportunities for learning. This is a fundamental shift from a fixed mindset, which sees intelligence and abilities as static and unchangeable. When faced with obstacles, remind yourself that every setback is a steppingstone to success. Adopt a curious attitude toward challenges, asking yourself what lessons can be learned rather than focusing solely on the outcome. What can you learn from this experience that will make you stronger, wiser, or more resilient? This shift in perspective fosters resilience and encourages you to persist, ultimately enhancing your confidence and self-esteem. It allows you to see failures not as a reflection of your worth, but as valuable learning opportunities. Embrace the discomfort of pushing yourself beyond your comfort zone, knowing that growth happens when you step outside of what feels familiar. Celebrate your progress, no matter how small, as each step forward is a testament to your growth. Acknowledge the effort you put in, regardless of the outcome. Focusing on the process rather than just the result can help you maintain motivation and build a stronger sense of self-efficacy. Keep a record of your achievements, both big and small, to remind yourself of your progress and build confidence in your ability to overcome challenges.

Lastly, surround yourself with positivity. The people you engage with, the content you consume, and the environments you inhabit all influence your mindset, often in subtle but profound ways. Seek out supportive relationships that inspire and uplift you. Distance yourself from negative or toxic individuals who drain your energy and undermine your self-belief. Engage with motivational literature, podcasts, or workshops that resonate with your journey. Fill your mind with inspiring ideas and perspectives that challenge your limiting beliefs. By immersing yourself in positive influences, you reinforce your commitment to personal growth and create a nurturing environment where your newfound mindset can flourish. Consider the impact of your physical environment on your mindset as well. Create a space that is conducive to positivity and productivity, filled with things that inspire and uplift you. Declutter your surroundings to eliminate distractions and create a sense of calm. Remember, shifting your mindset is not a one-time fix, but rather an ongoing process of self-awareness, intentional action, and consistent reinforcement. The journey of shifting your mindset is ongoing, but with determination and the right strategies, you can unlock your true potential and create a life filled with purpose, fulfillment, and joy. Be patient with yourself, celebrate your progress, and continue to cultivate a mindset that supports your growth and allows you to thrive.

Embracing Challenges as Opportunities

Embracing challenges as opportunities is a transformative mindset that can propel you toward personal growth and confidence. Life is replete with obstacles that can either deter you or serve as steppingstones to greater achievements. When you shift your perspective to view these challenges as opportunities for learning and growth, you unlock a powerful resource within yourself. Each challenge you face is a chance to discover your resilience, enhance your skills, and build a stronger foundation for your future.

Start by reframing your thoughts when encountering difficulties. Instead of seeing a setback as a roadblock, view it as a pivotal moment in your journey. This shift in thinking allows you to tap into positive affirmations, reinforcing your belief in your ability to overcome adversity. Remind yourself that every successful individual has faced challenges, and it is their response to these situations that sets them apart. Embrace the discomfort that comes with challenges; it is often the catalyst for profound personal growth.

Visualization practices can also play a crucial role in embracing challenges. Picture yourself navigating through a tough situation successfully; see yourself emerging stronger and more capable. This mental rehearsal not only prepares you for real-life encounters but also fosters a sense of confidence that you can draw upon when faced with adversity. Visualization helps you establish a clear goal and instills the belief that you can achieve it, regardless of the hurdles in your path.

Developing a growth mindset is essential in this journey. Understand that intelligence and abilities are not fixed traits but can be developed through dedication and hard work. When you adopt this mindset, you become more willing to take risks and step outside your comfort zone. Challenges will no longer intimidate you; instead, they will excite you as opportunities for improvement. Embrace the notion that failures are simply learning experiences that contribute to your overall development, leading you closer to your true potential.

Building confidence and self-esteem is a natural byproduct of embracing challenges. As you confront and overcome obstacles, you cultivate a sense of achievement and self-worth. Celebrate your victories, no matter how small, and acknowledge the progress you make along the way. This practice will reinforce your belief in your capabilities and encourage you to tackle even bigger challenges. By embracing challenges as opportunities, you embark on a journey of self-discovery that ultimately leads to a more fulfilling and confident life.

BUILDING CONFIDENCE FROM WITHIN

Identifying Your Strengths and Weaknesses

The process of identifying one's strengths and weaknesses is a fundamental aspect of personal growth and development. It involves an honest and courageous exploration of our own abilities, traits, and shortcomings. This journey, when undertaken with sincerity and commitment, can lead to profound self-awareness, empowerment, and improved performance in various aspects of life.

To begin the process, it is essential to reflect on moments in your life when you felt confident, empowered, and successful. These instances often serve as indicators of your strengths, as they highlight the unique qualities and skills that you possess. By identifying these strengths, you can gain a clearer understanding of your abilities, enabling you to build upon them and leverage them to your advantage in different situations. Celebrating your strengths is also crucial, as it reinforces your confidence and self-esteem, allowing you to approach challenges with a positive mindset.

Equally important is acknowledging your weaknesses, which should not be viewed as failures but rather as opportunities for growth. Each weakness presents a chance to learn, evolve, and develop new skills or mindsets that can help you overcome challenges. Instead of shying away from your weaknesses, confront them with curiosity and a willingness to learn. Ask yourself what specific skills, knowledge, or attitudes you lack that could help you address these challenges more effectively. By shifting your perspective from one of deficiency to one of possibility, you can begin to view weaknesses not as limitations but as areas for potential improvement.

Positive affirmations and visualization techniques can be powerful tools to aid in this process. Create a list of affirmations that reinforce your strengths and address your weaknesses constructively. For instance, if you struggle with time management, an affirmation could be, "I am becoming increasingly skilled at prioritizing tasks and managing my time effectively." Visualize yourself successfully navigating situations where your weaknesses may arise. This practice can help build confidence, prepare your mind for challenges, and foster a growth mindset.

A growth mindset is crucial in the journey of identifying and addressing your strengths and weaknesses. Understanding that strengths can be nurtured and developed, while weaknesses can be transformed into skills through dedicated practice and persistence, is essential. Embrace the belief that you can improve with effort and perseverance. This mindset fosters resilience, allowing you to face setbacks with determination and a commitment to continued growth.

Moreover, it is important to remember that the process of identifying your strengths and weaknesses is an ongoing journey. Embrace it with an open heart, a willingness to learn, and a growth mindset. Surround yourself with supportive individuals who encourage your growth and celebrate your achievements. With every step taken in awareness, you come closer to unleashing your full potential and becoming a more confident and empowered individual.

Recognizing and addressing your strengths and weaknesses is an essential component of personal growth and development. By reflecting on past experiences, acknowledging both your abilities and areas for improvement, utilizing positive affirmations and visualization techniques, and fostering a growth mindset, you can embark on a transformative journey of self-discovery and improvement. Embrace this process, and remember that each step taken in awareness brings you closer to realizing your full potential and becoming the best version of yourself.

Setting Achievable Goals

Setting achievable goals is a crucial step in the journey of personal growth and self-discovery. When we articulate our ambitions clearly, we create a roadmap that guides us toward realizing our fullest potential. The key to effective goal setting lies in understanding that aspirations must be grounded in reality, allowing us to stretch our capabilities without overwhelming ourselves. By breaking down our larger dreams into smaller, manageable tasks, we set ourselves up for success, building momentum and confidence along the way.

To begin this process, it's essential to reflect on what truly matters to you. Take a moment to visualize your ideal life—what does it look like? What feelings does it evoke? This mental imagery serves as inspiration, but the real magic happens when you translate that vision into specific, actionable goals. Use positive affirmations to reinforce your commitment to these goals, reminding yourself daily of your ability to achieve them. Affirmations act as powerful tools that reshape your mindset, fostering a belief in your potential and encouraging you to pursue your dreams relentlessly.

As you set these goals, remember the importance of making them SMART: Specific, Measurable, Achievable, Relevant, and Time-bound. Each element plays a vital role in ensuring that your objectives are not only clear but also attainable. For instance, instead of saying, "I want to be fit," articulate it as, "I will exercise three times a week for thirty minutes." This clarity eliminates ambiguity and allows you to track your progress effectively. Each small victory you achieve will boost your confidence and serve as a reminder of your capability to overcome challenges.

Embracing a growth mindset is essential in this goal-setting journey. Understand that setbacks and failures are not indications of your inadequacy but rather stepping stones toward growth. When you encounter obstacles, reflect on them as learning opportunities. Adjust your approach, if necessary, and keep your eyes on the prize. This resilience and adaptability will not only enhance your confidence but will also reinforce your commitment to the goals you've set. Remember, every great achievement was once considered impossible until someone dared to pursue it.

Celebrate your achievements, no matter how small they may seem. Each step forward is an affirmation of your progress and a testament to your dedication. Take the time to acknowledge your hard work, and allow these moments of celebration to fuel your motivation for the next goal. By continuously setting and achieving goals, you will cultivate a deeper sense of self-esteem and confidence, empowering you to unleash your full potential. The journey toward personal growth is ongoing, and with each goal you set, you take another step toward the extraordinary life you envision.

Celebrating Small Wins

In the journey of personal growth, celebrating small wins is an essential practice that can significantly boost motivation and confidence. Often, we set grand goals and envision monumental achievements, but in the day-to-day hustle, we may overlook the importance of acknowledging the smaller steps that lead us to our ultimate aspirations. Each minor accomplishment—whether it's completing a task, overcoming a fear, or making a new connection—deserves recognition.

By taking a moment to celebrate these small victories, we cultivate a positive mindset that reinforces our belief in our capabilities and propels us forward.

The act of celebrating small wins is more than just a fleeting moment of joy; it acts as a powerful affirmation of progress. When we recognize the effort we've put into a task, no matter how trivial it may seem, we reinforce our growth mindset. This practice encourages us to reflect on our journey rather than solely focusing on the end goal. By shifting our perspective to appreciate the small steps, we create a habit of gratitude, which in turn fosters resilience. This resilience becomes our ally, helping us navigate the inevitable challenges that arise in our pursuit of personal development.

Incorporating rituals to celebrate these small victories can enhance their impact. Consider setting aside time at the end of each week to review what you have achieved, jotting down moments that made you feel proud. Whether it's treating yourself to a favorite snack, sharing your accomplishments with a friend, or simply taking a moment to smile and acknowledge your progress, these rituals reinforce your commitment to growth. They remind you that every step, no matter how small, is a vital part of your journey and deserves recognition.

As you celebrate your small wins, take a moment to visualize your future. Picture the culmination of your efforts and the person you are becoming. This exercise not only boosts your confidence but also aligns your mindset with your goals. By imagining the positive outcomes of your hard work, you create a powerful mental framework that drives you to continue pushing forward. This dual practice of celebrating the present while envisioning the future can ignite your passion and determination.

Embracing the practice of celebrating small wins transforms your approach to personal growth. It allows you to see setbacks as steppingstones rather than obstacles, reinforcing the belief that you are capable of achieving your dreams. Every small win is a testament to your dedication and resilience, and acknowledging them fuels your journey toward greater confidence and self-esteem. In this process, you learn to appreciate the richness of your journey, reinforcing the notion that every day is an opportunity to grow, evolve, and become the best version of yourself.

OVERCOMING FEAR AND SELF DOUBT

Understanding the Roots of Fear

Fear is an innate human emotion, a primal response ingrained within us since the dawn of our existence. It serves a crucial and often understated purpose, acting as a protective mechanism that alerts us to potential danger, whether physical, emotional, or social. This internal alarm system has ensured our survival, guiding our ancestors away from predators and towards safety. However, in the complex tapestry of the modern world, where threats are often less tangible and more psychological, this primal instinct can manifest in ways that hinder our personal growth, stifle our creativity, and ultimately prevent us from realizing our full potential. To truly understand fear, we must first acknowledge its multifaceted roots, which often lie deeply buried within our past experiences, subtly shaped by societal conditioning, and sometimes even inherited through ancestral trauma. Recognizing that fear is not merely an enemy to be vanquished, but an intrinsic and complex part of the human experience, allows us to approach it with curiosity and compassion rather than immediate resistance or judgment. By understanding its origins and nuances, we can begin to dismantle its power over us and learn to harness its energy for growth and transformation.

Many fears are learned behaviors, often instilled during the formative years of childhood or through significant, sometimes traumatic, life events. From a young age, we absorb information and emotional cues from our environment, particularly from our parents, caregivers, and peers. These early interactions shape our perceptions of the world and, crucially, our beliefs about ourselves. A child who is repeatedly told, directly or indirectly, that they are not good enough, that they are incapable, or that they are prone to making mistakes, may grow into an adult who fears failure — a fear that then stifles their ambitions, limits their willingness to take risks, and ultimately hinders their dreams. Similarly, a traumatic event, such as a car accident or a public speaking disaster, can imprint a lasting fear that manifests as anxiety in similar situations in the future. As we navigate through life, these experiences accumulate, forming intricate patterns of fear and avoidance that dictate our choices and shape our identities. By actively reflecting on the origins of our individual fears, by tracing them back to the specific moments and messages that triggered them, we can begin to unravel the complex narratives that hold us back from living authentically and fulfilling our potential. This process requires a courageous and honest examination of our past, acknowledging the pain and vulnerability that may have been buried deep within. It also necessitates recognizing that, while these fears may have served a protective function at one point in our lives, perhaps even keeping us physically or emotionally safe, they are no longer serving our best interests, and in fact, are actively preventing us from thriving.

It is essential, therefore, to differentiate between rational fears and irrational ones, to discern between the genuine threats that warrant a cautious response and the phantom menaces conjured by our own anxieties. Rational fears, such as the fear of crossing a busy street without looking or touching a hot stove, are critical for our survival. They are based on real and present dangers and prompt us to take necessary precautions. On the other hand, irrational fears, often rooted in unfounded beliefs, past traumas, or societal pressures, can paralyze us, hindering our ability to make rational decisions and live fulfilling lives. These fears often manifest in the form of anxiety, phobias, or avoidance behaviors, and are frequently rooted in our imagination rather than grounded in reality. The fear of public speaking, for example, may stem from a fear of judgment or a fear of making mistakes, rather than from a realistic assessment of the potential consequences. These irrational fears can create significant barriers to our success, inhibiting our ability to pursue promising career opportunities, connect with others on a deeper level, or even simply enjoy everyday experiences. As we learn to consciously confront and challenge these irrational fears, by questioning their validity and exposing ourselves to the situations that trigger them in a controlled and supportive environment, we open the door to a more fulfilling and empowered life, allowing our deepest aspirations to flourish instead of being perpetually stifled by the weight of anxiety.

Visualization practices can be a remarkably powerful tool in overcoming fear, allowing us to reprogram our subconscious mind and create new, more positive associations with previously feared situations. By vividly envisioning ourselves successfully navigating a challenging scenario, whether it's delivering a compelling presentation, engaging in a difficult conversation, or simply trying something new, we can actually rewire the brain to associate positive outcomes with situations that previously triggered anxiety and avoidance. This practice reinforces the belief that we are capable, competent, and worthy of achieving greatness, despite the presence of fear. Positive affirmations, when used consistently and with genuine intention, further bolster this empowering mindset, reminding us that fear does not define us, nor does it dictate our fate. Instead, it is a temporary emotion, a stepping stone on our ongoing journey toward self-discovery, personal growth, and ultimately, profound empowerment. By consistently incorporating visualization and affirmations into our daily routine, we consciously shift our focus from what we fear might happen to what we are capable of achieving, thereby reclaiming our agency and fostering a sense of inner strength.

Understanding the roots of fear is about reclaiming our power, taking ownership of our emotional landscape, and choosing to live a life driven by courage and authenticity rather than by the constraints of anxiety. It is a call to recognize that fear is not an insurmountable barrier, but rather a challenge to be faced, an opportunity for growth, and a pathway to deeper self-understanding. As we peel back the layers of our fears, one by one, examining their origins and questioning their validity, we inevitably discover the inner strength and resilience to confront them head-on, to move beyond our comfort zones, and to embrace new possibilities. This ongoing journey of self-exploration fosters a deep sense of self-awareness, allowing us to cultivate a growth mindset that embraces challenges with open arms, viewing them not as threats, but as opportunities for learning and expansion. By transforming our relationship with fear, by shifting from a position of avoidance and resistance to one of acceptance and curiosity, we unlock the limitless potential within ourselves, paving the way for a life filled with confidence, joy, genuine connection, and unbounded possibility. The courage to face our fears is not the absence of fear, but the triumph over it. It is the unwavering commitment to living a life aligned with our values and aspirations, even in the face of uncertainty and discomfort. And it is within this courageous embrace of our fears that we discover the true essence of our strength and resilience.

Techniques for Confronting Your Fears

Facing your fears is a crucial step in the journey towards personal growth and self-discovery. It begins with acknowledging your fears rather than avoiding them. By identifying what truly scares you, you create a pathway to understanding and overcoming those fears. This recognition is not a sign of weakness; rather, it is an empowering act that allows you to take control of your life. Embrace this first step with a sense of curiosity and determination, knowing that every journey begins with a single decision to confront the unknown.

- Visualization is a powerful technique that can transform your relationship with fear. Picture yourself in situations that typically induce anxiety or discomfort. Imagine handling these scenarios with confidence and grace. As you visualize, engage all your senses; see the environment, hear the sounds, and feel the emotions associated with your success. This mental rehearsal prepares your mind to face real-life situations with a sense of calm. Over time, these positive images will replace negative thoughts, reinforcing your belief in your ability to overcome challenges. Trust in the power of your imagination to build a more confident version of yourself.

- Incorporating positive affirmations into your daily routine can also serve as a vital tool in confronting your fears. By repeating affirmations that resonate with your goals and desires, you program your subconscious mind to believe in your capabilities. Statements such as "I am capable of overcoming my fears" or "I embrace challenges as opportunities for growth" can shift your mindset. The more you affirm these beliefs, the more they become ingrained in your psyche. This practice not only boosts your self-esteem but also cultivates resilience, enabling you to tackle your fears head-on.

- Another effective technique is gradual exposure to your fears. Start by confronting them in small, manageable doses. If public speaking terrifies you, begin by speaking in front of a mirror, then to a trusted friend, and eventually work your way up to larger audiences. Each step you take reinforces your courage and builds confidence. Celebrate your progress, no matter how small, as each victory is a testament to your strength and commitment to personal growth. Remember, the journey is as important as the destination, and every step forward is a triumph.

- Finally, surround yourself with a supportive community that encourages your growth. Share your fears with trusted friends or join groups focused on personal development. Engaging with others who are on similar journeys can provide motivation and accountability. Their encouragement will remind you that you are not alone in your struggles. Together, you can celebrate successes and navigate setbacks, reinforcing the belief that confronting fears is a shared experience. In this collective journey, you will find strength, inspiration, and the confidence needed to unleash your true potential.

-

Developing Resilience through Adversity

Adversity is an inevitable part of life, weaving its way into our personal narratives and challenging our resolve. Like the relentless tides shaping the coastline, adversity sculpts our character, revealing hidden strengths and forcing us to confront our limitations. However, it is in these moments of struggle that we often discover the depths of our strength and resilience. Embracing adversity as a teacher rather than an adversary can transform the way we perceive our challenges. Each setback, every obstacle, can serve as a catalyst for growth, offering valuable lessons that shape our character and fortify our spirit. By shifting our mindset to view difficulties as opportunities for learning, we lay the groundwork for resilience, a crucial attribute for navigating the complexities and uncertainties of life.

Building resilience starts with acknowledging our feelings and experiences during tough times. It's easy to fall into despair when faced with trials; the weight of a seemingly insurmountable problem can feel crushing. However, suppressing these emotions is counterproductive. Recognizing and validating these emotions is crucial. Allow yourself to feel the pain, frustration, and disappointment, but do not dwell in negativity. Acknowledge these feelings without judgment, understanding that they are a natural response to challenging circumstances. Then, consciously shift your focus towards proactive coping mechanisms. Use positive affirmations to counter any self-doubt that arises. Phrases like "I am capable," "I can overcome this," and "I am learning and growing from this experience" can serve as powerful reminders of your inherent strength and potential. This practice not only bolsters self-esteem but also creates a mental environment conducive to problem-solving and growth, allowing you to approach challenges with a clearer perspective and a renewed sense of hope.

Visualization plays a vital role in cultivating resilience. The power of the mind to shape reality is profound, and visualization allows us to harness this potential. Picture yourself overcoming challenges and emerging stronger on the other side. By vividly imagining successful outcomes, you prepare your mind to navigate real-life obstacles with confidence and determination. This technique can help rewire your brain to respond positively when faced with adversity, creating new neural pathways that support resilience. The more you visualize triumph, the more likely you are to manifest those outcomes in your reality. Creating a mental blueprint of success encourages you to take proactive steps toward your goals, reinforcing the belief that you are capable of enduring and thriving. Consider visualizing not only the end result but also the steps you will take to achieve it, further solidifying your resolve and preparing you for the journey ahead. This proactive mental rehearsal allows you to anticipate potential challenges and develop strategies to overcome them, fostering a sense of control even in the face of uncertainty.

Adopting a growth mindset is essential in developing resilience. This mindset, championed by Carol Dweck, embraces the idea that our abilities and intelligence can be developed through dedication and hard work. It stands in stark contrast to a fixed mindset, which assumes that our talents and abilities are innate and unchangeable. When faced with adversity, those with a growth mindset view challenges as opportunities to expand their skills and understanding. Instead of feeling defeated, they ask themselves what lessons can be learned and how they can improve. This perspective not only enhances resilience but also fosters a sense of curiosity and a love for learning, making it easier to navigate life's ups and downs. Embracing a growth mindset means reframing failures and setbacks as valuable learning experiences, providing opportunities for growth and improvement. It also encourages you to seek out challenges and embrace experimentation, knowing that even if you don't succeed immediately, you will gain valuable knowledge and experience in the process.

Building a strong support network is crucial for fostering resilience. Connecting with friends, family, or mentors can provide invaluable emotional support and practical advice during challenging times. Sharing your experiences with others who understand and empathize can help you feel less alone and more empowered to cope with adversity. Seeking guidance from individuals who have successfully navigated similar challenges can provide valuable insights and strategies for overcoming obstacles. Remember that seeking help is a sign of strength, not weakness, and that leaning on others can provide the emotional and practical support you need to persevere.

Resilience is about bouncing back and moving forward with renewed vigor. It's not about avoiding adversity altogether, but about developing the ability to learn, adapt, and grow in the face of challenges. Each experience of overcoming adversity becomes a building block for your confidence and self-esteem. As you navigate through life's challenges, remember that you are not alone; many have walked this path and emerged transformed. Embrace your journey, trust in your ability to adapt, and remind yourself that resilience is not just about surviving but thriving. It's about emerging from the crucible of adversity stronger, wiser, and more compassionate. By developing this vital trait, you unlock the potential within yourself to face anything life throws your way, emerging stronger and more empowered than ever before. By embracing adversity as a catalyst for growth and cultivating the tools to navigate challenges effectively, you can transform obstacles into opportunities and unlock your full potential for a fulfilling and resilient life.

THE JOURNEY TOWARD PERSONAL GROWTH

Defining Personal Growth

Personal growth is a multifaceted concept that encompasses the continuous process of self-improvement and self-discovery. It involves an individual's journey to develop their potential, enhance their capabilities, and enrich their understanding of themselves and the world around them. This process is often driven by the desire for greater fulfillment and a deeper sense of meaning in life. While personal growth can take many forms—emotional, intellectual, social, and spiritual—it is defined by the commitment to evolve and adapt in pursuit of one's goals and values. This ongoing evolution is not a destination but rather a lifelong journey, characterized by continuous learning, adaptation, and a willingness to embrace change.

The philosophical underpinnings of personal growth can be traced back to existentialist thought, which emphasizes the importance of individual agency and the quest for meaning. This philosophical framework encourages individuals to confront their own existence and make conscious choices that align with their true selves. Through this lens, personal growth is not merely about achieving external success, measured by societal standards, but rather about cultivating an inner sense of purpose and authenticity. As individuals reflect on their values and beliefs, they become more equipped to navigate life's challenges, fostering resilience and emotional intelligence. This introspection allows for a deeper understanding of one's motivations and desires, guiding individuals to make choices that are genuinely aligned with their authentic selves, rather than being driven by external pressures or expectations. The emphasis on individual responsibility within existentialism highlights the active role each person plays in shaping their own growth and development.

An essential component of personal growth is the cultivation of emotional intelligence, which involves recognizing, understanding, and managing one's emotions as well as empathizing with others. This skill set not only enhances interpersonal relationships but also contributes to overall well-being. By developing emotional intelligence, individuals can better navigate the complexities of their feelings and the feelings of those around them, leading to more meaningful connections and experiences. The interplay between emotional intelligence and personal growth underscores the importance of self-awareness and self-regulation in achieving a more satisfying life. Furthermore, the development of emotional intelligence allows individuals to build stronger and more supportive relationships, fostering a sense of belonging and connection that is crucial for personal growth. Learning to effectively communicate emotions, resolve conflicts constructively, and demonstrate empathy can significantly enhance the quality of life and pave the way for deeper, more fulfilling interactions.

Beyond emotional intelligence, personal growth is also intrinsically linked to continuous learning and the expansion of one's intellectual horizons. Actively seeking knowledge, whether through formal education, self-directed study, or simply engaging in conversations with others, broadens perspectives and challenges pre-conceived notions. This intellectual curiosity fosters adaptability and critical thinking skills, allowing individuals to respond effectively to new and complex situations. Embracing a growth mindset, which emphasizes the belief that abilities and intelligence can be developed through dedication and hard work, is also crucial. This mindset encourages individuals to embrace challenges, learn from failures, and persist in the face of setbacks, ultimately leading to greater personal and professional achievements.

Moreover, the social aspect of personal growth should not be overlooked. Engaging in acts of service, contributing to the community, and building meaningful relationships with others not only enriches the lives of those around us but also provides valuable opportunities for self-reflection and growth. By stepping outside of our own comfort zones and connecting with people from diverse backgrounds, we gain new perspectives and challenge our own biases, ultimately expanding our understanding of the world and our place within it. Furthermore, engaging in collaborative endeavors and working towards a common goal can foster leadership skills, teamwork, and a sense of purpose that extends beyond individual achievements.

For many, personal growth also incorporates a spiritual dimension, which may involve exploring philosophical questions, engaging in religious practices, or simply cultivating a sense of connection to something larger than themselves. This spiritual exploration can provide a framework for understanding life's big questions, such as the meaning of existence, the nature of good and evil, and the search for ultimate truth. Whether through meditation, prayer, or contemplation of nature, cultivating a spiritual practice can foster inner peace, resilience, and a sense of purpose that transcends the material world. Inspirational stories of everyday heroes often serve as powerful reminders of the potential for growth within each person. These narratives highlight the transformative journeys of individuals who have overcome adversity, embraced change, and pursued their passions. Such stories inspire others to embark on their own paths of self-discovery, reinforcing the notion that personal growth is attainable and can lead to profound changes in one's life. The resilience demonstrated by these heroes exemplifies the human capacity for growth, encouraging individuals to confront their fears and strive for their aspirations.

The impact of gratitude on personal growth cannot be overlooked. Gratitude fosters a positive mindset and enhances life satisfaction, allowing individuals to appreciate their journey and the lessons learned along the way. By cultivating a practice of gratitude, people can shift their focus from what they lack to what they have, promoting a more optimistic outlook on life. This shift not only supports personal growth but also enriches relationships and overall well-being. As individuals embrace gratitude, they create a fertile ground for personal transformation, paving the way toward a more joyful and fulfilled existence.

Personal growth is a dynamic and multifaceted process that encompasses emotional, intellectual, social, and spiritual development. It is a journey of self-discovery and self-improvement, driven by the desire for a more fulfilling and meaningful life. By embracing continuous learning, cultivating emotional intelligence, nurturing meaningful relationships, and exploring our values and beliefs, we can unlock our full potential and navigate the complexities of life with greater resilience, purpose, and authenticity. This continuous pursuit of self-improvement not only benefits the individual but also contributes to a more compassionate, understanding, and thriving society.

Overcoming Obstacles to Growth: A Journey Towards Joy and Fulfillment

Overcoming obstacles to growth is a crucial aspect of the pursuit of joy, encapsulating the challenges that often accompany personal development. Life is replete with obstacles, whether they manifest as external circumstances or internal doubts. Understanding these barriers is the first step to transcending them. Many individuals grapple with fear of failure, self-doubt, and societal expectations, all of which can impede their journey toward happiness. Recognizing these obstacles not only validates our experiences but also allows us to confront them with a more informed and resilient mindset. This acknowledgment is not merely a passive acceptance of hardship, but an active engagement with the complexities of the human experience. It allows us to identify patterns in our reactions, understand the roots of our anxieties, and ultimately, develop strategies to navigate future challenges with greater ease and confidence. Without this initial recognition, we remain trapped in a cycle of avoidance, hindering our potential for growth and hindering our ability to truly experience joy.

Emotional intelligence plays a pivotal role in navigating the complexities of personal growth. It involves being aware of our emotions and understanding how they influence our thoughts and actions. By cultivating emotional intelligence, we can better manage our reactions to obstacles. This self-awareness fosters a greater capacity for empathy, enabling us to connect with others who may be facing similar challenges. Such connections can provide support and encouragement, reinforcing the idea that we are not alone in our struggles. This shared experience can be a powerful motivator, propelling us forward even when the path seems steep. Cultivating emotional intelligence isn't a solitary endeavor. It often requires actively seeking feedback from trusted friends, family, or mentors. Learning to identify our emotional triggers and understanding the subconscious narratives that drive our behavior can be a transformative process. Furthermore, it allows us to develop healthier coping mechanisms for dealing with stress and adversity, moving beyond reactive responses to more thoughtful and constructive actions. Through mindful practices like meditation or journaling, we can cultivate a deeper understanding of our inner landscape, fostering resilience and adaptability in the face of challenges.

Inspirational stories of everyday heroes serve as reminders that overcoming obstacles is not only possible but often leads to profound personal transformation. These narratives highlight individuals who have faced significant adversity and emerged stronger, embodying resilience and hope. Their journeys often illuminate the importance of perseverance and the power of a positive mindset. By sharing these stories, we can inspire others to recognize their own potential for growth, even in the face of daunting challenges. Such examples serve as beacons of possibility, encouraging us to embrace our struggles and view them as opportunities for development. These narratives aren't just about grand, sweeping victories; they often showcase the quiet courage of individuals who persevere through daily struggles, demonstrating that even small acts of resilience can lead to significant transformations. Whether it's the story of a single parent working multiple jobs to provide for their children, or an individual battling a chronic illness while pursuing their passions, these accounts serve as powerful reminders that the human spirit is capable of enduring immense hardship and emerging stronger on the other side. By internalizing these stories, we can develop a greater sense of self-efficacy, believing in our own ability to overcome obstacles and achieve our goals.

The philosophy of happiness emphasizes the importance of perspective when confronted with obstacles. Rather than viewing challenges as insurmountable barriers, they can be reframed as essential components of the growth process. This shift in perspective is integral to fostering a positive attitude, which can significantly impact our overall well-being. By practicing gratitude for the lessons learned through hardship, we can cultivate a mindset that values growth over comfort. This approach not only enhances personal satisfaction but also deepens our understanding of what it means to lead a fulfilling life. This reframing process requires conscious effort and a willingness to challenge our preconceived notions about what it means to face adversity. Practicing mindfulness and focusing on the present moment can help us detach from negative thoughts and emotions, allowing us to see challenges with greater clarity. By acknowledging the opportunities for learning and growth that arise from difficult experiences, we can begin to view obstacles not as roadblocks, but as steppingstones on the path to a more meaningful and purposeful life. Cultivating gratitude, even in the face of hardship, can further amplify this shift in perspective, fostering a sense of contentment and appreciation for the blessings we already possess. Ultimately, overcoming obstacles to growth requires a commitment to self-reflection and a willingness to embrace change. Engaging with existential questions about purpose and meaning can provide clarity in our pursuit of joy. As we navigate our journeys, we must remember that obstacles are often the catalysts for profound change. By embracing our struggles with courage and optimism, we can transform our challenges into stepping stones toward a more enriched and meaningful existence.

This journey not only enhances our own lives but also inspires those around us to pursue their paths with renewed vigor and hope. Embracing change requires stepping outside of our comfort zones and being willing to experiment with new approaches and perspectives. This might involve seeking out new challenges, taking risks, or even re-evaluating our values and beliefs. Engaging in self-reflection, through journaling, meditation, or therapy, can help us gain a deeper understanding of our motivations, fears, and aspirations. By confronting existential questions about our purpose and meaning, we can gain clarity on what truly matters to us, allowing us to align our actions with our values and live a more authentic and fulfilling life. In doing so, we not only pave the way for our own personal growth but also inspire those around us to embrace their own journeys of self-discovery and transformation, creating a ripple effect of positive change in the world. The pursuit of joy is not a destination, but a continuous process of overcoming obstacles, embracing change, and striving for a more meaningful and fulfilling existence.

Lifelong Learning and Happiness

Lifelong learning is an essential component in the quest for happiness, serving as a pathway to personal growth and fulfillment. As adults navigate their lives, the acquisition of knowledge and skills does not cease with formal education; instead, it becomes a continuous process that enriches both the mind and spirit. Engaging in lifelong learning fosters a sense of curiosity and wonder about the world, which can lead to greater emotional intelligence. This emotional growth allows individuals to better understand themselves and others, enhancing relationships and paving the way for deeper connections that contribute significantly to overall happiness.

The philosophy of happiness emphasizes that joy is not a destination but a journey, one that is greatly enhanced by a commitment to learning. By embracing new experiences, whether through formal classes, workshops, or self-directed study, individuals can cultivate a growth mindset. This mindset encourages resilience in the face of challenges and transforms setbacks into opportunities for learning. As adults face the complexities of life, adopting such an approach can lead to a greater sense of agency and control, fostering contentment and satisfaction in their everyday lives.

Furthermore, the power of positive thinking plays a crucial role in lifelong learning. When individuals approach learning with an optimistic outlook, they are more likely to embrace challenges and view failures as steppingstones rather than roadblocks. This positivity not only enhances the learning experience but also contributes to emotional well-being. Research indicates that a positive mindset can significantly impact one's overall life satisfaction, suggesting that the act of learning itself can serve as a source of joy and fulfillment.

The impact of gratitude on life satisfaction cannot be overstated in the context of lifelong learning. As individuals engage in new learning experiences, they often encounter moments of insight and growth that can foster a sense of appreciation for their journey. By practicing gratitude, learners can enhance their emotional resilience and develop a more profound sense of happiness. This reflective practice encourages individuals to recognize and celebrate their achievements, no matter how small, reinforcing the idea that happiness is cultivated through awareness and appreciation of one's experiences.

In exploring existential questions and the meaning of life, lifelong learning emerges as a vital tool for self-discovery. As adults seek to understand their place in the world, the knowledge gained through continuous learning can provide clarity and direction. This process not only contributes to personal growth but also enhances philosophical reflections on love and relationships. By understanding diverse perspectives and ideas, individuals can deepen their connections with others, contributing to a richer, more satisfying life. Ultimately, the pursuit of lifelong learning is intricately linked to the pursuit of happiness, revealing that joy is found in the journey of acquiring knowledge and embracing the world around us.

THE ROLE OF GRATITUDE IN PERSONAL GROWTH

The Benefits of a Gratitude Practice

Gratitude is a transformative practice that has the power to change our perspective on life and significantly enhance our overall well-being. When we cultivate gratitude, we shift our focus from what we lack to what we have, fostering a mindset that appreciates the abundance in our lives. This simple yet profound practice encourages us to recognize and celebrate the small joys and significant milestones alike, laying the groundwork for a more positive and fulfilling existence. By embracing gratitude, we open our hearts and minds to possibilities, allowing us to connect with our true selves and the world around us.

One of the most remarkable benefits of a gratitude practice is its ability to reduce stress and anxiety. When we take a moment each day to reflect on the things we appreciate, we create a mental buffer against negative thoughts and feelings. This shift not only helps to alleviate the burdens of daily life but also empowers us to respond to challenges with a calm and centered mindset. As we replace worry with gratitude, we find that we are better equipped to handle setbacks and obstacles, ultimately contributing to our resilience and emotional strength.

In addition to fostering resilience, gratitude enhances our relationships with others. Acknowledging the contributions and kindness of those around us strengthens our connections and encourages a spirit of reciprocity. When we express appreciation to friends, family, and colleagues, we not only uplift their spirits but also cultivate a positive environment that promotes collaboration and support. This ripple effect of gratitude can transform our social circles, leading to deeper bonds, improved communication, and a sense of belonging that enriches our lives.

Incorporating gratitude into our daily routines can significantly boost our self-esteem and confidence. By recognizing our achievements and the positive aspects of ourselves, we counteract the inner critic that often holds us back. Acknowledging our strengths and the progress we make toward our goals fosters a sense of accomplishment and self-worth. As we become more attuned to our positive attributes, we develop a growth mindset that encourages exploration, learning, and the pursuit of our dreams without the fear of failure.

The practice of gratitude ignites our motivation and inspires us to visualize a brighter future. When we focus on the abundance in our lives, we naturally become more optimistic about what lies ahead. This optimism fuels our ambitions and drives us to set and pursue meaningful goals. By envisioning our dreams while grounded in gratitude, we align our actions with our values and aspirations, creating a powerful synergy that propels us toward personal growth. Embracing gratitude as a daily practice not only enriches our lives but also empowers us to unleash our full potential, transforming our journey into one of boundless possibilities.

Creating a Daily Gratitude Ritual

Creating a daily gratitude ritual can be a transformative experience, allowing you to cultivate a mindset that embraces positivity and self-empowerment. By consciously acknowledging the things you are grateful for, you create a powerful shift in your perspective. This ritual doesn't require elaborate setups or extensive time commitments; it can be as simple as taking a few moments each day to reflect on what brings you joy and fulfillment. Embracing this practice can enhance your personal growth journey, providing you with a solid foundation of appreciation that fuels your confidence and self-esteem.

Start by setting aside a specific time each day dedicated to your gratitude ritual. This could be first thing in the morning, as you sip your coffee, or right before bed, reflecting on the day's experiences. Consistency is key; establishing a routine helps reinforce the habit and allows you to integrate gratitude into your daily life seamlessly. During this time, allow yourself to truly feel the gratitude for each item on your list. Whether it's a supportive friend, a delicious meal, or a moment of peace, savor these feelings. This practice not only highlights the positives but also trains your mind to seek out the good in every situation.

As you engage in this daily ritual, consider journaling your thoughts. Writing down your gratitude helps solidify these feelings and gives you a tangible record of your journey. You may find that as you write, new insights and reflections arise, deepening your understanding of what truly matters to you. Over time, this written record becomes a treasure trove of positivity that you can revisit whenever you need a boost of confidence or inspiration. The act of writing itself can be cathartic, allowing you to express emotions and thoughts that may otherwise go unacknowledged.

Incorporate visualization techniques into your gratitude ritual for an even more profound impact. As you reflect on the things you are grateful for, take a moment to visualize them in your mind. Picture the warmth of a loved one's embrace or the vibrant colors of a beautiful sunset. This practice not only enhances the emotional connection to your gratitude but also reinforces a positive mental image that can uplift your spirit. Visualization paired with gratitude fosters a deeper appreciation for your life, encouraging you to embrace the abundance surrounding you.

Share your gratitude with others. Expressing appreciation can strengthen relationships and create a ripple effect of positivity. Whether you send a heartfelt message to a friend or share your gratitude in a group setting, this act of acknowledgment can boost your confidence and inspire others to embrace their own gratitude rituals. By fostering an environment of appreciation, you not only benefit personally but also contribute to a collective shift towards positivity and growth. As you continue on your journey, remember that cultivating gratitude is a powerful tool that can help you unleash your potential and thrive in all areas of your life.

Shifting Perspectives *through* Thankfulness

In the journey of personal growth, one of the most transformative tools at our disposal is the practice of thankfulness. Shifting our perspectives through thankfulness enables us to move beyond the constraints of our current situations and tap into the abundance that life offers. When we consciously choose to focus on gratitude, we begin to change the narrative of our lives. Instead of viewing challenges as insurmountable obstacles, we start recognizing them as opportunities for growth and learning. This shift allows us to cultivate resilience and embrace a mindset that is open to new possibilities.

Thankfulness acts as a powerful lens through which we can view our experiences. When we express gratitude, we are not merely acknowledging what we have; we are also affirming our worth and the value of our journey. Each moment of appreciation serves as a reminder of our achievements, no matter how small. This practice reinforces our self-esteem and builds our confidence. Every time we recognize and celebrate our successes, we reinforce the belief that we are capable of greatness, fostering a growth mindset that propels us forward.

Visualization, intertwined with thankfulness, enhances our ability to manifest our desires and aspirations. When we visualize our goals while expressing gratitude for what we already have, we create a powerful synergy. This combination allows us to attract more positive experiences into our lives. Instead of fixating on what is lacking, we focus on abundance. By doing so, we rewire our brains to seek out opportunities rather than dwell on limitations. Our thoughts become aligned with our intentions, paving the way for us to realize our dreams and ambitions.

Incorporating positive affirmations into our practice of thankfulness further amplifies the shift in perspective. By affirming our strengths and capabilities, we foster a mindset that is not only resilient but also optimistic. Each affirmation is a declaration of our belief in ourselves, reinforcing the notion that we have the power to create the life we desire. When combined with gratitude, these affirmations serve as daily reminders that we deserve success and happiness. They become the foundation upon which we build our confidence and self-esteem.

Shifting perspectives through thankfulness is a deliberate choice that requires practice and commitment. It invites us to see the beauty in every aspect of our lives, transforming even the most mundane moments into opportunities for growth. As we cultivate a habit of gratitude, we discover that our potential is not defined by our circumstances but by our mindset. Embracing thankfulness empowers us to unleash our true potential, guiding us on a path toward greater fulfillment and self-discovery. As we continue this journey, let us remember that the power to transform our lives lies within us, waiting to be unlocked through the simple yet profound act of being thankful.

BUILDING SUPPORTIVE RELATIONSHIPS

The Importance of Community

Community is a vital component in the journey of personal growth and transformation. It serves as a nurturing environment where individuals can flourish and reach their fullest potential. When we surround ourselves with like-minded people who encourage and uplift us, we create a powerful support network that propels us forward. This collective energy ignites motivation and fosters resilience, reminding us that we are not alone in our endeavors. Embracing the strength of community allows us to share our struggles and victories, creating bonds that deepen our understanding of ourselves and others.

In a community, we find a wealth of perspectives and experiences that can challenge and expand our own worldview. Engaging with others encourages us to think critically and embrace diverse ideas, which in turn nurtures a growth mindset. When we actively participate in discussions, listen to different narratives, and remain open to feedback, we cultivate a richer understanding of our own beliefs and capabilities. This process not only enhances our personal development but also builds our confidence as we learn to articulate our thoughts and feelings in a supportive setting.

A strong community acts as a catalyst for accountability. When we declare our intentions within a group, we are more likely to follow through on our commitments. The encouragement and support we receive from others help us stay focused on our goals, even in the face of challenges. This accountability fosters a sense of responsibility not only to ourselves but also to those who believe in us. As we witness each other's progress, we cultivate an atmosphere of trust and encouragement, further enhancing our self-esteem and belief in our capabilities.

The importance of community in our personal growth journey cannot be overstated. It provides us with the tools, support, and inspiration we need to break through barriers and embrace our true potential. By surrounding ourselves with individuals who share our aspirations, we create a powerful environment that nurtures our dreams and amplifies our successes. Together, we can uplift one another, transform our lives, and build a future filled with confidence and self-belief. Embrace your community, for it is a vital part of your journey towards unleashing your potential.

Identifying Toxic Relationships

A Pathway to Personal Empowerment

Identifying toxic relationships is a crucial step on the path to personal growth, confidence, and overall well-being. These relationships, characterized by negativity, manipulation, and a consistent erosion of self-worth, can drain your energy, distort your self-perception, and ultimately, hinder your ability to pursue your dreams and live a fulfilling life. Understanding the subtle yet pervasive signs of toxicity empowers you to take decisive action, cultivate healthier emotional landscapes, and reclaim control over your happiness. As you embark on this journey of self-awareness, remember that acknowledging these damaging dynamics is not a sign of weakness or failure; rather, it is an empowering act of self-preservation, a testament to your strength and a commitment to prioritizing your own mental and emotional health. It's about recognizing your inherent value and refusing to settle for less than you deserve.

One of the first and most telling indicators of a toxic relationship is a persistent feeling of negativity or discomfort that lingers long after the interaction has ended. You may find yourself inexplicably feeling anxious, drained, emotionally depleted, or even fearful in anticipation of or following interactions with certain individuals. This feeling is often subtle, a nagging sense that something is amiss, but it's vital to pay attention to these internal signals. Keep a mental or even a physical journal to track how you feel after spending time with different people. If you consistently leave interactions feeling worse about yourself, your abilities, or your life in general – if you feel small, inadequate, or guilty – it is essential to reflect deeply on the nature of that relationship. This heightened awareness is a powerful affirmation of your intuition, a guiding force leading you toward healthier connections that uplift, inspire, and nourish your soul. It's about trusting your gut feeling, that inner voice that often whispers the truth long before your conscious mind catches up.

Another hallmark of toxicity, often more insidious and damaging, is the presence of manipulation or control. In a healthy relationship, both parties should feel safe, respected, and free to express their thoughts, feelings, and needs without fear of retaliation, judgment, or manipulation. There is an inherent sense of equality and mutual respect. However, in toxic relationships, power dynamics are often skewed, with one person exerting control over the other. This can manifest in various forms: consistently belittling your opinions, dismissing your feelings as invalid, pressuring you to conform to their desires or expectations, using guilt trips to manipulate your actions, or even resorting to threats or intimidation. Remember, you deserve relationships built on mutual respect, trust, and understanding, where your voice is valued and your boundaries are honored. Embrace the empowering belief that you have the inherent right to set boundaries that protect your well-being and to enforce those boundaries without guilt or apology. Learning to say "no" is not selfish; it's an act of self-love and a crucial step in reclaiming your personal power.

Communication, the cornerstone of any healthy relationship, plays a vital role in identifying toxicity. Healthy relationships thrive on open, honest, and respectful dialogue, where both parties feel heard, understood, and validated. In contrast, toxic relationships are often characterized by misunderstandings, blame-shifting, defensiveness, passive-aggressiveness, and a general lack of empathy. If conversations frequently devolve into arguments, leaving you feeling unheard, invalidated, or even gaslighted, it's a significant red flag. Reflect honestly on whether your concerns are acknowledged and addressed with respect or if they are consistently dismissed, minimized, or turned back on you. Does the other person actively listen to your perspective, or are they more focused on defending their own position? By committing to positive affirmations about your inherent right to be heard, respected, and understood, you can cultivate the confidence to address these communication issues directly and assertively. You can choose to seek healthier communication patterns, perhaps through couples counseling or individual therapy, or, if the toxicity persists, distance yourself from those who consistently disregard your voice and invalidate your feelings.

Lastly, and perhaps most importantly, consider the overall impact of the relationship on your personal growth and well-being. A supportive and healthy relationship should encourage you to pursue your goals and dreams, celebrate your successes, provide comfort during setbacks, and inspire you to become the best version of yourself. It should be a source of strength, encouragement, and positive energy. However, if you find that someone consistently undermines your aspirations, discourages your growth, criticizes your efforts, or makes you feel inadequate, it's essential to critically evaluate their influence in your life. Surround yourself with individuals who uplift you, believe in you, and share your vision for a brighter future. Consciously cultivate relationships with people who inspire you to reach your full potential and who support you unconditionally on your journey of self-discovery. By consciously choosing to invest in positive, nurturing relationships, you not only enhance your journey of self-discovery and personal growth but also reinforce your commitment to living a fulfilling, empowered, and authentic life, free from the harmful influence of toxic individuals. Remember, you deserve to be surrounded by people who celebrate your strengths, support your dreams, and love you for who you truly are. Protecting your emotional well-being is not selfish; it's a fundamental act of self-preservation and a necessary step towards creating a life filled with joy, purpose, and genuine connection.

Cultivating Positive Connections: The Foundation of Growth and Confidence

Cultivating positive connections is an essential aspect of personal growth and confidence, acting as the very bedrock upon which we construct meaningful and fulfilling lives. Relationships serve as the foundation upon which we build our experiences, shaping our perspectives, influencing our emotional well-being, and ultimately defining the narrative of our existence. When we consciously surround ourselves with supportive and encouraging individuals, we actively create an environment that is undeniably conducive to growth, resilience, and profound self-discovery. This environment acts as a fertile ground, nourishing our potential and allowing us to flourish. Embracing the power of positive connections, therefore, allows us to not only survive but to truly thrive, encouraging us to courageously pursue our dreams, confront challenges with renewed strength and optimism, and navigate the complexities of life with a supportive network at our side.

The cultivation of these invaluable connections requires a deliberate and multifaceted approach, prioritizing active listening and genuine communication as foundational elements. By being truly present and fully attentive to others during our interactions, we communicate a powerful message: that we genuinely value their thoughts, their feelings, and their experiences. This act of mindful attention fosters trust, a critical component of any meaningful relationship, and subsequently opens the door for deeper, more substantial conversations. These conversations allow us to vulnerably share our aspirations, our hopes, and even our fears, forging bonds built on authenticity and mutual understanding. When we express ourselves authentically, without the fear of judgment, and encourage others to reciprocate in kind, we collectively create a safe space for mutual growth, a sanctuary where vulnerability is celebrated and personal evolution is supported. Remember, every conversation, every interaction, presents a unique opportunity to build a bridge of understanding, connecting us to those who inspire us, challenge us to be our best selves, and ultimately enrich our lives. The quality of these connections directly influences our sense of belonging and our overall well-being.

Furthermore, the seemingly simple, yet profoundly powerful, practice of gratitude can significantly transform our relationships and dramatically enhance our connections with others. By consciously acknowledging the contributions, both large and small, that others make to our lives, we not only uplift and validate them but also actively reinforce our own positivity and appreciation for the good in our world. A simple, heartfelt "thank you" or a sincere compliment, offered with genuine intention, can strengthen existing bonds and encourage a cyclical pattern of kindness, support, and mutual respect. As we consistently express gratitude for the people and experiences that enrich our lives, we actively cultivate an atmosphere of appreciation, inviting more positive interactions, fostering deeper connections, and nourishing our spirits. This positive feedback loop naturally boosts our self-esteem and overall sense of well-being. In this way, gratitude becomes far more than just a polite social gesture; it evolves into a powerful tool for fostering meaningful, lasting connections that contribute significantly to our personal growth.

It is crucially important to remember that nurturing these valuable connections requires ongoing effort, consistent intention, and a proactive commitment to maintaining the relationships that enrich our lives. It is essential to consciously invest time and energy into these bonds, understanding that like any living thing, relationships require consistent care and attention to flourish. We must celebrate milestones together, both big and small, offering support and encouragement during times of triumph and providing a comforting presence and a helping hand during tough times and moments of adversity. Consistently checking in with those who truly matter, offering a listening ear, and simply letting them know you are thinking of them can make a world of difference. As you actively build, nurture, and maintain these positive connections, you will find that your overall confidence and self-esteem naturally flourish. By consciously surrounding yourself with individuals who uplift, inspire, and support you, you not only unlock your own inherent potential but also actively create a vibrant and dynamic community that wholeheartedly supports your journey toward continuous personal growth and enduring happiness. This community, built on mutual respect, shared values, and genuine connection, will serve as a powerful source of strength, resilience, and unwavering support throughout the ever-evolving landscape of life.

TAKING ACTION
THE KEY TO TRANSFORMATION

Setting Intentions and Taking Steps

Setting intentions is a powerful practice that serves as the foundation for personal growth and transformation. When we articulate our desires and aspirations with clarity, we create a roadmap that guides our actions and decisions. Intentions are not mere wishes; they are commitments to ourselves that align our thoughts and behaviors with our goals. By taking the time to truly reflect on what we want to achieve, we empower ourselves to move beyond limitations and step into our fullest potential. Each intention acts as a beacon, illuminating the path forward and reminding us of the values and outcomes we hold dear.

Once we've established our intentions, the next crucial step is taking action. Intentions without action remain dormant dreams. It is through the act of setting specific, measurable, and achievable goals that we begin to bridge the gap between where we are and where we want to be. Breaking down intentions into smaller, manageable steps allows us to track our progress and celebrate our achievements along the way. Each step forward, no matter how small, is a testament to our commitment and determination, reinforcing our belief in our capabilities and building the confidence we need to tackle even greater challenges.

Visualization practices play an integral role in this journey. By vividly imagining our desired outcomes, we engage our minds in a way that fosters creativity and motivation. Visualization is more than daydreaming; it is a technique that primes our subconscious to recognize opportunities and solutions that align with our goals. As we visualize our success, we not only strengthen our intention but also cultivate a mindset that embraces possibility. This practice encourages us to see ourselves in the light of our aspirations, instilling a sense of certainty that what we desire is within reach.

Developing a growth mindset is essential in this process. It allows us to view challenges as opportunities for learning rather than as roadblocks. By embracing this mindset, we shift our focus from the fear of failure to the excitement of growth. Each setback is merely a stepping stone on our journey, providing invaluable lessons that enhance our resilience and adaptability. This perspective fosters an environment where experimentation and exploration are celebrated, nurturing our self-esteem and reinforcing our belief that we are capable of achieving greatness.

Setting intentions and taking steps is a transformative practice that requires patience, dedication, and self-compassion. As we navigate our personal growth journey, it's vital to acknowledge our progress and appreciate the journey itself. Each intention set and each step taken brings us closer to the person we aspire to be. By committing to this ongoing process, we not only unleash our potential but also inspire those around us to embark on their own journeys of self-discovery and empowerment. In this shared growth, we cultivate a supportive community that thrives on positivity, encouragement, and the collective belief that we can achieve extraordinary things.

The Importance of Consistency

Consistency is the bedrock of personal growth, serving as the thread that weaves through the fabric of our aspirations and achievements. When embarking on a journey of self-improvement, it is easy to be swept away by the excitement of new goals and dreams. However, it is the steady and unwavering commitment to these goals that truly transforms aspirations into realities. Each small, consistent action taken day after day builds momentum, propelling us toward our desired outcomes. In this process, we not only nurture our ambitions but also cultivate a discipline that becomes a powerful ally in our pursuit of personal transformation.

Embracing consistency is akin to planting seeds in fertile soil. Just as a gardener tends to their plants with care and dedication, we must nurture our personal growth with the same level of attention. Each time we engage in positive affirmations, practice visualization, or challenge limiting beliefs, we are watering those seeds of potential. The results may not be immediately visible, but with patience and persistence, they will eventually flourish. This growth is not merely about reaching a destination; it is about the evolution of our mindset and the fortification of our self-esteem through the consistent practice of self-care and self-belief.

Consistency fosters resilience. Life is filled with ups and downs, moments of triumph and setbacks. In times of challenge, those who have cultivated a habit of consistent action are far more equipped to navigate adversity. When we commit to our journey to growth, we develop a robust foundation that helps us stay grounded, even when faced with obstacles. This resilience becomes a source of strength, reminding us that every effort contributes to our progress. Each challenge becomes less daunting, as we learn to trust in the process and in our ability to rise again, fortified by our consistent efforts.

Consistency also plays a vital role in building confidence. As we witness the cumulative effects of our dedicated actions, we naturally begin to believe in our capabilities. Each small victory reinforces our self-worth, creating a positive feedback loop that encourages us to keep pushing forward. This burgeoning confidence spills over into various aspects of our lives, allowing us to approach new challenges with a mindset rooted in possibility. By establishing a routine that embraces consistency, we empower ourselves to step outside our comfort zones, knowing that our efforts will yield growth and development.

The importance of consistency in our personal growth journey cannot be overstated. It is the unwavering commitment to our goals that allows us to unlock our potential and take bold strides toward self-improvement. As we cultivate this habit, we not only transform our external circumstances but also undergo profound internal changes. In the dance of life, let us remember that it is the rhythm of consistency that leads to the most beautiful melodies of growth, confidence, and fulfillment. Embrace it, nurture it, and watch as your journey unfolds with grace and purpose.

Measuring Your Progress

Measuring your progress is a vital aspect of personal growth that often goes overlooked. It is essential to recognize that growth is not always linear; it comes in waves, with peaks and valleys. Understanding where you are on your journey allows you to celebrate your achievements, no matter how small, and to recalibrate your path when necessary. By establishing clear metrics for your personal development, you empower yourself to track your evolution and maintain motivation. This awareness fosters a deeper connection to your goals and a heightened sense of purpose.

As you embark on this journey, begin by defining what progress means to you. Progress can manifest in various forms, from achieving specific milestones to embodying a mindset shift. Embrace the idea that growth is multi-faceted. It may involve enhancing your skills, cultivating emotional resilience, or expanding your comfort zone. Take time to reflect on your aspirations and identify tangible indicators of success. For instance, if your goal is to build confidence, you might measure progress by noting how frequently you step outside your comfort zone or how your self-talk has transformed.

Incorporating positive affirmations into your routine is another powerful method for measuring progress. Affirmations serve as daily reminders of your capabilities and the progress you have made. Craft affirmations that resonate with your personal goals and aspirations. For example, if you are working on boosting your self-esteem, repeat affirmations that reflect your worth and abilities. By actively engaging with these positive statements, you reinforce a growth mindset and create a supportive internal narrative that celebrates your journey.

Remember that progress is not only about reaching the end goal but also about the lessons learned along the way. Embrace the challenges and setbacks as integral components of your growth. Reflect on your experiences, gathering insights that can guide you in the future. Celebrate not just the accomplishments but the resilience you've built and the wisdom you've gained. By measuring your progress through these varied lenses, you create a holistic understanding of your development, fostering a deeper sense of confidence and a commitment to your ongoing journey of personal growth.

SUSTAINING YOUR GROWTH JOURNEY

Developing Lifelong Learning Habits

Developing lifelong learning habits is a transformative journey, a dynamic process that unlocks potential, fosters resilience, and ultimately propels individuals toward continuous personal and professional growth. Embracing the fundamental principle that learning transcends the boundaries of formal education is vital for adults seeking to enhance their skills, deepen their knowledge, and navigate the complexities of an ever-evolving world. This necessitates a conscious shift in mindset, a deliberate cultivation of the belief that learning is not a finite task but rather an ongoing, enriching endeavor. By cultivating a mindset that values continuous learning, individuals open themselves up to a kaleidoscope of new experiences, diverse perspectives, and boundless possibilities. This mindset shift forms the bedrock of a more fulfilling life, instilling confidence, promoting self-discovery, and fostering a sense of purpose that extends far beyond the traditional confines of career advancement.

To effectively foster these essential habits, the first step lies in nurturing a curious spirit. Curiosity serves as the powerful engine driving lifelong learning; it fuels the inherent desire to explore, question, and ultimately understand the intricate tapestry of the world around us. Instead of passively accepting information, cultivating curiosity encourages active engagement and critical thinking. Allow yourself to ask "why" and "how" in everyday situations, transforming mundane occurrences into opportunities for discovery. Whether it's delving into the pages of a new book, attending thought-provoking workshops, engaging in stimulating conversations with diverse individuals, or even exploring a new hobby, every interaction and experience becomes a potential learning opportunity. By actively pursuing knowledge, individuals not only enhance their skills and expand their understanding but also build a strong foundation for self-esteem, confidence, and a deeper sense of intellectual fulfillment. Moreover, cultivating curiosity fosters adaptability, a crucial skill in a rapidly changing world, enabling individuals to embrace new ideas and navigate unfamiliar situations with greater ease and resilience.

Incorporating positive affirmations into your daily routine can significantly reinforce your commitment to lifelong learning, acting as a powerful internal compass guiding you along your path. Affirmations are carefully crafted statements that help reshape ingrained beliefs and attitudes, influencing your subconscious mind to embrace a more positive and growth-oriented perspective. By consciously repeating phrases such as "I am capable of learning anything I set my mind to," or "Every day brings new opportunities for growth and development," you instill a sense of empowerment and self-efficacy within yourself. These affirmations serve as potent reminders that you are on a continuous journey of improvement, constantly evolving and expanding your capabilities. They encourage you to embrace challenges not as insurmountable obstacles, but as invaluable stepping stones leading to greater knowledge, understanding, and personal mastery. Furthermore, consistent use of affirmations helps to combat negative self-talk and limiting beliefs that may have previously hindered your learning potential.

Visualization practices can further enhance your learning journey, transforming abstract goals into tangible realities. Visualization involves creating a vivid mental image of yourself successfully acquiring new skills, mastering a challenging subject, or achieving any learning goal you set. This mental rehearsal not only motivates you by providing a clear vision of success, but also helps to create a positive mental environment that is conducive to learning and reduces anxiety. Picture the joy of understanding a complex concept finally clicking into place, the satisfaction of completing a demanding project, or the pride of sharing your newly acquired knowledge with others. This mental imagery reinforces your belief in your capabilities, making the pursuit of knowledge more appealing and ultimately more achievable. By regularly visualizing your success, you prime your mind for positive outcomes, increasing your motivation and fostering a greater sense of confidence in your ability to learn and grow.

Remember that developing lifelong learning habits is rarely a solitary endeavor. While individual effort is undoubtedly crucial, surrounding yourself with a supportive community that values personal growth and encourages continuous learning can significantly amplify your progress and sustain your motivation. Engage in stimulating discussions, share valuable resources, and celebrate one another's achievements, creating a collaborative environment where learning thrives. This collective energy can be incredibly motivating, providing accountability, inspiration, and a sense of belonging. Seek out mentors who can offer guidance and support, and connect with peers who share your passion for learning. Embrace the understanding that learning is a collaborative process, and that sharing knowledge and experiences with others can deepen your understanding and broaden your perspective. Finally, embrace the idea that learning is a lifelong process, a continuous cycle of exploration, discovery, and growth. Commit to nurturing these habits, understanding that they will not only enrich your own life but also inspire those around you to embark on their own paths of growth and self-discovery, creating a ripple effect of intellectual curiosity and personal fulfillment. By embracing lifelong learning, you unlock the potential to live a more meaningful, purposeful, and empowered life.

Revisiting Your Goals and Aspirations

Revisiting your goals and aspirations is an essential practice for anyone on a journey of personal growth. Life is a dynamic process, and as we evolve, so too should our ambitions and dreams. Taking the time to reflect on what truly matters to you can reignite your passion and purpose. This reflection is not merely an exercise in nostalgia; it is a powerful opportunity to align your current actions with your deepest desires. As you sit quietly and contemplate where you want to go, remember that your aspirations are not set in stone. They are living entities that can grow and transform alongside you.

As you delve into this introspective journey, consider the goals you set in the past. Were they influenced by societal expectations or external pressures? Or did they stem from your authentic self? Gently evaluate whether these objectives still resonate with your values and aspirations today. If they do, fantastic! If not, it might be time to let go of what no longer serves you and welcome in new visions that reflect your current self. This process of reassessment allows you to shed the weight of outdated goals and embrace a future that is vibrant and true to who you are.

Picture yourself achieving your dreams and the feelings that accompany those successes. By visualizing your aspirations, you create a mental blueprint that guides your actions and decisions. This practice not only enhances your motivation but also helps you to cultivate a growth mindset. Embrace the possibility that your dreams are within reach, and reaffirm your belief in your ability to achieve them.

As you redefine your aspirations, create affirmations that resonate with your journey. These affirmations should inspire confidence and remind you of your worth. Repeating them daily can help solidify your commitment to your new goals. By consistently affirming your potential, you build a strong foundation of self-esteem that empowers you to take the necessary steps toward your aspirations. This practice transforms doubt into determination, allowing you to face challenges with resilience.

Revisiting your goals and aspirations is an act of self-love. It is a commitment to living authentically and pursuing what truly fulfills you. Embrace this journey with an open heart and a willingness to adapt. Celebrate your progress, no matter how small, and trust that every step you take is a step toward unleashing your potential. As you navigate this path, remember that the journey itself is just as important as the destination. With each reflection, visualization, and affirmation, you are not only redefining your goals but also empowering yourself to shine brighter than ever before.

Keeping the Momentum Going

Keeping the momentum going in your journey of personal growth is essential to achieving lasting change and fulfillment. It is easy to feel inspired and motivated when you first embark on this path, but maintaining that drive requires intentionality and commitment. Embracing practices that reinforce your goals and aspirations can keep your enthusiasm alive. This involves establishing routines that nurture your mind and spirit, allowing you to stay focused on your objectives and continually push beyond your comfort zone.

One powerful way to sustain your momentum is through the consistent use of positive affirmations. These affirmations serve as daily reminders of your worth and potential, helping to counter negative self-talk that may arise during challenging times. By repeating affirmations that resonate with your goals, you create a positive mental environment that fosters growth. For instance, saying "I am capable of achieving my dreams" can reinforce a sense of agency and encourage you to take actionable steps toward your ambitions. The more you affirm your strengths and capabilities, the more resilient you become in the face of adversity.

Embrace the belief that your abilities and intelligence can be cultivated through effort and learning. When faced with setbacks, view them as opportunities for growth rather than insurmountable obstacles. This shift in perspective encourages resilience and adaptability, essential qualities for anyone seeking personal development. Celebrate your progress, no matter how small, and recognize that every step forward is a victory. This mindset fosters a sense of purpose and keeps you energized as you pursue your goals.

Engaging with like-minded individuals can provide encouragement and inspiration, reminding you that you are not alone on this journey. Whether it's through group activities, workshops, or online forums, connecting with others who are also focused on personal development can reignite your passion and keep you accountable. As you share your experiences and learn from each other, you create a powerful network that propels everyone involved toward greater heights. By fostering these connections, you ensure that your momentum continues to build, empowering you to unleash your full potential.

THE PURSUIT OF JOY A PHILOSOPHICAL JOURNEY TO HAPPINESS

The pursuit of joy is one of humanity's most enduring quests. It transcends cultures, religions, and epochs—an innate desire embedded within the human spirit. Yet, what does it mean to pursue joy, and more critically, how do we define it? Happiness has often been construed as the ultimate goal of human existence, yet its fleeting nature often leaves us grappling with our own desires. This essay embarks on a philosophical journey to unravel the complexities of joy and happiness, exploring historical perspectives and contemporary understandings, ultimately seeking to illuminate the paths we can traverse to foster a deeper sense of fulfillment in our lives.

Defining Joy and Happiness

A Deeper Exploration of Contentment and Flourishing

To embark on this exploration of the human condition, we must first delineate the concepts of joy and happiness. While often used interchangeably in everyday conversation, a closer examination reveals nuances that distinguish these two desirable states. Happiness, in its common understanding, is frequently viewed as a temporary emotional response, often dependent on external circumstances. It's the surge of pleasure upon receiving a gift, the elation after achieving a goal, or the contentment of a delicious meal. These moments, while delightful, are often fleeting, tied to specific events and sensory experiences. Joy, in contrast, is often perceived as a more profound and lasting state of contentment rooted in the soul. It is a deeper sense of well-being that persists even in the face of adversity, a quiet strength that anchors us in the present moment.

This subtle but significant difference is further illuminated by philosophical perspectives. Aristotle's notion of eudaimonia—usually translated as "happiness"—is better understood as "human flourishing." He argued that true happiness is not simply the accumulation of pleasurable experiences, but rather a state of living well and doing well. According to Aristotle, eudaimonia is achieved through the cultivation of virtue, the development of character, and the fulfillment of one's potential. It is about striving to be the best version of oneself, contributing to the common good, and living a life of purpose and meaning. This suggests that the pursuit of joy is not merely about the fleeting pleasures of life but is intrinsically tied to a deeper understanding of one's self and one's role in the grand tapestry of existence.

Consider, for instance, the difference between winning the lottery and dedicating one's life to a meaningful cause. Winning the lottery might bring an immediate rush of happiness, a temporary boost in mood driven by the anticipation of newfound wealth and the possibilities it unlocks. However, this happiness can be fragile, easily eroded by the pressures of managing such wealth, the complexities of newfound relationships, and the inevitable return to the mundane aspects of everyday life. On the other hand, dedicating oneself to a cause, such as environmental conservation or social justice, might not always bring immediate gratification. There will be challenges, setbacks, and moments of frustration. Yet, the sense of purpose and meaning derived from contributing to something larger than oneself can cultivate a deeper, more enduring sense of joy. This joy stems from the knowledge that one is living a life of value, aligned with their principles and contributing to the betterment of the world.

Furthermore, the distinction between joy and happiness can be understood through their relationship to adversity. Happiness, being externally driven, is often susceptible to being diminished or extinguished by negative circumstances. Loss, disappointment, or suffering can easily shatter the fleeting bubble of happiness. Joy, however, possesses a resilience that happiness often lacks. Rooted in inner strength and a deeper sense of purpose, joy can coexist with sorrow. It is not the absence of pain, but rather the presence of meaning and hope amidst the pain. It is the ability to find beauty and solace even in the darkest of times, knowing that life's challenges are an integral part of the human experience and an opportunity for growth and understanding.

While happiness and joy are both desirable states of being, they represent different dimensions of human experience. Happiness, often tied to external circumstances, provides fleeting moments of pleasure and satisfaction. Joy, rooted in a deeper understanding of self, purpose, and connection, offers a more profound and enduring sense of contentment and well-being. By striving for eudaimonia, cultivating virtue, and aligning our lives with our values, we can move beyond the pursuit of ephemeral happiness and embark on a journey towards lasting joy, a journey that ultimately leads to a more meaningful and fulfilling life. It is in this pursuit of meaning, in the connection to something larger than ourselves, and in the cultivation of inner strength that we truly discover the essence of lasting and profound joy.

Historical Perspectives on Joy

Throughout history, philosophers have grappled with the question of joy and its relationship to happiness, often exploring its source, its nature, and its role in the human condition. These inquiries have yielded diverse perspectives, ranging from the disciplined pursuit of virtue to the radical acceptance of existential absurdity. In the works of the Stoics, joy is viewed not as a fleeting emotion to be chased, but as a byproduct of living in accordance with nature and reason. They believed that aligning oneself with the natural order of the cosmos and cultivating inner resilience were the keys to a fulfilling life. Epictetus, a prominent figure in Stoicism, posited that true happiness is derived not from external goods, which are inherently transient and unreliable, but from the mastery of one's mind—a concept resonating within the idea of personal responsibility. This mastery involved controlling one's emotions, managing expectations, and focusing on what is within one's power to influence. For the Stoics, joy was the serenity and contentment that arose from this inner control and virtuous living, a state independent of external circumstances.

As we turn to the Eastern philosophies, such as Buddhism, we find a markedly different approach to understanding joy. Central to Buddhist teachings is the principle of 'dukkha'—a recognition of the intrinsic unsatisfactoriness of life, acknowledging the prevalence of suffering, impermanence, and dissatisfaction in the human experience. However, unlike a pessimistic worldview, 'dukkha' serves as a crucial starting point for a path towards liberation. Buddhism posits that joy emerges not from eliminating suffering, which is seen as an inherent part of existence, but from the cessation of desire and attachment. This involves detaching oneself from cravings and aversions, which are seen as the root causes of suffering. It emphasizes mindfulness and awareness as pathways to inner peace, suggesting that joy is found not in the pursuit of transient pleasures, which are ultimately fleeting and unsatisfying, but in the acceptance of life's impermanence and the cultivation of equanimity. Through meditation and ethical conduct, one can gradually reduce the power of desires and attain a state of inner tranquility, leading to a more profound and lasting joy. This joy isn't a boisterous, ecstatic emotion, but a quiet, pervasive contentment rooted in understanding and acceptance.

Furthermore, the 20th century saw the rise of existentialist thinkers, such as Jean-Paul Sartre and Albert Camus, who offered a radical perspective on the nature of existence and the pursuit of joy. They illuminated the absurd nature of life, devoid of inherent meaning or purpose. In a universe indifferent to human concerns, existentialists argued, individuals are faced with the daunting task of creating their own meaning and values. They contend that joy can be cultivated not through adherence to external norms or pre-ordained paths, but through authenticity and the embrace of personal freedom. The act of finding meaning in an indifferent universe itself becomes a source of joy, a testament to the human capacity for self-definition. This joy is not a passive state, but an active construction, created by the individual's choices and commitment to live a life of their own design. This requires confronting the anxieties and uncertainties of existence, acknowledging the burden of responsibility that comes with freedom, and embracing the inherent ambiguity of life. Thus, joy is intricately connected to the authentic human experience, the willingness to confront the void, and the choices we make in the face of that void. It echoes the sentiment that while life may inherently lack meaning, it is through our actions, our passions, and our relationships that we carve our own narrative, creating our own unique and meaningful existence, and ultimately, finding our own version of joy.

The perspectives of the Stoics, Buddhists, and Existentialists, while distinct in their approaches, offer valuable insights into the complex and multifaceted nature of joy. They underscore the importance of inner resilience, mindful awareness, and authentic self-expression in the pursuit of a fulfilling life. Ultimately, the search for joy remains a deeply personal journey, shaped by individual values, experiences, and perspectives.

Contemporary Understandings

In our contemporary society, the path to joy has often been obscured by the relentless pursuit of material wealth, social status, and validation. We are bombarded with messages suggesting that happiness is a commodity to be bought—a mirage available through consumption. This misinterpretation has led to a pervasive sense of dissatisfaction among individuals, even in the midst of affluence.

Sadly, the pursuit of material possessions and societal recognition has led many to believe that happiness can be bought or attained through external means. This perspective, however, often leaves individuals feeling unfulfilled and unsatisfied, even in the midst of abundance. The rise of positive psychology has challenged this notion, providing a more holistic understanding of what truly fosters joy in one's life.

Positive psychology, as propounded by researchers such as Martin Seligman, posits that happiness is a multifaceted construct, encompassing several components that work together to create a sense of fulfillment and well-being. These components, often referred to as PERMA, include positive emotion, engagement, relationships, meaning, and accomplishment. By focusing on these aspects, individuals can cultivate joy through intentional practices that nurture both their inner selves and their connections with others.

Engaging in activities that promote a state of flow is essential to achieving joy. Flow refers to the experience of being fully immersed in an activity, leading to a heightened sense of enjoyment and satisfaction. By pursuing such activities, individuals can tap into their innate talents and passions, fostering a sense of purpose and engagement that goes beyond mere material gain.

Relationships play a crucial role in cultivating joy. The support, companionship, and love provided by others serve as a foundation for emotional well-being. By nurturing connections with family, friends, and community, individuals can tap into a reservoir of positive emotions that bolster their overall sense of happiness. Furthermore, engaging in acts of kindness and altruism has been shown to boost one's own happiness while also positively impacting those on the receiving end.

Meaning is another critical component of joy. Individuals who find purpose in their lives, whether through work, volunteering, or personal pursuits, are more likely to experience happiness than those who approach life from a solely transactional perspective. By identifying and pursuing endeavors that align with their values and passions, individuals can create a sense of fulfillment that transcends material possessions and societal status.

Lastly, achievement is an essential aspect of joy. The satisfaction derived from setting and accomplishing goals contributes to a sense of self-efficacy and self-worth. By recognizing and celebrating their accomplishments, individuals can build confidence and resilience, which, in turn, fosters a positive outlook on life.

Gratitude has emerged as a powerful catalyst for joy. By regularly practicing gratitude, individuals can learn to appreciate the simple joys of life, cultivating a mindset that focuses on abundance rather than scarcity. Research has demonstrated that people who engage in gratitude exercises, such as journaling or expressing thanks to others, exhibit higher levels of well-being and emotional resilience.

The path to joy in our contemporary society involves much more than the mere pursuit of material wealth and social status. By nurturing positive emotions, engagement, relationships, meaning, and achievement (PERMA), individuals can cultivate a state of being that fosters happiness and fulfillment. Furthermore, the practice of gratitude can significantly enhance one's emotional landscape, leading to a greater appreciation for the beauty and simplicity of everyday experiences. By embracing these principles, individuals can redefine joy, transforming it from a distant goal into a present reality.

The Path to Joy:

An Individual *and* Collective Responsibility

As we navigate the intricacies of the pursuit of joy, it becomes evident that our journey is both an individual and collective endeavor. On an individual level, the responsibility lies within us to cultivate self-awareness, embrace vulnerability, and engage in authentic relationships. This journey entails confronting the inner narratives that confine us and dismantling the barriers that prevent us from experiencing joy. Practicing mindfulness and self-compassion, we can foster an internal environment conducive to joy—a sanctuary within that remains unshaken amidst life's tumult.

Collectively, we bear the responsibility to create spaces that nurture joy. Societies that prioritize mental health, accessibility to resources, and community-building initiatives provide fertile ground for collective flourishing. When we honor diversity and inclusivity, affirming the experiences of every individual, we foster a sense of belonging that is critical for joy to flourish. Schools, workplaces, and communities should emphasize emotional intelligence, compassion, and connection, nurturing the collective spirit essential for joy.

The pursuit of joy is a profound philosophical journey that invites us to explore the depths of our being and the richness of our relationships. It beckons us to seek meaning beyond material success and to cultivate a mindset that embraces gratitude, vulnerability, and authenticity. By integrating historical insights, contemporary understandings, and our personal agency into this quest, we can weave a tapestry of joy that transcends transient happiness.

Joy is found not in the absence of suffering but in our capacity to navigate the complexities of existence with grace, resilience, and love. Let us embark on this journey with open hearts, for in the pursuit of joy, we not only enrich our own lives but also illuminate the paths of those around us. In the end, it is through collective joy that we shall find true happiness, which is fused together in the beautifully intricate fabric of human experience.

UNDERSTANDING HAPPINESS

The Definition of Happiness

Happiness, a concept universally sought yet uniquely experienced, resists any singular, definitive explanation. Its meaning is fluid, shaped by cultural nuances, philosophical underpinnings, and the deeply personal narratives of individuals. While traditionally viewed as a state of well-being characterized by contentment, joy, and fulfillment, a deeper exploration reveals a tapestry woven with threads of virtue, subjective experience, existential inquiry, and the transformative power of gratitude.

Philosophers throughout history have grappled with the essence of happiness. Aristotle, a towering figure in this intellectual pursuit, posited that happiness, or *eudaimonia*, transcends mere pleasure and represents the highest good achievable by humans. He argued that *eudaimonia* is not a fleeting emotion but rather a state of flourishing achieved through virtuous living and the diligent cultivation of one's potential. This perspective emphasizes the importance of moral character and purposeful action in the pursuit of a truly fulfilling life. Modern interpretations often equate happiness with emotional states and life satisfaction, suggesting a broader understanding encompassing both ephemeral moments of joy and a more enduring sense of contentment. This contemporary view acknowledges the spectrum of human experience and recognizes that happiness can manifest in diverse forms and intensities.

However, the subjective nature of happiness introduces a significant layer of complexity. What brings profound joy to one individual may hold little significance for another. The sources of happiness are as varied as the individuals who seek it. Some may find it in the tangible accomplishments of their careers, while others derive it primarily from the intangible bonds of their relationships. Still others might discover profound happiness in spiritual exploration or the quiet contemplation of nature. This inherent subjectivity underscores the crucial role of emotional intelligence in not only understanding one's own happiness but also in appreciating the diverse paths to happiness pursued by others. By acknowledging and respecting these individual differences, we can foster more compassionate and empathetic interpersonal relationships, building connections based on mutual understanding and shared experiences, even when the specific sources of joy differ.

Furthermore, the philosophical exploration of happiness inevitably leads to an intersection with profound existential questions about meaning and purpose. Many individuals grapple with the understanding that happiness is not merely the absence of suffering or the constant pursuit of pleasure; rather, it involves a deeper, more meaningful engagement with the complexities of life. This perspective challenges the often-simplistic notion of happiness as a constant state of bliss and invites a critical reflection on the role of struggle, challenge, and even adversity in the pursuit of a truly fulfilling existence. It suggests that true fulfillment may arise not from avoiding discomfort or hardship, but from navigating life's inherent complexities with resilience, courage, and a unwavering commitment to personal growth. In this context, happiness is not a destination to be reached, but a transformative journey of self-discovery and continuous becoming.

The conscious cultivation of gratitude stands as a powerful tool in shaping our understanding and experience of happiness. Empirical research consistently demonstrates a strong correlation between gratitude and increased life satisfaction, emotional well-being, and overall happiness. By consciously shifting our focus from what we lack to what we already possess, we can fundamentally alter our perception of happiness, moving it away from dependence on external circumstances and grounding it in internal attitudes and perspectives. This shift encourages a more profound appreciation for the seemingly mundane aspects of daily life – the simple act of sharing a meal with loved ones, the beauty of a sunset, the comfort of a warm home. By recognizing and cherishing these everyday moments and relationships, we cultivate a deeper sense of joy and fulfillment, enhancing our overall sense of well-being.

The relentless pursuit of happiness, often fueled by societal pressures and unrealistic expectations, can ironically lead to dissatisfaction and a diminished sense of contentment. The constant striving for an idealized state of happiness can create a sense of inadequacy and prevent us from appreciating the present moment. Learning to embrace impermanence, to accept the inevitable ebb and flow of emotions, and to find meaning even in moments of sadness or disappointment is crucial for cultivating a sustainable and authentic sense of happiness.

In the end, the definition of happiness remains a dynamic and evolving concept, influenced by individual experiences, cultural contexts, philosophical reflections, and the ever-changing circumstances of life. It encompasses not only the pursuit of pleasure and the avoidance of pain, but also the quest for meaning, purpose, and connection to something larger than oneself. As individuals navigate their own unique paths to happiness, engaging with these varied dimensions can inspire profound personal growth and a deeper understanding of what it truly means to live a joyful, meaningful, and fulfilling life. Embracing the inherent complexity of happiness allows for a richer exploration of our own values, aspirations, and the very essence of our humanity, paving the way for a more authentic and profoundly rewarding existence. The journey towards understanding and experiencing happiness is a lifelong endeavor, one that demands self-reflection, empathy, and a willingness to embrace the full spectrum of human experience.

Historical Perspectives on Happiness

From ancient philosophies to modern psychological theories, the understanding of happiness has evolved significantly, undergoing a metamorphosis shaped by cultural shifts, intellectual revolutions, and the enduring human quest for a fulfilling life. In ancient Greece, philosophers such as Aristotle proposed that true happiness, or *eudaimonia*, is achieved through virtuous living and fulfillment of one's potential. This concept of happiness was not merely about pleasure or transient joy but was deeply intertwined with moral character and the pursuit of a meaningful existence. Aristotle emphasized the importance of developing virtues like courage, justice, temperance, and wisdom, arguing that consistent practice of these virtues would lead to a life of flourishing and genuine happiness. This perspective moves beyond fleeting gratification and emphasizes the development of a well-rounded, ethical character. Aristotle's emphasis on virtue as a path to happiness continues to resonate in contemporary discussions about personal growth and emotional intelligence, particularly in fields like leadership development and character education, where the cultivation of ethical behavior is seen as integral to long-term success and fulfillment. Furthermore, the concept of *eudaimonia* has found its way into modern positive psychology, influencing interventions aimed at promoting psychological well-being by fostering meaning, purpose, and engagement in life.

In contrast, the Stoics, another influential school of thought in ancient times, offered a different approach to happiness, one rooted in self-sufficiency and inner peace. They posited that true contentment comes from within and is cultivated through self-control, rationality, and acceptance of one's circumstances. Stoicism teaches that while external events are beyond our control, our responses to those events are within our power. This philosophy encourages individuals to focus on what they can control – their thoughts, emotions, and actions – and to accept what they cannot. By mastering their inner selves, Stoics believed that individuals could achieve a state of tranquility and freedom from suffering, regardless of external circumstances. This perspective fosters resilience and encourages individuals to find peace in their inner selves, a notion that aligns closely with modern practices of mindfulness and positive thinking. The Stoic belief that happiness is a state of mind rather than a result of external validation invites us to explore our emotional responses and personal growth. Techniques like cognitive restructuring, derived from Cognitive Behavioral Therapy (CBT), echo Stoic principles by encouraging individuals to challenge negative thoughts and adopt more rational and adaptive perspectives. The renewed interest in Stoicism in the 21st century reflects a growing desire for strategies to cope with the stresses and uncertainties of modern life, highlighting the enduring relevance of this ancient philosophy.

The Enlightenment era brought about a shift in the understanding of happiness, as philosophers like John Locke and Jean-Jacques Rousseau began to connect it with individual rights and societal structures. Happiness was increasingly seen as an inalienable right, linked to life, liberty, and the pursuit of personal fulfillment. This period marked a move away from purely individualistic or religiously determined notions of happiness toward a more socially and politically embedded understanding. Locke's emphasis on natural rights and Rousseau's concept of the social contract emphasized the role of government in ensuring the well-being of its citizens. This perspective placed a greater emphasis on the importance of social justice, equality, and access to opportunities as preconditions for individual happiness.

The notion that societal frameworks can either enhance or hinder well-being is a concept that remains relevant today, as we navigate the complexities of modern life and seek to cultivate environments that foster joy and satisfaction. Debates about income inequality, healthcare access, and educational opportunities are all fundamentally linked to the Enlightenment ideal of creating a society that promotes the happiness and well-being of all its members. Furthermore, the Universal Declaration of Human Rights, adopted by the United Nations in 1948, reflects the enduring influence of Enlightenment ideals by affirming the right to life, liberty, and the pursuit of happiness as fundamental human rights.

In the 19th and 20th centuries, the advent of psychology introduced new dimensions to the exploration of happiness, providing empirical tools to study and understand this complex phenomenon. Thinkers like William James, a pioneer of American psychology, explored the role of emotions and subjective experiences in shaping individual well-being. Later, positive psychologists such as Martin Seligman, Mihaly Csikszentmihalyi, and Ed Diener shifted focus to empirical studies of well-being, moving beyond the traditional focus on mental illness to explore the factors that contribute to human flourishing. This scientific approach sought to quantify happiness and identify the factors that contribute to it, from gratitude and relationships to purpose and engagement. The impact of gratitude on life satisfaction, for instance, has been extensively studied, demonstrating that recognizing and appreciating the positive aspects of life can significantly enhance one's overall sense of happiness. Studies have shown that practicing gratitude can lead to increased positive emotions, improved physical health, and stronger social connections. Similarly, research on flow, a state of complete absorption and engagement in an activity, has revealed its profound impact on happiness and well-being. This intersection of philosophy and psychology underscores the multifaceted nature of happiness, inviting individuals to draw from both realms in their pursuit of joy. Positive psychology has also led to the development of various interventions aimed at promoting happiness and well-being, such as gratitude journaling, mindfulness meditation, and acts of kindness, providing practical tools for individuals to cultivate more fulfilling lives.

Today, as we reflect on historical perspectives on happiness, it becomes clear that the journey toward understanding this elusive state is ongoing, a continuous dialogue between diverse disciplines and perspectives. The increasing awareness of the limitations of solely focusing on material success has led to a renewed interest in the philosophical and spiritual dimensions of happiness. Philosophical reflections on love, relationships, and the existential questions surrounding meaning continue to shape our views and experiences of happiness. The recognition of the importance of social connections and community engagement has also highlighted the interconnectedness of individual happiness with the well-being of others. The stories of everyday heroes who embody resilience, gratitude, and positivity serve as powerful reminders of the potential for joy in the human experience. These narratives offer inspiration and practical guidance, demonstrating how individuals can overcome adversity, cultivate positive emotions, and find meaning in their lives. By integrating insights from history, philosophy, and psychology, we can aspire to cultivate a deeper understanding of happiness that transcends mere pleasure, fostering a more profound sense of fulfillment and connection in our lives. This integrated approach recognizes the multifaceted nature of happiness, acknowledging the importance of both inner states and external factors in shaping our overall well-being. Ultimately, the pursuit of happiness is a lifelong journey, requiring ongoing reflection, self-awareness, and a commitment to cultivating virtues, fostering meaningful relationships, and contributing to the well-being of the wider community.

Modern Philosophical Approaches

Modern philosophical approaches to happiness and well-being have evolved significantly, integrating insights from various disciplines such as psychology, sociology, neuroscience, and even economics. At the forefront of this evolution is the recognition that happiness is not merely a fleeting emotion, a momentary burst of pleasure, but a complex and multifaceted state influenced by a myriad of factors. These factors range from deeply personal choices and ingrained habits to the intricate web of social connections and the often-overlooked impact of environmental conditions. Philosophers today are increasingly interested in understanding not just the individual components of happiness, but also how these elements interact and contribute to a holistically fulfilling life. This exploration often leads to a more nuanced and comprehensive view of happiness, where emotional intelligence plays a critical role in navigating life's inevitable challenges, fostering deeper and more meaningful relationships, and ultimately shaping our perception of ourselves and the world around us.

One prominent modern approach, and perhaps the most influential in recent decades, is the positive psychology movement. This framework emphasizes the importance of identifying, cultivating, and leveraging our inherent strengths, virtues, and positive experiences in leading a happy and flourishing life. Rather than dwelling solely on pathology and dysfunction, positive psychology encourages individuals to actively cultivate qualities such as resilience in the face of adversity, gratitude for the good things in their lives, empathy towards others, and the capacity for forgiveness, both of themselves and others. It also underscores the profound significance of personal growth, continuous learning, and the unwavering pursuit of self-improvement, not as a means to achieve some external ideal, but as a way to unlock one's full potential and live a more authentic and meaningful existence. By focusing on what actively enhances well-being, rather than merely addressing what causes distress or alleviates suffering, positive psychology provides practical tools and actionable strategies for individuals seeking to enhance their emotional intelligence, cultivate a more optimistic outlook, and ultimately increase their overall life satisfaction. This proactive approach shifts the focus from problem-solving to strength-building, empowering individuals to take control of their own happiness trajectory.

Beyond the practical application of positive psychology, philosophers have also turned their attention to the fundamental existential questions surrounding meaning and purpose in life, recognizing that happiness is often inextricably intertwined with our intrinsic human need for significance. This profound inquiry invites individuals to engage in deep reflection on their core values, their underlying beliefs about the world, and their most cherished aspirations for the future. It prompts us to ask ourselves: What truly matters to me? What impact do I want to have on the world? What legacy do I hope to leave behind? By confronting existential dilemmas such as the inevitability of death, the burden of freedom, and the inherent uncertainty of the universe, people can forge a deeper and more authentic understanding of their own existence, leading to more fulfilling and meaningful experiences. This process of self-discovery can be challenging, even painful, but it can also be incredibly liberating and empowering, allowing us to live with greater intentionality and purpose. These profound reflections can spur inspirational stories of everyday heroes, showcasing how ordinary individuals, faced with extraordinary circumstances, navigate their struggles and triumphs in pursuit of joy, meaning, and a well-lived life. Consider the stories of individuals who dedicate their lives to social justice, environmental conservation, or artistic expression – their relentless pursuit of a cause larger than themselves often provides a profound sense of purpose and contributes significantly to their overall well-being.

The power of positive thinking, often dismissed as mere wishful thinking, is another modern philosophical approach that has gained considerable traction, particularly as research in cognitive-behavioral therapies (CBT) continues to shed light on its efficacy. Rooted in cognitive-behavioral theories, this perspective posits that our thoughts, beliefs, and interpretations of events exert a powerful influence on our emotions, behaviors, and ultimately, our overall well-being. By consciously cultivating a more positive and optimistic mindset, individuals can actively reshape their experiences, build resilience against adversity, and develop a more hopeful outlook on the future.

This approach is not about ignoring or denying negative emotions, but rather about learning to challenge negative thought patterns, reframe challenging situations, and focus on the positive aspects of life, even in the midst of difficulty. This proactive mindset not only enhances personal well-being but also has a significant impact on our relationships, as positivity can foster deeper connections, promote a more supportive and collaborative environment, and enhance our ability to empathize with and understand others. The ripple effects of positive thinking create environments where gratitude flourishes, appreciation for the present moment increases, and overall life satisfaction is significantly enhanced.

Lastly, the philosophical reflections on love and relationships remain absolutely central to modern discussions on happiness and well-being. The enduring recognition that human connections are fundamental to our well-being and our ability to thrive has led to a renewed and intensified focus on the transformative role of love in enriching our lives. Philosophers today examine the intricate dynamics of various types of relationships – romantic partnerships, familial bonds, friendships, and even our connection to wider communities. They explore the multifaceted nature of love, delving into its different forms (agape, eros, philia, storge), its potential pitfalls, and its unparalleled capacity for growth, healing, and transcendence. By understanding the complexities of love, learning to communicate effectively, and fostering healthy and mutually supportive relationships, individuals can cultivate a deeper sense of belonging, enhance their emotional resilience, and ultimately experience a more profound and lasting sense of happiness. This includes understanding the importance of self-love and the role it plays in forming healthy relationships with others. Recognizing one's own worth, setting healthy boundaries, and practicing self-compassion are crucial elements in building a fulfilling and meaningful life, both individually and in connection with others. In conclusion, modern philosophical approaches to happiness and well-being offer a rich tapestry of insights and perspectives, highlighting the multifaceted nature of this elusive yet universally desired state. By integrating philosophical inquiry with empirical research from various disciplines, we can gain a deeper understanding of what truly contributes to a flourishing life and develop practical strategies for cultivating greater happiness and well-being in ourselves and in the world around us.

THE ROLE OF EMOTIONAL INTELLIGENCE

Defining Emotional Intelligence

Emotional intelligence, often abbreviated as EI, is a multifaceted concept that plays a crucial role in our daily interactions and overall well-being. At its core, emotional intelligence refers to the ability to recognize, understand, and manage our own emotions while also being attuned to the emotions of others. This dual awareness allows individuals to navigate complex social environments, fostering deeper connections and enhancing personal growth. In the pursuit of joy, emotional intelligence serves as a foundational pillar, enabling us to respond to life's challenges with resilience and empathy.

One of the key components of emotional intelligence is self-awareness. This involves not only recognizing one's own emotional states but also understanding how these emotions influence thoughts and behaviors. Those who possess high levels of self-awareness are better equipped to reflect on their experiences and make informed decisions that align with their values and aspirations. This reflective practice is essential in the philosophical journey toward happiness, as it encourages individuals to confront their inner realities and make choices that promote fulfillment.

Another critical aspect of emotional intelligence is self-regulation. This ability allows individuals to manage their emotional responses, particularly in stressful or challenging situations. By cultivating self-regulation, one can maintain composure, think clearly, and respond thoughtfully rather than react impulsively. This skill is particularly beneficial in personal relationships, where emotional outbursts can lead to misunderstandings and conflict. Through self-regulation, individuals can create a more harmonious environment, contributing to both their own well-being and that of others.

Empathy, a vital element of emotional intelligence, involves understanding and sharing the feelings of others. It goes beyond mere sympathy, as it requires a genuine effort to perceive situations from another's perspective. Empathy fosters deeper connections and strengthens relationships, making it an essential component of love and companionship. In philosophical discussions about relationships, the role of empathy cannot be overstated; it cultivates trust and intimacy, allowing individuals to engage in meaningful dialogues that enhance emotional bonds and contribute to overall life satisfaction.

Emotional intelligence encompasses social skills, which facilitate effective communication and collaboration. Individuals with strong social skills are adept at building networks, resolving conflicts, and inspiring others. These abilities are crucial not only for personal growth but also for creating supportive communities that promote collective well-being. By harnessing the power of emotional intelligence, we can transform our interactions, leading to a more compassionate and understanding world. Thus, in the pursuit of joy, cultivating emotional intelligence is not merely an individual endeavor but a shared journey towards a more harmonious existence.

Emotional Intelligence and Personal Growth

Emotional intelligence (EI) plays a pivotal role in personal growth, shaping our ability to navigate the complexities of life and fostering a deeper understanding of ourselves and others. At its core, emotional intelligence encompasses the awareness of one's own emotions, the ability to manage them effectively, and the capacity to empathize with the emotions of others. This multifaceted skill set not only enhances interpersonal relationships but also contributes significantly to overall well-being and happiness. As adults strive to cultivate a more fulfilling life, fostering emotional intelligence becomes an essential endeavor that can lead to profound personal transformation.

The journey toward enhancing emotional intelligence begins with self-awareness, the cornerstone of personal growth. By engaging in reflective practices such as mindfulness and journaling, individuals can gain insights into their emotional patterns and triggers. This increased awareness allows for better emotional regulation, which is crucial when confronting life's challenges. As individuals learn to recognize and articulate their emotions, they become equipped to respond thoughtfully rather than react impulsively. This shift in perspective empowers adults to take charge of their emotional landscape, creating space for growth and resilience in the face of adversity.

Emotional intelligence fosters empathy, a vital quality that enriches our relationships. Understanding the emotions of others enables individuals to connect on a deeper level, forging meaningful bonds based on compassion and support. This connection is instrumental in building strong personal and professional networks, which are essential for sustained happiness. By actively practicing empathy, individuals can cultivate an environment of trust and collaboration, enhancing both their own well-being and that of those around them. These enriched relationships not only provide emotional support but also serve as a source of inspiration and motivation in the pursuit of personal goals.

In the realm of gratitude, emotional intelligence plays a significant role in how we perceive and appreciate our experiences. Individuals with high emotional intelligence are often more adept at recognizing the positive aspects of their lives, even amid challenges. This ability to focus on gratitude can dramatically enhance life satisfaction, as it encourages a shift from a scarcity mindset to one of abundance. By regularly reflecting on what they are thankful for, people can reinforce positive thinking patterns that contribute to a greater sense of happiness and fulfillment, thereby accelerating personal growth.

The interplay between emotional intelligence and personal growth is a dynamic and ongoing process. As adults invest time in developing their emotional skills, they not only enrich their own lives but also create a ripple effect that can positively influence their communities. This journey of self-discovery and emotional evolution not only deepens one's understanding of happiness but also aligns with the broader philosophical inquiries into the meaning of life and relationships. In embracing emotional intelligence, individuals embark on a transformative path that leads to a more joyful, connected, and meaningful existence.

Cultivating Emotional Intelligence in Daily Life

Cultivating emotional intelligence in daily life is an essential pursuit for anyone seeking to enhance their happiness and well-being. Emotional intelligence, the ability to recognize, understand, and manage our own emotions while also empathizing with the emotions of others, serves as a foundation for building meaningful relationships and fostering personal growth. In the chaotic tapestry of modern life, honing these skills not only contributes to individual fulfillment but also enriches the communities we inhabit, creating a ripple effect of positivity and connection.

One practical approach to cultivating emotional intelligence is through self-awareness. This involves regularly pausing to reflect on one's own emotional state and identifying the triggers that influence feelings and reactions. Journaling can be a powerful tool in this regard, allowing individuals to articulate their thoughts and emotions, recognize patterns, and gain insights into their behavior. By fostering self-awareness, adults can learn to respond more thoughtfully rather than react impulsively, leading to healthier relationships and a greater sense of internal harmony.

Another crucial aspect of emotional intelligence is empathy, which can be nurtured through active listening and genuine engagement with others. Taking the time to truly understand the perspectives and feelings of those around us not only deepens our connections but also enhances our capacity for compassion. Practicing empathy can transform everyday interactions—whether in the workplace, with friends, or in family settings—into opportunities for building trust and mutual respect. This practice encourages us to look beyond our own experiences, fostering a sense of shared humanity that contributes to overall well-being.

Mindfulness techniques also play a significant role in enhancing emotional intelligence. By incorporating mindfulness into daily routines, individuals can cultivate a greater awareness of their emotions as they arise. Techniques such as meditation, breathing exercises, or mindful walking allow for a pause in the hustle and bustle of life, providing space to process emotions without judgment. This intentional practice helps in developing resilience, making it easier to navigate challenges with a balanced perspective. As one becomes more attuned to their emotional landscape, the capacity to manage stress and cultivate joy increases significantly.

Expressing gratitude is a powerful practice that can enhance emotional intelligence and overall life satisfaction. By acknowledging and appreciating the positive aspects of life, individuals can shift their focus from negativity to abundance. Gratitude journaling or sharing moments of gratitude with others fosters a culture of appreciation that can strengthen bonds and promote a positive outlook. As adults actively incorporate these practices into their daily lives, they not only elevate their own emotional intelligence but also contribute to a more compassionate and joyful world, embodying the essence of the philosophical journey toward happiness.

Understanding Emotional Intelligence

Emotional intelligence, a concept gaining increasing recognition in both personal and professional spheres, can be defined as the capacity to recognize, understand, and manage our own emotions. More than simply being "nice" or "sensitive," it involves a nuanced understanding of the internal emotional landscape and the ability to navigate it effectively. Simultaneously, emotional intelligence extends outward, fostering healthy relationships by empathizing with the emotions of others and responding with appropriate sensitivity and understanding. Pioneered by psychologists like Daniel Goleman, who popularized the concept in his seminal book, this vital intelligence encompasses five crucial domains: self-awareness, self-regulation, motivation, empathy, and social skills. These dimensions do not merely enhance personal relationships; they also serve as foundations for meaningful engagement with the world around us, influencing everything from leadership effectiveness to conflict resolution and overall well-being.

Let's delve deeper into each of these five components. **Self-awareness**, the cornerstone of emotional intelligence, involves recognizing and understanding our own emotions as they arise. It's about being attuned to the subtle shifts in our feelings, identifying the triggers that provoke specific emotional responses, and understanding how these emotions impact our thoughts and behaviors. A person with high self-awareness can accurately identify when they are feeling stressed, anxious, or frustrated, and understand the root causes of these feelings. This awareness allows them to proactively manage their emotional state and prevent negative emotions from spiraling out of control. For example, someone self-aware might recognize that presentations trigger anxiety and take steps to prepare thoroughly, practice relaxation techniques, or even seek feedback to alleviate their fears.

Building upon self-awareness, **self-regulation** refers to the ability to control and manage our emotions and impulses effectively. This doesn't mean suppressing or denying emotions, but rather channeling them in a healthy and productive manner. It involves taking responsibility for our actions and reactions, thinking before we speak, and adapting to changing circumstances with composure. Someone with strong self-regulation skills is less likely to react impulsively in stressful situations, instead choosing to respond thoughtfully and strategically. They can manage their frustration, delay gratification, and remain calm under pressure, allowing them to navigate challenging situations with grace and resilience.

Motivation, the third key dimension, encompasses the drive and passion to pursue goals with energy and persistence. It's not just about external rewards or recognition, but rather an intrinsic desire to achieve, improve, and excel. Highly motivated individuals are driven by a sense of purpose and are resilient in the face of setbacks. They are proactive, set challenging goals, and remain committed to achieving them despite obstacles. This internal drive fuels their efforts and allows them to maintain a positive and optimistic outlook, even when confronted with adversity.

Moving from the internal to the external, **empathy** is the ability to understand and share the feelings of others. It involves putting yourself in another person's shoes, recognizing their emotional state, and responding with compassion and understanding. Empathy is crucial for building strong relationships, fostering collaboration, and resolving conflicts effectively. An empathetic person can accurately perceive nonverbal cues, listen attentively, and understand diverse perspectives. They can connect with others on a deeper level and build trust and rapport, creating a more supportive and harmonious environment.

Finally, **social skills** encompass the ability to effectively manage relationships and interact with others in a constructive manner. This involves communication skills, conflict resolution skills, leadership skills, and the ability to build rapport and influence others. Socially skilled individuals are adept at navigating social situations, building strong networks, and working effectively in teams. They communicate clearly and persuasively, listen actively, and are able to resolve conflicts peacefully and effectively. They are able to build consensus, inspire others, and create a positive and collaborative environment.

Emotional intelligence is far more than just a desirable trait; it is a fundamental skill set that empowers individuals to navigate their internal world and engage effectively with the external world. By cultivating self-awareness, mastering self-regulation, harnessing motivation, practicing empathy, and developing social skills, we can unlock our full potential, build stronger relationships, and contribute meaningfully to our communities and the world around us. As research continues to highlight the importance of emotional intelligence in various domains, from leadership effectiveness to personal well-being, its cultivation promises to be an increasingly valuable investment in our personal and professional lives.

The Importance of Self-Regulation *in* Finding Purpose

Once we cultivate self-awareness, the next step is self-regulation—the ability to manage our emotions and reactions in various situations. Self-regulation is critical in the search for meaning, as it equips us with the resilience and composure required to navigate life's inevitable challenges.

Life is fraught with unexpected turns, and our emotional responses to these events can significantly influence our sense of purpose. For instance, consider a setback in one's career or a personal loss. Those equipped with high emotional intelligence are more likely to approach these circumstances with a balanced mindset. They acknowledge their feelings of disappointment or grief while determining to grow from the experience and seek new avenues for fulfillment.

Self-regulation fosters a sense of agency, allowing individuals to respond thoughtfully rather than react impulsively. This reflective approach opens doors to more significant opportunities and, ultimately, a more profound sense of purpose. A life driven by purpose is one grounded in long-term goals and aspirations rather than fleeting emotions. Thus, the development of self-regulation becomes essential in our evolutionary narrative.

Motivation: The Engine of Purpose

While self-awareness and self-regulation lay the groundwork for emotional intelligence, motivation—driven by our intrinsic values and passions—serves as the engine propelling us toward our life's meaning. Individuals with high emotional intelligence possess a natural inclination to pursue goals aligned with their values, fostering a sense of fulfillment and satisfaction.

Intrinsic motivation, fueled by genuine interests and feelings of connection to our goals, often leads to a more profound sense of meaning than extrinsic motivation, which relies on external recognition or rewards. For example, a teacher driven by a passion for imparting knowledge and inspiring students finds deeper significance in their role than one merely performing for accolades or financial gain.

As we harness our motivational energies, we acknowledge that our unique paths contribute to the greater tapestry of existence. This realization not only strengthens our resolve but also encourages us to cultivate resilience in the face of adversity, keeping our eyes fixed on the horizon of personal significance.

Empathy: Bridging the Divide

While the journey inward is essential, the quest for meaning extends beyond the self. Empathy, the ability to understand and share the feelings of others, serves as a connective tissue in the broader human experience. It is through empathy that we foster relationships, build communities, and recognize our shared humanity.

In a world increasingly marked by isolation and division, emotional intelligence becomes a beacon that illuminates the importance of understanding others. Empathy invites us to listen deeply, to see the world through the lens of another's experience, and to recognize the intertwined destinies that shape our lives.

Witnessing suffering or joy in others can prompt reflection on our own experiences, leading to significant insights into what we truly value and strive for in life. The development of empathy fosters a sense of community and belonging—two essential components of a meaningful existence. As we learn to connect with those around us, our individual purpose often expands to encompass a greater societal role, thereby enriching our understanding of the tapestry of human life.

Social Skills: The Art of Connection

Finally, the ability to navigate social environments effectively is an extension of emotional intelligence. Strong social skills enable us to communicate effectively, resolve conflicts, and collaborate with others, all of which are essential in our search for meaning. In an interdependent world, our interactions shape not only our lives but also the lives of those we encounter.

The capacity to constructively engage with others fosters richer relationships and creates environments where collective meaning can flourish. The influence of collaboration and shared purpose cannot be overstated. Organizations and communities built on principles of emotional intelligence exhibit greater innovation, resilience, and fulfillment.

For instance, consider the transformative power of teams that prioritize emotional awareness and support within their ranks. When individuals feel valued, understood, and emotionally safe, their collective potential is unleashed, and they are more inclined to pursue challenges with vigor and a sense of purpose.

INSPIRATIONAL STORIES OF EVERYDAY HEROES

Acts of Kindness

Acts of kindness are not merely altruistic gestures; they serve as powerful catalysts for joy and well-being in both the giver and the receiver. In the context of happiness and personal growth, these acts create ripples of positivity that extend far beyond the immediate interaction. When individuals engage in kindness, they often experience a surge of emotional satisfaction, which can lead to improved mental health and a greater sense of purpose. This phenomenon aligns with the philosophical underpinnings of happiness, suggesting that our interactions with others play a crucial role in our overall sense of fulfillment.

Moreover, acts of kindness can significantly enhance emotional intelligence. Understanding the feelings of others and responding with compassion requires a keen awareness of one's own emotions. When individuals practice kindness, they hone their ability to empathize and connect with others on a deeper level. This emotional growth not only enriches personal relationships but also fosters a more profound understanding of oneself. By recognizing the impact of kindness, individuals can learn to navigate their emotional landscape more effectively, leading to enhanced resilience and greater overall happiness.

The narratives of everyday heroes often illuminate the transformative power of kindness. These stories serve as inspiration, showcasing how simple acts can lead to extraordinary outcomes. Whether it's a stranger helping someone in need or a friend offering support during difficult times, these moments highlight the interconnectedness of human experience. Such accounts remind us that each act of kindness, no matter how small, contributes to the tapestry of community and belonging. This sense of connection is essential for cultivating a meaningful life, reinforcing the idea that our well-being is intricately linked to our relationships with others.

The power of positive thinking is amplified through acts of kindness. Engaging in generous behavior not only uplifts those around us but also reinforces a positive mindset within ourselves. When we focus on the good we can do in the world, we shift our perspective from one of scarcity to one of abundance. This shift fosters a more optimistic outlook on life, further enhancing our capacity for joy. By cultivating a habit of kindness, we create a feedback loop that encourages more positive thoughts and actions, thereby enriching our experience of life.

The impact of gratitude on life satisfaction cannot be overlooked in discussions of kindness. When we engage in acts of kindness, we often find ourselves on the receiving end of gratitude, creating a cycle of appreciation that enhances our sense of well-being. This reciprocal relationship reinforces the importance of love and connection in our lives, encouraging us to reflect on the meaning we derive from our interactions. As we explore these existential questions, it becomes clear that kindness is not just a moral obligation; it is a pathway to deeper happiness, fulfillment, and a richer understanding of what it means to be human.

Overcoming Adversity

Overcoming adversity is a fundamental and inescapable theme in the human narrative, inextricably linked to the pursuit of joy and happiness. Life, in its unpredictable and often turbulent nature, presents a myriad of challenges, ranging from profoundly personal losses and debilitating health crises to widespread societal upheavals and crippling economic struggles. Each individual, irrespective of background or circumstance, faces their own unique set of difficulties, and the manner in which we respond to these challenges often profoundly shapes our trajectory towards fulfillment, or conversely, towards despair. The ability to navigate through hardship not only strengthens our emotional resilience, acting as a buffer against future difficulties, but also deepens our understanding of ourselves, fostering a greater sense of self-awareness and a more nuanced perspective on the world around us. Engaging with adversity, rather than passively enduring it, can serve as a powerful catalyst for personal growth, encouraging us to critically examine our values, beliefs, and priorities, ultimately leading to a more authentic and meaningful existence.

Philosophically, the concept of overcoming adversity aligns closely with the core tenets of existentialism, a school of thought that emphasizes individual freedom and responsibility. Existentialism posits that individuals are ultimately responsible for creating meaning in their lives, even — and perhaps especially — in the face of suffering and the inherent absurdity of existence. This perspective actively invites us to confront the inevitable challenges of existence head-on, rather than shying away from them or seeking solace in escapism. By embracing the struggle, by acknowledging the inherent difficulty of being, we can uncover hidden layers of strength, resilience, and resourcefulness that we may not have even realized we possessed. This arduous journey through difficulty, marked by moments of doubt, fear, and perhaps even despair, often leads to profound insights about ourselves, our relationships, and our place in the cosmos, fostering a deeper and more genuine appreciation for joy and happiness when they do eventually arrive. It is through this enlightened lens of understanding that we can reframe our perception of adversity, viewing it not as a mere obstacle to overcome, a frustrating impediment to an otherwise smooth path, but as a necessary and integral component of the complete human experience, a crucible in which character is forged and wisdom is gleaned.

Furthermore, the specific strategies employed to navigate adversity significantly impact the outcome. Emotional intelligence, a multifaceted set of skills that encompasses self-awareness, self-regulation, social awareness, and relationship management, plays a crucial role in how we handle adversity and ultimately emerge from it stronger. The ability to recognize, understand, and manage our own emotions, as well as empathize with the emotions of others, allows us to respond to challenges in a constructive and proactive manner, rather than reacting impulsively or defensively. Emotional intelligence enables us to maintain a sense of perspective during difficult times, preventing us from being overwhelmed by negative emotions and fostering an attitude of resilience and hope. By actively cultivating this crucial skill through introspection, mindfulness practices, and intentional self-improvement, we learn to navigate our feelings and reactions with greater awareness and control, transforming potentially destructive emotions such as anger, fear, and sadness into opportunities for growth, learning, and self-discovery. Moreover, this heightened emotional awareness can lead to increased empathy and compassion for others facing similar struggles, fostering a sense of community, shared experience, and mutual support that can bolster our collective resilience and provide a vital safety net during times of crisis. Sharing our experiences and offering support to others not only alleviates their suffering but also reinforces our own sense of purpose and meaning, further strengthening our resolve to overcome adversity.

When faced with seemingly insurmountable challenges, it can be all too easy to succumb to feelings of inadequacy, focusing on what we lack, what has been taken from us, or what we believe we deserve but have not received. However, practicing gratitude, a conscious and deliberate effort to appreciate the positive aspects of our lives, allows us to fundamentally shift our perspective, recognizing the blessings and opportunities that still exist, even amidst turmoil and hardship. Numerous research studies have consistently demonstrated that individuals who cultivate a sense of gratitude, who actively seek out and acknowledge the good things in their lives, experience significantly higher levels of life satisfaction, emotional well-being, and overall happiness. This practice encourages us to find joy in seemingly small moments, to appreciate the beauty of nature, the warmth of human connection, and the simple pleasures of everyday life. It also reinforces our awareness of the support systems around us, including family, friends, and even our community, reminding us that we are not alone in our struggles and that there are people who care about us and are willing to offer assistance. By embracing gratitude as a daily practice, we can fundamentally transform our relationship with adversity, viewing it not only as a daunting hurdle to be overcome but also as an invaluable opportunity for profound growth, deeper fulfillment, and a more profound appreciation for the preciousness and fragility of life. Ultimately, it is through this combination of resilience, emotional intelligence, and gratitude that we can not only survive adversity but also thrive in its wake, emerging stronger, wiser, and more compassionate individuals.

The Ripple Effect of Small Actions

The concept of the ripple effect illustrates how small actions can lead to significant changes, resonating far beyond their initial context. This phenomenon is particularly relevant in the pursuit of happiness and well-being. A simple act of kindness, such as holding the door for someone or offering a compliment, can create a chain reaction, uplifting those around us and fostering a more positive environment. When individuals engage in these small, thoughtful gestures, they not only enhance their own emotional state but also contribute to a collective atmosphere of goodwill. This interconnectedness emphasizes the idea that our actions, no matter how minor they may seem, hold the potential to impact the broader community.

In the realm of emotional intelligence, understanding the ripple effect of our actions can lead to personal growth and improved relationships. When we consciously choose to respond with empathy and compassion, we model these behaviors for others. This creates a nurturing cycle where emotional awareness flourishes. As individuals witness the constructive outcomes of their actions, they are more likely to engage in similar behaviors. This transformation fosters an environment where emotional intelligence thrives, ultimately enhancing interpersonal connections and creating a supportive community that prioritizes well-being.

Inspirational stories of everyday heroes often highlight the power of small actions in generating meaningful change. Consider a neighbor who consistently checks in on an elderly resident, providing companionship and assistance. This seemingly small commitment not only enriches the lives of those directly involved but also inspires others to engage in similar acts of kindness. These narratives serve as powerful reminders that heroism does not always manifest in grand gestures; sometimes, it is the cumulative effect of small, consistent actions that leads to profound change. By sharing these stories, we encourage a culture of gratitude and recognition for the everyday contributions that enhance collective happiness.

Positive thinking is another crucial element intertwined with the ripple effect of small actions. When individuals focus on the positive aspects of their experiences and express gratitude, they contribute to a more optimistic atmosphere. This positivity can spread like ripples in a pond, influencing the attitudes and behaviors of those around us. Research shows that expressing gratitude not only enhances personal satisfaction but also promotes resilience and emotional stability. By adopting a mindset that values the power of small, positive actions, individuals can create a supportive network that uplifts everyone involved, reinforcing the idea that joy can be cultivated through intentional choices.

Exploring existential questions about meaning and relationships often reveals the importance of connection and shared experiences. The ripple effect serves as a reminder that our lives are intertwined; our actions do not exist in isolation. Engaging with others in meaningful ways—through small acts of kindness, expressions of love, or moments of shared joy—creates ripples that foster deeper relationships and a greater sense of belonging. As we reflect on our connections, we realize that the pursuit of joy is not merely an individual endeavor, but a collective journey that is enriched by the small actions we take. Embracing this interconnectedness can lead to a more fulfilling existence, where happiness is not just a personal achievement but a shared reality.

THE POWER OF POSITIVE THINKING

The Science Behind Positive Thinking

The science behind positive thinking encompasses a range of psychological and neurological studies that reveal how our thoughts can significantly influence our emotional and physical well-being. Research in cognitive psychology has established that our mindset affects our perception of reality, shaping how we respond to challenges and interact with the world around us. Positive thinking, characterized by an optimistic outlook and the expectation of favorable outcomes, has been linked to various health benefits, including reduced stress levels, improved immunity, and enhanced overall life satisfaction. This growing body of evidence underscores the importance of cultivating a positive mindset as a fundamental aspect of personal growth and emotional intelligence.

Neuroscience has shed light on how positive thinking impacts brain function. When individuals engage in positive thoughts, the brain releases neurotransmitters such as dopamine and serotonin, which are associated with feelings of happiness and well-being. These chemicals not only elevate mood but also improve cognitive processes such as decision-making, creativity, and problem-solving. Studies have demonstrated that individuals who practice positive thinking are more resilient in the face of adversity and are better equipped to manage stress. This resilience is not merely a matter of attitude; it is rooted in the brain's capacity to adapt and reorganize itself in response to experiences, a phenomenon known as neuroplasticity.

The impact of positive thinking extends beyond individual health; it influences social relationships and community dynamics. When individuals adopt a positive outlook, they tend to engage more constructively with others, fostering an environment of support and encouragement. This social aspect is vital, as strong relationships have been shown to enhance emotional well-being and provide a buffer against life's challenges. The interconnectedness of positive thinking and social support highlights the role of community in personal growth and happiness. Everyday heroes, who exemplify resilience and optimism, often inspire those around them to adopt similar attitudes, creating a ripple effect of positivity.

The practice of gratitude is closely intertwined with positive thinking and has been shown to significantly enhance life satisfaction. Research indicates that individuals who regularly express gratitude experience increased levels of positive emotions, reduced symptoms of depression, and a stronger sense of connection to others. Gratitude shifts focus from what is lacking to what is present, encouraging a mindset that values the good in life. This practice can be cultivated through simple daily rituals, such as keeping a gratitude journal or sharing moments of appreciation with loved ones. By integrating gratitude into our lives, we not only boost our own happiness but also contribute to a more positive atmosphere for those around us.

In reflecting on the philosophical dimensions of positive thinking, it becomes clear that this practice is not merely a psychological tool but a profound approach to living a meaningful life. Embracing positivity invites individuals to confront existential questions with hope and resilience rather than despair. This perspective allows for a deeper understanding of love, relationships, and the pursuit of happiness as interconnected elements of the human experience. By prioritizing positive thinking, we embark on a journey that not only enhances our personal well-being but also enriches the lives of those we touch, ultimately contributing to a more compassionate and joyful world.

Techniques for Cultivating Positivity

Cultivating positivity is an essential practice for enhancing overall well-being and achieving a deeper sense of happiness. One effective technique is the **regular practice of gratitude**. Research has shown that individuals who consistently express gratitude experience lower levels of stress and depression, as well as higher levels of emotional resilience. This can be achieved through simple actions such as maintaining a gratitude journal, where one records daily instances of appreciation, or by sharing expressions of thanks with others. By consciously focusing on positive experiences and acknowledging the contributions of people in our lives, we can shift our mindset away from negativity and foster a more optimistic outlook.

Another powerful technique is **the cultivation of mindfulness**. Mindfulness encourages individuals to remain present and fully engaged with their current experiences, rather than dwelling on past regrets or future anxieties. Techniques such as meditation, deep-breathing exercises, and mindful walking can help individuals develop a heightened awareness of their thoughts and feelings. By observing these mental patterns without judgment, individuals can create space for positivity to emerge. As mindfulness becomes a regular practice, it can lead to a greater appreciation for life's simple pleasures, allowing joy to flourish in the everyday moments that might otherwise go unnoticed.

Engaging in acts of kindness and service can also significantly enhance one's sense of positivity. When individuals help others, they not only contribute to the well-being of their communities but also experience an increase in their own happiness. This reciprocal relationship between helping and feeling good about oneself is supported by various studies indicating that altruistic behavior leads to improved mental health outcomes. Simple acts such as volunteering, offering support to friends, or even small gestures of kindness can create a ripple effect that uplifts both the giver and the receiver, reinforcing the idea that connection and compassion are fundamental to human happiness.

Building and nurturing strong relationships is another vital technique for fostering positivity. Social connections provide emotional support, enhance our sense of belonging, and contribute to our overall happiness. Investing time and energy into relationships, whether with family, friends, or colleagues, can lead to more fulfilling interactions.

Regular communication, shared experiences, and expressing appreciation for one another can strengthen these bonds. As individuals cultivate positive relationships, they create a network of support that can buffer against life's challenges, enabling them to maintain a positive outlook even in difficult times.

Embracing a growth mindset can significantly influence one's ability to cultivate positivity. This philosophy, popularized by psychologist Carol Dweck, suggests that individuals who view challenges as opportunities for growth are more likely to persevere through adversity and maintain a positive attitude. By reframing setbacks as learning experiences, individuals can reduce fear of failure and increase their resilience. This shift in perspective not only fosters a more optimistic outlook but also encourages personal development and self-improvement. By adopting these techniques, individuals can actively engage in the pursuit of positivity, creating a foundation for a more joyful and fulfilling life.

The Impact of Positivity on Well-being

The impact of positivity on well-being is a topic that resonates deeply within the realms of philosophy, psychology, and personal development. Positivity, often manifesting as an optimistic outlook, significantly influences an individual's mental and emotional health. Research has consistently shown that maintaining a positive attitude can lead to a range of benefits, from improved physical health to enhanced relationships. In the pursuit of joy, understanding how positivity shapes our experiences is crucial in navigating life's complexities and challenges.

One of the most profound effects of positivity is its ability to foster resilience. Individuals who cultivate a positive mindset are better equipped to face adversity and bounce back from setbacks. This resilience stems from a belief in one's capacity to overcome difficulties and an expectation that good outcomes are possible. When people approach life with a positive lens, they are more likely to view obstacles as temporary and surmountable. This shift in perspective not only alleviates stress but also empowers individuals to take proactive steps toward their goals, reinforcing a cycle of achievement and fulfillment.

Moreover, positivity enhances emotional intelligence, a vital component of personal growth and effective interpersonal relationships. Individuals who are positive tend to exhibit greater empathy, better communication skills, and an ability to navigate social interactions with ease. This heightened emotional intelligence allows them to connect more deeply with others, fostering relationships built on understanding and support. As these connections deepen, they create a network of mutual encouragement that further amplifies positive feelings and experiences, contributing to overall life satisfaction.

The power of positive thinking also intersects with the practice of gratitude, which has been shown to significantly impact life satisfaction. When individuals focus on the good in their lives and express gratitude for their experiences, they cultivate a mindset that acknowledges abundance rather than scarcity. This practice not only shifts attention away from negative thoughts but also strengthens the appreciation for relationships and meaningful experiences. As gratitude becomes a regular part of one's routine, it reinforces positive thinking and creates a foundation for a more fulfilling and joyous existence.

The exploration of positivity's impact on well-being invites philosophical reflections on the nature of happiness itself. It challenges individuals to consider what it means to live a good life and how our thoughts influence our perceptions of reality. By embracing positivity, individuals not only enhance their own well-being but also contribute to a more compassionate and supportive community. In this pursuit of joy, the cultivation of a positive mindset emerges as an essential practice, shaping not only individual lives but also the collective experience of humanity.

EXPLORING EXISTENTIAL QUESTIONS

The Search for Meaning

The quest for meaning is a fundamental aspect of the human experience, influencing our decisions, relationships, and overall sense of well-being. As adults navigate through the complexities of life, the search for deeper significance becomes increasingly prominent. Philosophers throughout history have explored this existential question, suggesting that meaning is not inherently given but rather constructed through our experiences, choices, and reflections. The pursuit of meaning is intricately linked to the notion of happiness; understanding what gives life meaning can lead to greater fulfillment and joy.

Human existence is often characterized by a profound quest for understanding and purpose. From the dawn of consciousness, we have grappled with existential questions: Why are we here? What is the nature of reality? What does it mean to live a meaningful life? These inquiries transcend cultural, geographical, and temporal boundaries, resonating with individuals across varied backgrounds. At the core of our existence lies a tapestry woven with threads of philosophy, spirituality, science, and personal experience, each contributing to our understanding of the elusive concept of meaning. This essay endeavors to explore these existential questions, engaging with philosophical perspectives, psychological insights, and spiritual dimensions, ultimately advocating for a personal quest that illuminates one's unique path to meaning.

The Philosophical Perspective

Philosophy, the pursuit of wisdom, serves as a wellspring for existential exploration. Thinkers like Socrates, Nietzsche, and Camus have examined the nature of existence and meaning. Socratic thought emphasizes the importance of self-knowledge, encapsulated in his famous dictum, "The unexamined life is not worth living." Through introspection, we are urged to confront our beliefs, values, and motivations, facilitating a deeper understanding of our purpose.

In stark contrast, Friedrich Nietzsche articulated the notion of the "will to power" and the idea of eternal recurrence, prompting us to consider the implications of our choices and the manner in which we affirm our existence. Nietzsche challenges us to reject nihilism—the rejection of inherent meaning—and instead create our own values in a universe that may seem indifferent. He famously declared, "God is dead," suggesting that traditional sources of meaning had diminished, leaving humanity with the responsibility to forge meaning amidst absurdity.

Albert Camus, in his exploration of the absurd, recognized the struggle for meaning in a seemingly chaotic world. In "The Myth of Sisyphus," Camus likens human existence to the eternal struggle of Sisyphus, condemned to roll a boulder up a hill only for it to roll back down. Yet, he posited that true freedom and authenticity arise from embracing the absurd, finding solace in the journey itself rather than succumbing to despair. The existentialist framework offers a rich landscape for understanding the complexities of meaning, emphasizing personal accountability and the creation of one's purpose.

The Psychological Dimension

While philosophy addresses the fundamental nature of existence, psychology delves into the human experience, offering insights into our emotional and cognitive responses to existential questions. The work of Viktor Frankl, a Holocaust survivor and psychiatrist, exemplifies the intersection of psychology and meaning. In his seminal book, "Man's Search for Meaning," Frankl posits that the primary human drive is not pleasure, as Freud suggested, nor power, as Nietzsche proposed, but the pursuit of meaning.

Frankl's experiences in concentration camps illustrated that even in the most harrowing circumstances, individuals could find purpose through love, suffering, and the courage to transcend pain. He proposed that meaning can be derived from three sources: creating a work or doing a deed, experiencing something or encountering someone, and the attitude we take toward unavoidable suffering. This perspective underscores the notion that meaning is not simply given but is actively constructed through our experiences and choices.

Psychology informs us that the search for meaning is intimately linked to well-being. Studies indicate that individuals who identify a sense of purpose are more resilient, experience better mental health, and display greater life satisfaction. This suggests that cultivating meaning is not merely an existential pursuit but a vital component of thriving in our complex world.

The Spiritual Quest

Beyond philosophy and psychology, spirituality offers another dimension to our search for meaning, often intersecting with existential inquiries. Spirituality encompasses a wide spectrum of beliefs and practices that facilitate a connection to something greater than oneself, be it a divine presence, nature, or the universe. Spiritual traditions, from Buddhism to Christianity, provide frameworks for understanding life's purpose and the interconnectedness of all beings.

In Buddhism, the notion of impermanence and the interdependent nature of existence cultivate a profound appreciation for life as it unfolds. The practice of mindfulness encourages individuals to inhabit the present moment, fostering a sense of clarity and purpose. In this context, meaning is found not in external validation but in the depths of one's own awareness and experience.

Christianity offers a narrative of redemption and love, suggesting that meaning arises from serving others and cultivating compassion. The teachings of Jesus emphasize the importance of community, empathy, and the transformative power of love, offering a pathway to a purposeful life that resonates with many seekers.

Across spiritual traditions, the pursuit of meaning is often realized through the cultivation of virtues, the embrace of love, and a connection to the transcendent. This spiritual aspect of meaning underscores the idea that while our individual journeys may differ, the quest itself unites us in our shared humanity.

A Personal Journey

Ultimately, the search for meaning is a deeply personal journey. Each individual must grapple with their values, experiences, and beliefs to carve out their unique path. It is a dynamic process, one that evolves over time as we encounter new challenges, insights, and transformations.

Reflecting on existential questions enables us to confront our fears and uncertainties, fostering growth and resilience. Embracing the complexity of our experiences—including joy, suffering, love, and loss—affords us opportunities to weave a rich tapestry of meaning. Engaging in creative pursuits, forging connections with others, and seeking knowledge can deepen our understanding and reinforce a sense of purpose.

In a world that often feels chaotic and fragmented, the search for meaning remains an inspiration for hope. It calls us to explore the depths of our being, to engage with others, and to contribute to the greater good. The questions may remain unanswered, but the journey itself holds transformative potential.

The quest for meaning is a fundamental aspect of the human experience, resonating across the epochs of time and the breadth of existence. Through philosophical inquiry, psychological insight, and spiritual exploration, we are encouraged to confront the existential questions that shape our lives. In embracing this journey, we transcend the mundane and connect with the essence of what it means to be human.

As we navigate the complexities of existence, let us remember that the search for meaning is not a destination but a way of being in the world. It is an invitation to live fully, to love deeply, and to create a life that reflects our values and aspirations. In the tapestry of existence, we are both seekers and creators, as we navigate the intricate dance of life in search of understanding and purpose.

One of the key components in the search for meaning is the development of emotional intelligence. This involves recognizing one's own emotions and the emotions of others, fostering a deeper connection to the human experience. When individuals cultivate emotional intelligence, they become more adept at navigating their inner landscapes and understanding the emotional currents that influence their actions and relationships. Through this heightened awareness, they can identify what truly resonates with them, paving the way for a more meaningful life.

While philosophers, theologians, and thinkers throughout history have grappled with the essence of meaning, one key component has emerged as pivotal in this journey: emotional intelligence (EI). The evolution of our societies and the individual quest for purpose are intricately linked to our ability to understand, manage, and harness our emotions effectively, both within ourselves and in our interactions with others.

The Interplay of Emotional Intelligence *and* Meaning

The search for meaning is an intricate journey marked by the development of emotional intelligence. As we cultivate self-awareness, self-regulation, motivation, empathy, and social skills, we deepen our understanding not only of ourselves but also of the world in which we exist. This journey demands introspection and outward connection, weaving together personal and collective narratives of significance.

Emotional intelligence serves as both the compass guiding us toward our true purpose and the fuel propelling us forward in the face of adversity. By embracing the full spectrum of our emotional experiences, we unearth the richness of existence and contribute to a world imbued with meaning—transforming both ourselves and the communities we inhabit. The quest for meaning, deeply intertwined with emotional intelligence, is an odyssey that promises to illuminate our paths, reminding us that within the fragile beauty of our shared humanity lies the potential for profound significance.

The power of positive thinking plays a crucial role in the search for meaning. Optimism can shift one's perspective, allowing individuals to see opportunities for growth even in difficult circumstances. By focusing on what is possible rather than what is lacking, individuals can cultivate a mindset that fosters gratitude and enhances life satisfaction. This practice of gratitude not only enriches personal relationships but also reinforces a sense of connection to something larger than oneself, contributing to a more meaningful existence.

Exploring existential questions about love and relationships also enriches the search for meaning. Relationships are often cited as a primary source of joy, yet they can also be sources of conflict and confusion. Understanding the dynamics of love, compassion, and connection can lead to deeper insights into oneself and others. By reflecting on the nature of these relationships, individuals can uncover the underlying values that drive their actions and choices, ultimately guiding them toward a more fulfilling and meaningful life. Through this exploration, the pursuit of joy becomes not just an individual journey but a shared human experience, deeply intertwined with our connections to one another.

The Role of Self-Awareness
in the Search for Meaning

Self-awareness, the cornerstone of emotional intelligence, is the ability to introspect and understand our own emotions, motivations, and values. It is more than simply knowing *what* we feel; it's about understanding *why* we feel it, and how those feelings influence our thoughts and actions. To embark on the quest for meaning, a pursuit inherent to the human condition, we must first embark on the journey within. This self-exploration allows us to unearth our truest desires and aspirations, unveiling the essence of what we deem meaningful in life. Without this foundational understanding, we risk building our lives on shaky ground, chasing fleeting goals that ultimately leave us feeling empty and unfulfilled.

Consider the philosopher Socrates, who famously stated, "The unexamined life is not worth living." This assertion encapsulates the importance of self-awareness in our pursuit of significance. Socrates argued that a life lived passively, without critical reflection and conscious decision-making, is akin to sleepwalking. Without a profound understanding of ourselves, we cannot navigate the complexities of existence with intention and purpose. We become susceptible to external pressures, societal expectations, and the whims of immediate gratification, losing sight of our individual compass. As we delve into our emotions, we begin to recognize patterns in our behavior, the influences of our past experiences, and the beliefs that shape our understanding of the world. This clarity empowers us to make conscious choices aligned with our values, leading us away from superficial pursuits toward endeavors that resonate deeply within us.

This journey inward is not always easy or comfortable. It requires courage to confront our shadows — the aspects of ourselves we may have tried to suppress or ignore. It demands honesty to acknowledge our imperfections and shortcomings. We may uncover past traumas, limiting beliefs, or unhealthy patterns that have been holding us back. However, these discoveries are not meant to discourage us, but rather to provide us with the raw materials for growth and transformation. By understanding the roots of our anxieties, fears, and insecurities, we can begin to heal and cultivate a stronger, more resilient sense of self.

Furthermore, self-awareness extends beyond simply understanding our internal landscape. It also involves recognizing how we interact with the world around us and the impact we have on others. By understanding our own biases and prejudices, we can strive to be more empathetic and compassionate in our interactions. By recognizing our strengths and weaknesses, we can better contribute to our communities and pursue goals that align with our talents and passions.

The process of cultivating self-awareness is an ongoing one, a lifelong practice of introspection and reflection. It can be fostered through various techniques, such as mindfulness meditation, journaling, therapy, or even simply engaging in deep conversations with trusted friends or mentors. Each of these practices provides us with opportunities to pause, observe our thoughts and feelings, and connect with our inner selves.

The journey inward is not an end in itself, but rather a means to a more meaningful and fulfilling life. By understanding ourselves, we can better understand our place in the world and the impact we want to have. We can make choices that are aligned with our values, pursue goals that are truly meaningful to us, and build relationships that are authentic and supportive. The quest for meaning begins with the journey inward, and it is a journey worth taking. Only by knowing ourselves can we truly begin to know what it means to live.

The Intersection of Happiness *and* Existentialism

The intersection of happiness and existentialism presents a compelling landscape for understanding human experience. Existentialism, a philosophical movement emphasizing individual freedom and choice, delves into the complexities of existence, identity, and meaning. This exploration often leads to profound questions about what it means to live a fulfilling life. Happiness, traditionally viewed as a state of contentment or pleasure, takes on a richer meaning when examined through the lens of existential thought. Rather than being a fleeting emotion, happiness can be seen as a deeper, more enduring sense of fulfillment that arises from embracing one's freedom, confronting life's inherent uncertainties, and finding personal significance in one's choices.

Across cultures and epochs, it has transcended the constraints of geography, language, and time, emerging as a universal aspiration. Yet, paradoxically, happiness often appears elusive, slippery—an enigma that has prompted extensive philosophical inquiry and debate. One philosophical lens that offers profound insights into the nature of happiness is existentialism. This essay will delve into the intersection of happiness and existentialism, examining how the philosophy's core tenets illuminate the complex relationship between personal meaning, subjective experience, and the quest for fulfillment.

Understanding Existentialism

Existentialism is a philosophical movement that gained prominence in the 20th century, characterized by its emphasis on individual existence, freedom, and choice. Thinkers such as Søren Kierkegaard, Friedrich Nietzsche, Jean-Paul Sartre, and Simone de Beauvoir grappled with the implications of human autonomy in a world often devoid of inherent meaning. At its heart, existentialism posits that individuals must navigate their lives, make choices, and construct their own essence in an indifferent universe. In this context, happiness can be redefined—not as a transient emotion or a state to be pursued, but as a byproduct of authentic living.

The Quest for Authenticity

At the core of existentialist thought lies the pursuit of authenticity. To live authentically is to be true to oneself, to embrace one's freedom, and to accept responsibility for the choices made. In a world saturated with external expectations—societal norms, cultural traditions, and familial obligations—the challenge lies in discerning one's true desires and aspirations. Authenticity necessitates introspection and self-reflection, urging individuals to confront existential anxiety and the inherent absurdity of life.

From an existentialist perspective, happiness is not found in the accumulation of wealth, status, or superficial pleasures. Instead, it arises when individuals align their actions with their authentic selves. This alignment is often wrought with struggle and discomfort, as it requires a courageous confrontation with the self. Sartre famously underscored the burden of freedom and choice, suggesting that individuals often evade their responsibility through "bad faith"—the denial of one's freedom and the acceptance of external definitions imposed by society. In contrast, by acknowledging our freedom and the weight of our choices, we can cultivate a sense of ownership over our lives, leading to a deeper, more fulfilling happiness.

The Role of Meaning

Another vital aspect wherein happiness intersects with existentialist philosophy is the concept of meaning. Existentialists contend that life does not come pre-packaged with meaning; rather, we must create our own. Viktor Frankl, a notable figure in existential thought, articulated this notion in his seminal work "Man's Search for Meaning." Drawing from his experiences in Nazi concentration camps, Frankl emphasized that individuals can find meaning even in the direst circumstances. He posited that happiness emerges from a deep sense of purpose—from pursuing meaningful goals, fostering genuine connections with others, and engaging in acts that transcend oneself.

The pursuit of happiness, thus, is inextricably linked to the search for meaning. When individuals anchor their lives in causes and pursuits that resonate with their values, they experience a profound sense of fulfillment. Happiness, then, becomes less about fleeting moments of joy and more about the enduring satisfaction derived from living a life imbued with significance. This existential journey cultivates resilience—a critical virtue in facing life's inevitable adversities.

Embracing Ambiguity and Suffering

Existentialism reminds us that life is fraught with ambiguity and suffering. Traditional pursuits of happiness often emphasize positivity, success, and comfort, glossing over the complexities of the human experience. Yet, existential thinkers argue that embracing suffering is essential for growth and understanding. Nietzsche's concept of the "will to power" encourages individuals to harness challenges and struggles as catalysts for personal transformation.

In the existential framework, acknowledging and embracing the darker facets of existence—the pain, the confusion, the despair—can ultimately lead to a more profound appreciation of happiness. By confronting our limitations and suffering, we equip ourselves with the tools necessary for authentic living. Happiness, therefore, is not merely about the absence of discomfort but involves the acceptance of life's inherent challenges. It is through this acceptance that individuals can cultivate a richer, deeper existence.

Redefining Happiness

The intersection of happiness and existentialism offers a transformative lens through which we can reshape our understanding of fulfillment. Rather than perceiving happiness as an end goal or a fleeting state, we can view it as a byproduct of living authentically, seeking meaning, and embracing the full spectrum of human experience. Existentialism urges us to confront our freedom, make choices that resonate with our true selves, and cultivate resilience in the face of life's inevitable challenges.

In this journey, happiness becomes an inner state rooted in our ability to create meaning, nurture authentic relationships, and confront the complexities of our existence. As we navigate the intricate tapestry of life, we discover that happiness is not something to be chased but rather a companion that emerges as we engage deeply with our most authentic selves. By embracing existentialism, we embark on a journey toward a more resilient, meaningful, and profoundly fulfilling existence—a journey that celebrates the beauty of being alive, in all its messiness and wonder.

Existentialists argue that happiness cannot be pursued directly; instead, it emerges as a byproduct of living authentically. The notion of authenticity is central to existential philosophy, suggesting that true happiness arises when individuals align their actions with their values and beliefs. This alignment often requires a courageous confrontation with the self, acknowledging both strengths and vulnerabilities. By making conscious choices that reflect their true selves, individuals can cultivate an inner joy that is resilient against external circumstances. This perspective shifts the focus from external validation to internal fulfillment, encouraging adults to seek meaning and purpose in their everyday lives.

Furthermore, the existential exploration of happiness emphasizes the importance of grappling with life's fundamental uncertainties. Existential thinkers such as Jean-Paul Sartre and Albert Camus highlight that acknowledging the absurdity of life can lead to a more profound appreciation of existence. Instead of viewing challenges and dilemmas as obstacles to happiness, they can be reframed as opportunities for growth and self-discovery. This shift fosters emotional intelligence, as individuals learn to navigate their feelings and responses to adversity. By embracing the unpredictable nature of life, one can cultivate resilience and develop a more nuanced understanding of happiness that includes both joy and sorrow.

Recognizing and appreciating the transient moments of joy can enhance life satisfaction, allowing individuals to find beauty in the ordinary. Existentialism encourages a reflective practice of gratitude, prompting individuals to consider the significance of their experiences and relationships. This practice not only reinforces positive thinking but also deepens connections with others, as gratitude fosters empathy and understanding. By cultivating a grateful mindset, adults can enrich their lives with meaning and satisfaction, ultimately contributing to a more profound sense of happiness grounded in existential awareness.

The intersection of happiness and existentialism invites a transformative approach to understanding well-being. By embracing authenticity, confronting uncertainties, and practicing gratitude, individuals can cultivate a richer, more meaningful experience of happiness. This philosophical journey encourages adults to reflect on their values and choices, fostering personal growth and emotional intelligence. As they navigate the complexities of life, the insights gained from existential thought can inspire a deeper appreciation for the multifaceted nature of happiness, reminding us that true joy often lies in the acceptance of both the light and shadow of the human experience.

Embracing Uncertainty in Life

Embracing uncertainty is a vital aspect of the human experience that often goes unacknowledged in the quest for happiness. In an increasingly predictable world, the desire for stability and certainty can overshadow the inherent unpredictability of life. However, it is within this unpredictability that opportunities for growth, learning, and genuine joy reside. By accepting uncertainty, individuals can cultivate emotional resilience and a deeper understanding of themselves and their relationships. This acceptance not only fosters personal development but also enhances overall well-being, allowing individuals to navigate life's challenges with a positive mindset.

Uncertainty can evoke feelings of anxiety and fear, yet it also presents a fertile ground for exploration and discovery. When faced with the unknown, individuals are often pushed out of their comfort zones, which can lead to transformative experiences. Engaging with uncertainty encourages curiosity and creativity, essential components for personal growth. For instance, the act of pursuing a new career path or engaging in a challenging relationship can be daunting, but such endeavors often yield profound insights and enrich one's life. By reframing uncertainty as an opportunity rather than a threat, individuals can unlock new pathways to joy and fulfillment.

The power of positive thinking plays a significant role in how we perceive and react to uncertainty. When faced with ambiguous situations, adopting a positive outlook can mitigate feelings of fear and anxiety. This shift in perspective allows individuals to embrace challenges with a sense of optimism and hope. Emotional intelligence, which encompasses the ability to manage one's emotions and understand the emotions of others, is crucial in navigating uncertainty. By developing emotional intelligence, individuals can better cope with the complexities of life, fostering healthier relationships and enhancing their overall sense of happiness.

Acknowledging and appreciating the present moment, despite its unpredictability, fosters a sense of contentment. By focusing on what is good and working well in life, individuals can cultivate resilience and a more positive outlook. This practice not only enhances life satisfaction but also encourages a deeper connection to the world around them. Inspirational stories of everyday heroes who have faced adversity and uncertainty serve as reminders that joy can emerge from the most challenging circumstances, highlighting the importance of resilience and gratitude in the pursuit of happiness.

Embracing uncertainty invites individuals to reflect on the existential questions of life and their own personal journeys. It encourages a deeper exploration of meaning and purpose, challenging societal norms that prioritize certainty and stability. By accepting that life is intrinsically unpredictable, individuals can develop a more profound appreciation for the present moment. This philosophical reflection on uncertainty not only enriches one's understanding of happiness but also fosters a compassionate approach to love and relationships. In the end, embracing uncertainty can lead to a more fulfilling life, allowing individuals to navigate their paths with grace, resilience, and joy.

THE IMPACT OF GRATITUDE ON LIFE SATISFACTION

Understanding Gratitude

Gratitude is often described as a simple act of acknowledging and appreciating the kindness and support we receive from others. However, its implications are profound, extending far beyond mere politeness. Understanding gratitude involves examining its roots in human experience, its psychological benefits, and its role as a catalyst for personal growth and well-being. At its core, gratitude fosters a sense of connection, drawing individuals closer to those around them and reinforcing the bonds that constitute our social fabric. This connection is fundamental to our emotional intelligence, enabling us to navigate complex relationships with empathy and understanding.

Philosophically, gratitude can be viewed through various lenses, including existentialism and utilitarianism. Existentialists might argue that gratitude is a response to the absurdity of life, a means of finding meaning in an often chaotic world. In contrast, utilitarian perspectives emphasize the benefits of gratitude in promoting overall happiness and societal well-being. Studies have shown that individuals who practice gratitude regularly report higher levels of life satisfaction, lower levels of stress, and improved mental health. This evidence suggests that gratitude is not merely a passive response but an active choice that shapes our outlook on life and influences our behavior toward others.

The relationship between gratitude and emotional intelligence cannot be overstated. Individuals who cultivate gratitude are better equipped to recognize and respond to the emotional needs of themselves and others. This heightened awareness enhances interpersonal relationships, allowing for deeper connections and a greater appreciation for the people in our lives. Moreover, gratitude serves as a protective factor against negative emotions, such as envy and resentment. By focusing on what we have rather than what we lack, we can foster a positive mindset that promotes resilience in the face of adversity.

In the realm of personal growth, gratitude acts as a powerful tool for transformation. When individuals consciously practice gratitude, they shift their focus from external circumstances to internal attitudes. This shift can lead to profound changes in how one perceives challenges and opportunities. Inspirational stories of everyday heroes often highlight acts of gratitude in the midst of hardship, illustrating how a grateful mindset can empower individuals to overcome obstacles and find joy even in difficult times. These narratives serve as reminders that gratitude is not only a response to favorable conditions but also a proactive approach to living a fulfilling life.

Understanding gratitude involves recognizing its multifaceted nature and its impact on our overall well-being. It invites philosophical reflection on love and relationships, pushing us to consider how we express appreciation and cultivate bonds with those who matter most. As we explore the depths of gratitude, we uncover a pathway to greater happiness and fulfillment, enriching our lives and the lives of those around us. By embracing gratitude as a guiding principle, we can create a more joyful existence, grounded in connection, resilience, and a profound appreciation for the human experience.

Practices to Foster Gratitude

Practices to foster gratitude are essential in the pursuit of happiness and well-being. As research consistently shows, cultivating a mindset of gratitude can significantly enhance life satisfaction and emotional resilience. Individuals who engage in regular gratitude practices report higher levels of positive emotions, improved relationships, and even better physical health. This subchapter explores various practices that can be seamlessly integrated into daily life, encouraging readers to embrace gratitude as a fundamental aspect of their personal growth journey.

- One of the most effective methods for fostering gratitude is maintaining a **gratitude journal**. Taking just a few minutes each day to write down things for which one is thankful can shift focus away from negative experiences and cultivate a greater appreciation for life's simple pleasures. This practice encourages reflection on positive aspects of life, whether they are big achievements or small daily joys. Over time, individuals may find that their overall perspective changes, leading to a more optimistic outlook on life and increased emotional intelligence.

- Another powerful practice involves **expressing gratitude directly to others.** Writing thank-you notes or verbally acknowledging the contributions of friends, family, or colleagues can strengthen relationships and foster a sense of community. This expression not only uplifts the recipient but also reinforces the giver's sense of connection and belonging. Such acts of kindness can create a ripple effect, encouraging a culture of appreciation that enhances social bonds and contributes to overall happiness.

- **Mindfulness meditation** can also play a crucial role in developing a grateful mindset. By focusing on the present moment, individuals can become more aware of the positive aspects of their surroundings and experiences. Mindfulness encourages individuals to acknowledge and appreciate what is happening in their lives right now, rather than getting caught up in past regrets or future anxieties. This practice allows for a deeper connection to one's feelings and experiences, ultimately leading to a more profound appreciation for both the mundane and the extraordinary.

- **Engaging in acts of kindness** can serve as a catalyst for gratitude. Volunteering, helping a neighbor, or simply offering support to someone in need can enhance one's appreciation for life and its many blessings. These actions not only benefit others but also provide the giver with a sense of purpose and fulfillment. In recognizing the impact of their actions on others, individuals can cultivate a deeper gratitude for their own circumstances. The intertwined nature of gratitude and kindness highlights an essential truth: by fostering gratitude within ourselves, we can create a more compassionate and joyful world.

The Long-term Benefits of Gratitude

Gratitude, often viewed as a fleeting emotion, possesses profound long-term benefits that extend far beyond momentary appreciation. At its core, gratitude fosters a greater sense of connection to oneself and others, enhancing emotional intelligence and personal growth. By regularly acknowledging and appreciating the positive aspects of life, individuals cultivate a mindset that encourages resilience and optimism. This shift not only improves emotional well-being but also lays the groundwork for deeper interpersonal relationships, as gratitude promotes empathy and understanding, essential components of emotional intelligence.

Research indicates that practicing gratitude can lead to significant improvements in mental health. Individuals who regularly express gratitude report lower levels of depression and anxiety, and higher levels of overall life satisfaction. This connection between gratitude and mental well-being can be attributed to the way gratitude reorients the mind. Instead of dwelling on negative experiences or perceived injustices, grateful individuals focus on positive relationships and achievements, creating a more balanced perspective on life. Over time, this practice can lead to a more optimistic outlook, which is a cornerstone of positive thinking and an essential factor in the pursuit of happiness.

In addition to enhancing mental health, gratitude has a ripple effect on physical well-being. Studies have shown that grateful individuals tend to engage in healthier behaviors, such as regular exercise and proper nutrition. This correlation suggests that gratitude not only influences emotional states but also encourages proactive approaches to health. By fostering a sense of appreciation for one's body and its capabilities, individuals are more likely to take care of themselves, leading to improved physical health over the long term. This holistic approach to well-being emphasizes the interconnectedness of emotional and physical health, reinforcing the idea that gratitude can be a transformative force in one's life.

Gratitude also plays a pivotal role in shaping our relationships. When individuals express appreciation for their friends, family, and partners, they create an environment of support and love, which strengthens bonds and fosters deeper connections. This is particularly relevant in the context of love and relationships, as gratitude encourages individuals to recognize and acknowledge the contributions of others. By celebrating the small gestures and sacrifices made by loved ones, individuals not only enhance their relationships but also cultivate a shared sense of joy and fulfillment, creating a positive feedback loop that enriches both partners' lives.

The philosophical implications of gratitude extend into existential reflections on meaning and purpose. Engaging in gratitude prompts individuals to consider the larger picture of their lives, contemplating what truly matters to them and why. This reflective process can lead to a greater sense of purpose, as individuals begin to align their values with their actions and relationships. By recognizing the abundance in their lives, individuals can shift their focus from scarcity to gratitude, ultimately enriching their personal growth journey. In essence, the long-term benefits of gratitude are not just about feeling good; they encompass a deeper, more meaningful engagement with life that resonates across emotional, relational, and existential dimensions.

PHILOSOPHICAL REFLECTIONS ON LOVE

The Nature of Love

Love, in its myriad forms, transcends mere emotion; it is a profound force that shapes our existence and influences our pursuit of happiness. Philosophically speaking, love can be dissected into various categories, including romantic love, familial love, platonic love, and self-love. Each type possesses unique characteristics yet shares common threads that bind humans together. Understanding love's nature requires delving into its emotional, psychological, and social dimensions, revealing how it underpins our relationships and contributes to our overall sense of well-being.

Love, that most fundamental and enigmatic of human experiences, has captivated the hearts and minds of thinkers, poets, and everyday people from the dawn of civilization. Its complexities echo through our relationships, art, literature, and spiritual practices, acting as a mirror reflecting our deepest desires, fears, and aspirations. In the quest to understand love, we embark on a philosophical journey, traversing the realms of metaphysics, ethics, psychology, and sociology. This essay seeks to explore the multifaceted nature of love, offering insights that enrich our understanding and appreciation of its profound impact on our existence.

The Ontological Dimension of Love

At its core, love transcends mere emotion or infatuation; it embodies an ontological commitment to another being. Philosophers like Martin Buber have posited that love allows us to move from a "I-It" relationship—one characterized by objectification and detachment—to an "I-Thou" relationship, which emphasizes mutual recognition and authentic connection. This movement toward valuing the "Thou" in our lives fosters an acknowledgment of the intrinsic worth of others, promoting empathy and understanding.

To comprehend the ontological nature of love is to perceive it as a spiritual journey. In engaging with others through love, we dissolve egoistic boundaries, allowing for a profound interconnectedness that affirms our shared humanity. In this light, love is not merely a personal solace; it catalyzes our growth and nurtures a collective consciousness. The act of loving invites us to participate in the unfolding narrative of existence, wherein every relationship is a chapter contributing to a greater story.

Love as Ethical Imperative

Love also presents an ethical dimension vital to our moral lives. In an age marked by individualism and transactionality, love challenges us to adopt a framework where altruism, care, and responsibility take precedence. Philosophers like Emmanuel Levinas argue that love is grounded in an ethical obligation to the other, calling us to respond to their needs and vulnerabilities. In recognizing the other's suffering, we are inspired to act—not from a place of self-interest, but from a deep-seated compassion.

This ethical lens underscores that love is not passive; instead, it demands action. Love calls us to extend ourselves beyond our immediate circles and consider the wider implications of our relationships. It transforms how we navigate societal structures, compelling us to advocate for justice, equity, and the inherent dignity of all individuals. Love's ethical imperative extends into our everyday lives, nudging us toward acts of kindness and fostering a culture of care that uplifts rather than diminishes.

The Epistemological Quest of Love

If love embodies a relational ontology and an ethical imperative, it also presents an epistemological dimension, challenging our understanding of knowledge and truth. In love, we may encounter a paradox: the more intimately we know another person, the more we realize the vastness of what remains unknown. This mystery is what can make love so exhilarating yet so frightening. We strive to penetrate the depths of another's soul while simultaneously acknowledging our limitations in fully grasping another's experiences and perspectives.

The quest for knowledge through love prompts us to become attentive listeners, cultivating patience and vulnerability in our interactions. Love teaches us to embrace uncertainty, as the act of loving requires us to confront our insecurities and fears of rejection. The vulnerability inherent in loving is not merely a risk; it is a pathway toward richer understanding and connection. In reaching out to another with an open heart, we engage in an epistemological journey that can lead us to insights not only about our beloved but also about ourselves.

The Transformative Power of Love

In considering the transformative power of love, we recognize its ability to serve as a catalyst for personal and societal change. Love inspires acts of creativity and beauty, motivating us to express our innermost thoughts and feelings. Think of the timeless works of art, literature, and music birthed from love's presence; they speak to humanity's greatest triumphs and deepest sorrows. Love shapes our identities, encouraging growth and self-discovery. It ignites dreams, desires, and passions, driving us to pursue our aspirations and challenge the status quo.

Moreover, love possesses a revolutionary potential in its capacity to bridge divides, heal wounds, and foster reconciliation. History is filled with examples where love transcends boundaries—be it cultural, racial, or ideological—promoting dialogues that highlight our shared existence. Figures like Mahatma Gandhi and Martin Luther King Jr. espoused love as a powerful force for social change, preaching nonviolent resistance rooted in love for humanity. Their legacies remind us that love is not only an emotion but also a revolutionary force capable of dismantling oppressive systems and building a more just world.

The Eternal Quest for Love

The nature of love is a complex tapestry woven from various threads of philosophical inquiry. It encompasses ontology, ethics, epistemology, and a transformative vision for our lives and societies. As we reflect on love, we recognize its duality: it is both a journey inward, navigating our own hearts, and an outward expression, fostering connections with others. We find ourselves in a perpetual quest for love, a quest that challenges us to embrace vulnerability, cultivate empathy, and commit ourselves to the well-being of others.

As we navigate the intricacies of love, let us do so with an open mind and heart—willing to learn, to heal, and to transform. Love calls us to recognize our interconnectedness, urging us to embody its values in our everyday actions. In the end, love may well be the most profound and essential aspect of our lives, inviting us to celebrate existence in all its beauty, complexity, and imperfection. In the face of uncertainty, love remains our enduring guiding star, lighting the way toward a more compassionate and enriched existence.

Romantic love often garners the most attention in both literature and philosophy, celebrated for its intensity and passion. It can be exhilarating, yet it also carries the potential for heartache and disappointment. The duality of romantic love serves as a reminder of its complexity. This form of love encapsulates the joy of connection and intimacy, but it also challenges individuals to grapple with vulnerability and the fear of loss. The interplay between these contrasting emotions fosters personal growth, encouraging individuals to cultivate emotional intelligence and resilience, essential qualities in navigating both love and life's broader challenges.

Familial love represents another critical dimension of human connection, often characterized by unconditional support and deep-rooted bonds. This type of love fosters a sense of belonging and security, which is vital for emotional development and well-being. Families provide the first context in which individuals learn about love, shaping their subsequent relationships. The nurturing aspect of familial love often instills values such as compassion and gratitude, which can significantly influence one's approach to life and relationships. Recognizing the importance of familial love can lead to greater appreciation for the individuals who have shaped our lives, ultimately enhancing our happiness.

Platonic love, characterized by deep friendships and mutual respect, plays a crucial role in personal growth and emotional fulfillment. These relationships often serve as a source of support and encouragement, allowing individuals to explore their identities and aspirations. The power of positive thinking is amplified in the presence of genuine friendships, as these connections foster an environment where individuals can thrive. Friendships grounded in platonic love challenge us to be our authentic selves, cultivating a sense of belonging that is essential for overall happiness and life satisfaction.

At the heart of all forms of love lies the concept of gratitude. Recognizing and appreciating the love we receive from others can significantly impact our overall well-being. Gratitude fosters a positive mindset, enhancing our ability to connect with others and experience joy. Furthermore, philosophical reflections on love and relationships reveal that love is not merely an emotion but a conscious choice that impacts our actions and interactions. By embracing love in its various forms and expressing gratitude for these connections, we strengthen our emotional intelligence, enrich our lives, and ultimately foster a deeper sense of happiness.

Love as a Pathway to Happiness

Love serves as a fundamental pathway to happiness, intricately woven into the fabric of human existence. Philosophers throughout history have posited that love not only enriches our lives but also enhances our well-being. The emotional bonds we form with others can be a source of profound joy and fulfillment. This connection fosters a sense of belonging, purpose, and emotional security, which are essential components of a happy life. When we engage in loving relationships, whether romantic, familial, or platonic, we create a supportive network that nurtures our emotional health and helps us navigate the complexities of life.

The impact of love on our emotional intelligence cannot be overstated. Through loving relationships, we learn empathy, compassion, and understanding. These qualities are vital for personal growth and for cultivating deeper connections with others. When we experience love, we become more attuned to the emotions and needs of those around us. This awareness not only enhances our interpersonal skills but also bolsters our ability to manage our own emotions. In this way, love acts as both a catalyst for personal development and a foundation for emotional resilience, equipping us to face life's challenges with grace and optimism.

Exploring existential questions about the meaning of life often brings us back to love. Many philosophical traditions assert that love is one of the highest expressions of our humanity, providing meaning and direction in an otherwise chaotic world. Engaging in loving relationships allows us to confront our mortality and the transient nature of existence with a sense of comfort. By investing in love, we create lasting memories and legacies that transcend our individual lives. This pursuit of love ultimately enriches our understanding of existence, imbuing our journey with significance and joy.

Recognizing and appreciating the love we receive and give fosters a cycle of positivity. When we express gratitude for our relationships, we deepen our connections and cultivate an environment where love can flourish. This reciprocal relationship between love and gratitude amplifies our capacity for happiness. As we acknowledge the warmth and support from those we cherish, we become more open to giving love in return, creating a virtuous cycle that nourishes both ourselves and our loved ones. In essence, love not only acts as a pathway to happiness but also as a garden in which gratitude can thrive, leading us toward a richer, more joyful existence.

The Role of Relationships in Well-being

Relationships play a crucial role in our overall well-being, serving as a cornerstone for happiness and fulfillment in life. The connections we foster with others contribute significantly to our emotional and psychological health. Research consistently indicates that individuals with strong, supportive relationships report higher levels of happiness and lower levels of stress. These relationships provide not only companionship but also a sense of belonging, which is vital for emotional stability. As we navigate the complexities of life, the presence of trusted friends and family members can offer comfort and reassurance, helping us to face challenges with resilience.

The quality of our relationships matters profoundly. Positive interactions with others can enhance our emotional intelligence, allowing us to better understand and manage our own emotions while empathizing with those around us. This emotional interconnectedness fosters a supportive environment where individuals can thrive. Conversely, toxic relationships can undermine our well-being, leading to increased anxiety, depression, and a diminished sense of self-worth. It is essential to cultivate relationships that uplift and inspire us, as these connections are instrumental in fostering personal growth and a deeper understanding of our place in the world.

Expressing appreciation for the people in our lives not only strengthens bonds but also promotes a positive atmosphere that encourages open communication and mutual support. When we actively acknowledge the contributions of others, we create a cycle of positivity that can lead to greater satisfaction in our relationships. This practice of gratitude can transform ordinary interactions into meaningful exchanges, allowing us to experience deeper joy and fulfillment in our connections.

Moreover, the philosophical reflections on love and relationships highlight their existential significance. Love, in its various forms, challenges us to confront our vulnerabilities and desires, prompting profound questions about the nature of our existence. Engaging with these questions can lead to a richer understanding of ourselves and our relationships. The pursuit of meaningful connections invites us to explore not just the joys of companionship but also the complexities of intimacy, commitment, and the sacrifices often required to maintain healthy relationships. This exploration can be a source of inspiration and motivation, encouraging us to seek out authentic connections that resonate with our values and aspirations.

The role of relationships in our well-being cannot be overstated. They serve as a vital source of emotional support, facilitate personal growth, and provide opportunities for meaningful reflection on our lives. By nurturing positive relationships and practicing gratitude, we can enhance our happiness and overall life satisfaction. The journey toward joy is deeply intertwined with the connections we cultivate, reminding us that we are not alone in our quest for fulfillment. As we honor the relationships we build, we unlock doors to deeper understanding, resilience, and ultimately, a more profound experience of happiness.

BUILDING MEANINGFUL RELATIONSHIPS

The Importance of Connection

Connection plays a fundamental role in the pursuit of joy, serving as a bridge between individuals and the world around them. It is through connections—whether they are with family, friends, colleagues, or even strangers—that we cultivate a sense of belonging and purpose. Relationships provide us with emotional support, enrich our experiences, and foster resilience during challenging times. In a philosophical context, the value of connection extends beyond mere companionship; it shapes our understanding of happiness and well-being. By exploring the depth of our relationships, we can unlock pathways to a more fulfilling life.

The human experience is inherently social. From the earliest moments of our lives, we crave connection and seek out interaction with others. This innate desire stems from our evolutionary past, where cooperation and community were essential for survival. While the threats and challenges we face today may differ from those of our ancestors, the fundamental need for connection remains deeply ingrained within us. Without it, we risk isolation, loneliness, and a diminished sense of self-worth. Think of the newborn infant who thrives on the touch and voice of their caregiver, or the elderly individual who finds solace and comfort in the presence of loved ones. These are potent reminders of the enduring power of connection throughout the lifespan.

The importance of connection can also be understood through the lens of emotional intelligence, which emphasizes the ability to recognize and manage our own emotions while also empathizing with others. This emotional awareness is crucial for building strong, meaningful relationships. When we engage with others on a deeper level, we not only enhance our own emotional well-being but also contribute positively to the lives of those around us. The act of connecting with others allows us to share our joys and sorrows, creating a tapestry of experiences that enriches our understanding of life. Thus, fostering emotional intelligence through connection is a vital aspect of personal growth. Cultivating empathy, listening actively, and responding with compassion are all essential components of this process. These skills allow us to navigate the complexities of human interaction with grace and understanding, leading to stronger, more fulfilling relationships.

The benefits of connection extend beyond the individual level, impacting communities and societies as a whole. Strong social networks foster a sense of collective responsibility and encourage cooperation towards common goals. When individuals feel connected to their community, they are more likely to participate in civic engagement, contribute to charitable causes, and work towards a more just and equitable society. Consider the impact of social movements throughout history, where individuals united by a shared cause and a sense of collective identity have been able to bring about significant social change. These movements demonstrate the transformative power of connection when channeled towards a common purpose.

However, in our increasingly digital world, it is important to distinguish between superficial online interactions and genuine, meaningful connections. While social media platforms can provide a convenient way to stay in touch with friends and family, they can also contribute to feelings of isolation and anxiety if not used mindfully. The curated and often unrealistic portrayals of life online can create a sense of inadequacy and comparison, undermining our self-esteem and diminishing our sense of connection to the real world. Therefore, it is crucial to prioritize face-to-face interactions, actively listen to others, and engage in activities that foster genuine connection and shared experiences.

The pursuit of joy and well-being is intimately intertwined with our ability to connect with others. By cultivating meaningful relationships, fostering emotional intelligence, and engaging in activities that promote social connection, we can unlock pathways to a more fulfilling and meaningful life. It is through these connections that we find support, inspiration, and a sense of belonging, allowing us to navigate the challenges of life with greater resilience and embrace the joys of human existence with greater appreciation. As the poet John Donne famously wrote, "No man is an island, entire of itself; every man is a piece of the continent, a part of the main." This timeless sentiment underscores the fundamental truth that we are all interconnected, and that our individual happiness is inextricably linked to the well-being of others. Embracing this interconnectedness is key to unlocking a more joyful and fulfilling life for ourselves and for the world around us.

Communication and Empathy

Communication serves as the bridge that connects individuals, allowing for the exchange of thoughts, feelings, and experiences. It is through communication that we express our inner worlds and understand the perspectives of others. In the pursuit of joy, effective communication becomes a vital tool for fostering relationships that enrich our lives. It is essential to recognize that true communication involves not only the words we choose but also the emotional nuances that accompany them. Engaging in active listening and being attuned to non-verbal cues can significantly enhance our interactions, making them more meaningful and empathetic.

Empathy plays a crucial role in the communication process, as it allows us to resonate with the emotions and experiences of those around us. By striving to understand another person's feelings, we create a space where vulnerability can flourish. This mutual understanding lays the groundwork for deeper connections and enhances our capacity for compassion. When we practice empathy, we not only acknowledge the struggles of others but also validate their experiences, which can lead to a profound sense of belonging and acceptance. Such connections are fundamental to our well-being, as they foster a supportive environment that encourages personal growth.

The interplay between communication and empathy can be illustrated through everyday interactions. Consider a moment when a friend shares their challenges with you. If your response is rooted in empathy—reflecting their feelings and offering genuine support—you not only strengthen your bond but also contribute to their emotional healing. This exchange can lead to increased joy for both parties, as it reinforces the idea that we are not alone in our struggles. When individuals feel understood, they are more likely to engage in open dialogues, which can further enhance their self-awareness and emotional intelligence.

Moreover, the cultivation of empathy through communication can lead to a ripple effect in our communities. When we engage in empathetic conversations, we inspire others to do the same. This can create a culture of understanding and support, where individuals feel empowered to share their stories and vulnerabilities. Such environments can significantly impact overall life satisfaction, as they foster gratitude for the connections we build. Recognizing and appreciating the contributions of others to our happiness reinforces the idea that joy is often found in shared experiences rather than isolated achievements.

The philosophical exploration of communication and empathy reveals that our relationships are integral to our pursuit of joy. By embracing these practices, we not only enhance our own emotional intelligence but also contribute to a more compassionate world. The journey toward happiness is seldom a solitary one; it is through our interactions and the connections we forge that we uncover the true essence of well-being. As we cultivate empathy in our communication, we empower ourselves and those around us to live richer, more meaningful lives.

Nurturing Healthy Relationships

Nurturing healthy relationships is a cornerstone of personal happiness and well-being. The cultivation of these connections requires intention and effort, as relationships do not flourish by chance. They thrive on mutual respect, empathy, and understanding. When individuals prioritize emotional intelligence, they become more adept at recognizing and responding to the feelings of others. This awareness fosters deeper connections, allowing relationships to evolve from mere acquaintances to profound bonds that enhance the human experience.

Effective communication is vital in nurturing relationships. It involves not just the exchange of words, but also the ability to listen actively and engage with sincerity. By expressing thoughts and feelings transparently, individuals create an environment of trust. This open dialogue encourages vulnerability, allowing partners, friends, and family members to share their true selves without fear of judgment. Healthy relationships are marked by this ability to communicate openly, leading to a greater understanding of one another's needs and aspirations.

Recognizing and appreciating the contributions of others fosters a positive atmosphere. When people express gratitude, they not only acknowledge the actions of others but also reinforce their value within the relationship. This simple yet powerful act can transform interactions, turning moments of routine into opportunities for connection. By regularly practicing gratitude, individuals can enhance their emotional bonds and contribute to a culture of appreciation that uplifts everyone involved.

In exploring the philosophical implications of love and relationships, one can draw parallels between personal growth and the dynamics of connection. Relationships serve as mirrors, reflecting our strengths and weaknesses. They challenge us to confront our insecurities and cultivate resilience. Through these interactions, individuals learn valuable lessons about compromise, forgiveness, and unconditional support. Embracing these lessons allows for personal development, ultimately contributing to a deeper understanding of oneself and one's place in the larger tapestry of life.

Nurturing healthy relationships requires a commitment to positivity and mutual growth. It is essential to approach relationships with an optimistic mindset, focusing on shared goals and experiences rather than dwelling on conflicts. By fostering a culture of support and encouragement, individuals can inspire each other to reach new heights. This positive reinforcement not only enhances personal satisfaction but also enriches the relationship itself, creating a lasting partnership rooted in joy, understanding, and shared aspirations.

INTEGRATING PHILOSOPHY INTO DAILY LIFE

Practical Philosophical Exercises

Practical philosophical exercises serve as valuable tools for adults seeking to enhance their understanding of happiness and well-being. These exercises encourage individuals to engage with philosophical concepts in a tangible way, allowing for personal growth and reflection. By incorporating philosophical inquiry into daily life, individuals can cultivate emotional intelligence, develop a deeper appreciation for their relationships, and explore the existential questions that shape their experiences. This subchapter will outline several exercises designed to lead readers toward a more profound pursuit of joy.

Philosophy, often perceived as an abstract discipline reserved for lofty academic discussions, offers profound insights into the everyday challenges we face. Integrating philosophical concepts into our daily lives can lead to a more thoughtful, intentional existence. By harnessing the wisdom of the ages, we can navigate the complexities of modern life with enhanced clarity, purpose, and resilience. This essay explores practical philosophical exercises that can inspire individuals to embrace philosophical thinking in their daily routines, nurturing personal growth and enriching their interactions with the world.

The Importance of Philosophy *in* Everyday Life

In a world relentlessly charging forward, driven by technological advancements and the constant barrage of information, the importance of philosophy might seem relegated to dusty bookshelves and academic ivory towers. However, nothing could be further from the truth. Philosophy, far from being an esoteric pursuit, serves as an essential compass guiding us through the complexities of modern life. It teaches us to step back and reflect, to cultivate critical thinking, and to embrace the enduring questions that shape our understanding of ourselves and the world around us.

In a world inundated with information and distractions, the ability to think critically and contemplate our values is invaluable. We are constantly bombarded with opinions, advertisements, and narratives vying for our attention and acceptance. Without the tools of philosophical inquiry, we risk becoming passive consumers of these messages, blindly accepting them as truth. Philosophy equips us with the skills to analyze arguments, identify biases, and evaluate evidence, allowing us to form our own reasoned opinions. It enables us to question norms, to challenge the status quo, and to seek truths that lie beneath the surface of superficiality. By cultivating this critical lens, we move beyond simply accepting what we are told and begin to actively shape our own understanding of the world.

Philosophy allows us to embrace moral considerations that guide our decisions. In a society often driven by pragmatism and immediate gratification, ethical considerations can easily be overlooked. Philosophy provides a framework for navigating moral dilemmas, encouraging us to consider the consequences of our actions and the impact they have on others. From deciding how to allocate resources to navigating complex interpersonal relationships, philosophical ethics offers tools for thoughtful and principled decision-making. It challenges us to examine our own moral compass, to identify potential conflicts in our values, and to strive towards a more just and equitable world.

The practice of philosophy highlights the importance of self-examination—encouraging us to consider who we are, what we believe, and why we act as we do. Self-awareness is a cornerstone of personal growth and fulfillment. By delving into questions of identity, purpose, and meaning, philosophy helps us to understand our own motivations, strengths, and weaknesses. This deeper understanding allows us to make more conscious choices, aligning our actions with our values and pursuing a life that is authentic and meaningful. It empowers us to break free from ingrained habits and unconscious biases, enabling us to cultivate a more conscious and deliberate existence.

Beyond individual benefits, philosophy plays a crucial role in shaping a more just and compassionate society. By engaging with diverse philosophical perspectives, we develop a greater appreciation for the complexity of human experience and the validity of different viewpoints. This understanding fosters tolerance, empathy, and a willingness to engage in constructive dialogue, even with those who hold fundamentally different beliefs. Philosophy encourages us to consider the perspectives of marginalized groups, to challenge systems of oppression, and to advocate for a more inclusive and equitable society.

Embracing philosophical perspectives fosters emotional intelligence. As we engage with complex ideas about existence, ethics, and purpose, we become more adept at understanding ourselves and others. This doesn't just involve intellectual understanding; it cultivates a deeper emotional resonance. By grappling with universal human experiences like love, loss, and suffering through the lens of philosophical inquiry, we develop a greater capacity for empathy and compassion. We learn to recognize the shared humanity that binds us together, even across differences in culture, background, and belief. This skill is critical in building empathy and compassion, further enriching our relationships and community interactions. It allows us to connect with others on a deeper level, to offer genuine support, and to contribute to a more caring and supportive community.

The importance of philosophy in everyday life cannot be overstated. It is not merely an abstract academic pursuit, but a practical and essential toolkit for navigating the complexities of the modern world. By cultivating critical thinking, encouraging self-reflection, and fostering emotional intelligence, philosophy empowers us to live more meaningful, purpose-driven lives. In a world desperately seeking direction and understanding, philosophy offers a beacon of hope, guiding us towards a future grounded in reason, compassion, and a deeper appreciation for the shared human experience. As we embrace philosophical inquiry, we not only enrich our own lives but also contribute to a more just, equitable, and enlightened world for all.

PRACTICAL PHILOSOPHICAL EXERCISES

1. The Daily Reflection Journal

Beginning each day with a few moments of introspection can set a powerful tone for the hours ahead. Allocate time each morning to reflect on the following prompts:

- What values do I wish to embody today?

- How do my actions align with my beliefs?

- What challenges might arise, and how can I respond ethically?

By anchoring your thoughts in reflection, you can articulate intentions and align your actions with your philosophical tenets. Documenting these reflections in a journal not only solidifies insights but also allows for retrospective examination—tracking personal growth and understanding how philosophical inquiries manifest in daily life.

2. The Socratic Method in Conversations

Inspired by the ancient philosopher Socrates, who believed that the pursuit of knowledge begins with questioning, employ the Socratic method in your conversations. Rather than asserting opinions or truths, practice asking open-ended questions that encourage deeper exploration. For example:

- What evidence supports your viewpoint?

- How do you reconcile differing opinions on this topic?

This technique promotes critical thinking, nurtures empathy, and fosters healthy dialogue. Engaging in meaningful conversations rooted in inquiry cultivates a culture of respect and intellectual curiosity, allowing for diverse perspectives to emerge.

3. The Philosophy of Gratitude

Gratitude is a virtue deeply rooted in many philosophical traditions, including Stoicism and Buddhism. Take time each day to express gratitude, either verbally or in writing. Reflect on the following prompts:

- What experiences or interactions am I grateful for today?

- How do these moments contribute to my well-being and my values?

Fostering a gratitude practice shifts focus from scarcity to abundance, enhancing mental well-being and encouraging a positive outlook on life. By consistently acknowledging the contributions of others and the world around you, you reinforce connections and create a sense of community.

4. Ethical Dilemmas and Decision-Making

Philosophy often grapples with moral dilemmas. To integrate ethics into your daily choices, present yourself with hypothetical scenarios and reflect on your responses. For instance, consider a situation where you must choose between honesty and loyalty—a classic ethical quandary.

- What values are at stake?

- How might each choice affect yourself and others?

Explore the reasoning behind each potential action. By consciously engaging with ethical dilemmas, you develop a robust moral framework that informs your decisions, promoting integrity and accountability in your interactions.

5. Mindfulness and the Art of Presence

Many philosophical traditions, particularly existentialism and Eastern philosophies, emphasize the importance of being present. Engage in mindfulness practices that ground you in the current moment. Dedicate time to simple activities like mindful eating, walking, or breathing exercises, attentively observing sensations, thoughts, and emotions.

This practice not only enhances self-awareness but also cultivates appreciation for the present. Through mindfulness, you develop a richer understanding of your experiences and an appreciation for life's subtleties. The philosophical dimension transforms ordinary moments into profound encounters with existence.

6. Reading Philosophical Works

To cultivate philosophical thinking, incorporate readings from influential philosophers into your routine. Choose texts that resonate with you—whether the Stoics, existentialists, or modern ethical theorists. Take notes and reflect on key concepts, asking questions like:

- How does this philosophy relate to my life?

- What insights can I apply to current challenges?

Discussing philosophical ideas with others, whether in a book club or informal gatherings, further deepens your understanding. Engaging in discourse about philosophical works encourages exploration and expands perspectives.

Integrating philosophy into daily life is a journey of self-discovery, ethical development, and emotional growth. The practical exercises outlined above serve as compasses, guiding us through the complexities of existence and encouraging a more intentional approach to life. By fostering critical thinking, emotional intelligence, and a strong moral compass, we can navigate challenges with greater resilience.

Philosophy, far from being an esoteric pursuit, can enrich our daily experiences, offering powerful tools for self-exploration and interpersonal connection. As we cultivate these practices, we contribute to a more reflective, compassionate, and enlightened society—transforming not only our lives but also the world around us. Thus, let us embrace philosophy, not just as a discipline but as a way of life, realizing that the answers we seek are often found in the questions we dare to ask.

Exploration of personal values. Adults are invited to list their core values and reflect on how these values influence their decisions and behaviors. This exercise prompts self-examination and can lead to greater alignment between one's actions and beliefs. By identifying what truly matters to them, individuals can create a more meaningful life, enhancing their sense of purpose and direction. Additionally, this reflection can inform how they approach relationships, work, and personal challenges, ultimately contributing to their overall sense of happiness.

Engaging in philosophical dialogues is another practical exercise that fosters connection and understanding. Participants can form small discussion groups to explore philosophical questions related to happiness, love, and the meaning of life. These dialogues encourage open-mindedness and active listening, allowing individuals to gain diverse perspectives. Through sharing personal stories and insights, participants can inspire one another, recognizing the shared human experience in their quests for joy. This communal exploration not only enhances emotional intelligence but also strengthens social bonds.

Practicing mindfulness encourages individuals to observe their thoughts and feelings without judgment. This practice can help adults confront existential questions and embrace the uncertainties of life. By cultivating a non-reactive awareness, individuals can develop a deeper understanding of their emotions and improve their capacity for resilience. Integrating mindfulness into daily routines allows for a more profound engagement with the present moment, diminishing anxiety about the past or future.

Through these practical philosophical exercises, adults are empowered to embark on a transformative journey toward happiness and fulfillment. By embracing gratitude, clarifying values, engaging in dialogue, and practicing mindfulness, individuals can cultivate a richer understanding of themselves and their relationships. These exercises not only enhance personal growth but also foster a greater appreciation for the interconnectedness of life, ultimately leading to a deeper pursuit of joy.

Living with Intention

Living with intention means approaching life with a purposeful mindset, where each action aligns with one's core values and aspirations. It is about making conscious choices that reflect what truly matters to us, rather than drifting through the days on autopilot. This practice invites individuals to examine their motivations and desires, fostering a deeper understanding of their own emotional landscape. By cultivating awareness of our thoughts and behaviors, we can begin to steer our lives toward greater fulfillment and joy.

At the heart of living intentionally is the practice of self-reflection. This involves regularly assessing our goals, values, and the alignment between them. By asking ourselves critical questions—What do I truly value? Am I living in accordance with my beliefs?—we can identify areas of our lives that may require change. This introspective process not only enhances emotional intelligence but also encourages personal growth, enabling individuals to break free from societal pressures and external expectations that may cloud their judgment.

Incorporating gratitude into our daily routines is another powerful aspect of intentional living. Research consistently shows that gratitude significantly impacts life satisfaction, leading to improved mental well-being and stronger interpersonal relationships. By actively acknowledging and appreciating the positive aspects of our lives, we cultivate a mindset that focuses on abundance rather than scarcity. This shift in perspective not only enhances our current state of happiness but also builds resilience against life's inevitable challenges.

A Journey Toward Purpose

In the cacophony of modern existence, where distractions abound and the demands of daily life can lead us astray, the quest for a purpose-driven life has never been more vital. Living with intention is not merely a buzzword; it is a profound philosophy that beckons us to examine our values, align our actions accordingly, and, ultimately, create a life that resonates with our deepest aspirations.

The Essence of Intention

At its core, living with intention is about awareness and mindfulness. It involves recognizing that every decision we make, from the smallest choices of our daily routines to the larger decisions that shape our destinies, can either propel us toward our goals or divert us from them. This conscious approach transforms life from a series of passive occurrences into a dynamic journey marked by purpose and direction.

Awareness: The First Step

The first step toward living with intention is cultivating awareness. We must become attuned to our thoughts, feelings, and motivations. This self-reflection can unravel the layers of conditioning that obscure our true desires. Often, we find ourselves living in accordance with societal expectations, familial pressures, or historical lineage rather than our genuine aspirations. Intentional living urges us to peel back these layers and uncover our authentic selves.

Meditative practices, journaling, and mindful contemplation can pave the way for this self-discovery. By engaging with our inner landscape, we learn about what we truly value. This is not just an intellectual exercise; it is a courageous confrontation with our innermost beliefs and desires, and it lays the groundwork for living a life rooted in authenticity.

Alignment: Values and Actions

Once we achieve a clearer understanding of our core values, the next step is alignment. Living with intention requires that our actions mirror what we hold dear. This alignment is essential for maintaining integrity; when our daily choices are in harmony with our principles, we experience a sense of inner peace and fulfillment.

For instance, if one places high value on health and well-being, then intentional living may dictate lifestyle changes such as a commitment to fitness, nutrition, and mental wellness practices. Alternatively, someone who values creativity may choose to dedicate time to artistic pursuits, ensuring that their day-to-day existence nurtures rather than stifles their creative spirit.

Embracing this alignment can empower us to make difficult choices. It might involve leaving a job that no longer serves us, ending toxic relationships, or engaging in new experiences that inspire growth. The courage to make these choices springs from a deep-seated conviction that we are not mere spectators in our lives but active architects of our destinies.

The Ripple Effect of Intention

Living with intention extends beyond the individual. Intention is contagious and can inspire those around us. When we act with purpose, we create an aura of positivity and motivation that encourages others to reflect on their paths. This ripple effect fosters a community of intention, where collective aspirations and values drive shared growth.

Consider the story of individuals who choose to live sustainably. Their deliberate choices—such as reducing waste, supporting local economies, or embracing renewable energy—often inspire others to reconsider their practices. The impact of these intentions can gradually morph into broader societal change, as more people awaken to the potential of living purposefully.

Overcoming Challenges

Adopting a life of intention is not without its challenges. Often, we encounter obstacles that test our commitment to our values. Distractions, self-doubt, and societal norms can create significant friction. Yet, it is within these challenges that the true essence of intentional living is revealed.

Resilience becomes a crucial component of this journey. When faced with setbacks, individuals rooted in intention can pivot back to their core motivations, using adversity as an opportunity for growth. Each challenge navigated with intention fortifies our resolve and deepens our understanding of what truly matters.

Moreover, the practice of gratitude can act as an anchor during turbulent times. By recognizing and appreciating the successes, however small, we reaffirm our commitment to our values and objectives. Gratitude shifts our focus from perceived failures to opportunities, allowing us to maintain momentum on our intentional path.

Cultivating a Legacy

Ultimately, living with intention culminates in the legacy we create. Life is fleeting; the sands of time slip through our fingers, and what remains are the footprints we leave behind. Intentional living guides us to consider the impact of our actions on future generations. It propels us to ask questions such as: What do I wish to be remembered for? How can I contribute positively to the world around me?

In this context, our legacies are not merely about grand achievements. They are also about the kindness we extend, the wisdom we impart, and the love we share. Each intentional moment contributes to the tapestry of human experience, interweaving our stories with the stories of others.

Living with intention promotes deeper connections with others. It encourages individuals to engage authentically and openly in their relationships, facilitating meaningful interactions that enrich our lives. As we reflect on what we value in our connections, we become more aware of how love and empathy play crucial roles in our happiness. This understanding fosters a supportive community where individuals feel seen and valued, further enhancing our collective well-being.

The journey of living with intention is a philosophical exploration of existence itself. It invites us to confront existential questions and seek meaning beyond the superficial aspects of modern life. By embracing this journey, we not only enhance our joy but also inspire those around us. Through our intentional choices and actions, we become everyday heroes who exemplify the transformative power of positive thinking and the quest for a fulfilling life.

Embracing the Journey

Living with intention is a lifelong journey of discovery, alignment, and legacy-building. It invites us to engage actively with our lives, ensuring that our days are framed by purpose and meaning. By cultivating awareness, aligning our actions with our values, inspiring others, overcoming challenges, and considering our legacies, we embark on a transformative path.

In a world that often embraces the mundane over the meaningful, let us choose to live with intention. As we navigate our unique journeys, we not only enhance our lives but also contribute to a collective narrative that celebrates purpose, connection, and the beautiful complexity of the human experience. In the end, it is this journey that will define us and the impact we will have on those who follow in our footsteps.

Creating a Personal Happiness Philosophy

Creating a personal happiness philosophy involves a thoughtful exploration of what happiness means to you as an individual. This journey starts with introspection, where one must examine their values, beliefs, and experiences. Understanding the nuances of what brings joy and satisfaction can provide essential insights into shaping a personal framework for happiness. This process may include reflecting on significant moments in life that elicited feelings of joy or contentment, as well as the challenges that have shaped one's understanding of happiness. By identifying these key experiences, individuals can begin to construct a philosophy that resonates with their unique life narrative. Consider, for instance, a time when you felt truly alive and engaged. Was it during a creative endeavor, a moment of connection with loved ones, a personal achievement, or an act of service to others? Analyzing the common threads in these moments can reveal core values and needs that are fundamental to your personal sense of happiness. Furthermore, reflecting on periods of unhappiness can be equally illuminating. What circumstances contributed to those feelings? What coping mechanisms proved effective or ineffective? Understanding these patterns can help you proactively avoid situations that diminish your well-being and cultivate strategies for navigating difficult times with greater resilience.

Central to a personal happiness philosophy is the concept of emotional intelligence. This involves recognizing and understanding one's emotions, as well as the emotions of others. Developing emotional intelligence allows individuals to navigate their feelings more effectively and fosters deeper connections with those around them. By cultivating awareness of emotional responses, one can better manage stress, improve relationships, and enhance overall well-being. Embracing emotional intelligence as a cornerstone of happiness can lead to more authentic interactions and a greater sense of fulfillment in life. Practicing mindfulness techniques, such as meditation and mindful breathing, can significantly enhance emotional awareness. These practices allow you to observe your thoughts and feelings without judgment, creating space between your emotions and your reactions. This, in turn, allows you to respond to situations with greater clarity and composure. Moreover, actively listening to others, empathizing with their perspectives, and communicating your own feelings effectively are crucial components of emotional intelligence that strengthen relationships and foster a sense of belonging, a vital ingredient for sustained happiness. Cultivating empathy, in particular, allows us to transcend our own limited perspectives and connect with the shared human experience, fostering compassion and understanding.

Research consistently shows that individuals who practice gratitude report higher levels of happiness and life satisfaction. This can involve simple daily practices such as keeping a gratitude journal, where one notes things they are grateful for each day. By focusing on the positive aspects of life, individuals can shift their perspective, making it easier to appreciate the present moment. This practice not only enhances personal happiness but also fosters a sense of community and connection with others, reinforcing the idea that happiness is often found in shared experiences. Beyond simply listing things you are grateful for, consider delving deeper into the "why" behind your gratitude. For instance, if you are grateful for a friend, reflect on the specific qualities that make that friendship valuable and the impact it has on your life. This deeper engagement with gratitude can amplify its positive effects. Furthermore, expressing your gratitude to others can have a profound impact, strengthening relationships and fostering a reciprocal cycle of appreciation. A simple thank you note, a heartfelt expression of appreciation, or an act of kindness can go a long way in building a more supportive and joyful community.

Engaging with philosophical inquiries about existence, purpose, and the nature of happiness can provide clarity and direction. Individuals may find that their understanding of happiness evolves as they confront these profound questions. This exploration can lead to a more profound appreciation for the complexities of life and encourage a mindset that embraces uncertainty. In doing so, one may discover that happiness is not a fixed destination but rather a dynamic state of being that can shift with perspective and personal growth. Consider grappling with questions such as: What is the meaning of life for you? What values are most important to you? What legacy do you want to leave behind? Engaging with these questions forces you to confront your own mortality and priorities, leading to a more intentional and purpose-driven life. Exploring the works of philosophers such as Aristotle, Epicurus, and Nietzsche can provide valuable insights into different perspectives on happiness and help you refine your own understanding. Embracing the inherent uncertainties of life, rather than resisting them, can also foster a greater sense of peace and contentment. Recognizing that setbacks and challenges are inevitable parts of the human experience allows you to approach them with greater resilience and adaptability.

Integrating the power of positive thinking into a personal happiness philosophy can significantly enhance one's outlook on life. This approach emphasizes the importance of maintaining an optimistic perspective, even in the face of adversity. By consciously choosing to focus on positive thoughts and outcomes, individuals can foster resilience and enhance their overall well-being. This doesn't mean ignoring life's challenges; rather, it involves recognizing difficulties while maintaining hope and striving for improvement. A positive mindset can empower individuals to take proactive steps toward their happiness, reinforcing the belief that joy is not merely a fleeting emotion but a sustainable practice that can be cultivated through intention and effort. One practical way to cultivate positive thinking is through the practice of reframing negative thoughts. When faced with a difficult situation, challenge your initial negative reactions and try to identify alternative, more positive interpretations. For example, instead of thinking "I failed," try thinking "I learned something valuable from this experience." Furthermore, surrounding yourself with positive influences, such as supportive friends, uplifting books, and inspiring environments, can contribute significantly to a positive mindset. Cultivating a sense of humor and finding joy in everyday moments can also help to buffer against stress and enhance overall well-being. Ultimately, creating a personal happiness philosophy is an ongoing process of self-discovery, reflection, and intentional living. It requires a commitment to understanding yourself, nurturing your emotional well-being, practicing gratitude, engaging with philosophical inquiries, and cultivating a positive mindset. By embracing these practices, you can create a personalized roadmap for navigating life's challenges and cultivating a deeper, more sustainable sense of happiness.

THE ETHICS OF ME
NAVIGATING INDIVIDUALISM IN A COLLECTIVE WORLD

A Final Reflection

Having journeyed through the intricate landscapes of Western and Eastern philosophies, and explored the multifaceted concept of individualism, we arrive not at a definitive conclusion, but rather a fertile ground for continued reflection. This book, "The Ethics of Me," has sought to illuminate the tensions and harmonies inherent in navigating the individual's path within a world undeniably shaped by collective forces. We began by understanding individualism not as a monolithic doctrine, but as a dynamic interplay of autonomy, responsibility, and self-discovery — a philosophy that champions the inherent worth and unique potential residing within each person.

But simply *defining* individualism is insufficient. Instead, we must ask: what wisdom can we glean from the diverse perspectives of East and West to better understand its *application*? Is individualism merely a license for self-serving pursuits, or can it be a powerful catalyst for both personal flourishing and societal good? In a world grappling with interconnected challenges — from climate change to global inequality — can a focus on the individual truly contribute to collective solutions?

In this book we explored the intricate dance between the individual and the collective, a dance performed across millennia and continents, informed by the wisdom of both Western and Eastern philosophical traditions. We have dissected the concept of individualism, examined its virtues and potential pitfalls, and now, at the confluence of these explorations, we must ask: what have we learned? What ethical framework can we forge, one that acknowledges the inherent worth of the individual while simultaneously recognizing our interconnectedness and responsibility to the larger world?

The very definition of individualism, as we have seen, is not a simple matter. It is not synonymous with selfishness or isolation. Instead, it is a recognition of the individual as a locus of moral agency, a being endowed with the capacity for reason, self-reflection, and the right to self-determination. Western thought, from the stoic pronouncements of Marcus Aurelius to the Enlightenment ideals of John Locke, has championed this inherent dignity. It has asserted the primacy of individual rights against the encroachment of tyrannical power, be it political or societal. The emphasis on individual liberties, freedom of expression, and the pursuit of personal happiness has fueled innovation, creativity, and progress. Yet, the shadow side of this emphasis is the potential for fragmentation, a relentless pursuit of personal gain that can blind us to the needs of others and erode the very fabric of community.

Eastern philosophies, conversely, often highlight the interconnectedness of all beings. Concepts like *karma* in Hinduism and Buddhism emphasize the ripple effect of our actions on the entire universe. The Taoist principle of *wu wei* (effortless action) encourages us to align ourselves with the natural flow of existence, recognizing our place within a larger, harmonious order. Confucianism stresses the importance of social harmony and filial piety, emphasizing the responsibilities we have to our families and communities. While these traditions may sometimes appear to de-emphasize the individual, a closer examination reveals a nuanced understanding of the self. The goal is not the obliteration of individuality, but rather its integration into a larger context of interconnectedness and shared responsibility. The enlightened individual, in these traditions, is not someone who stands apart, but someone who is aware of their interdependence and acts with compassion and wisdom in the service of the greater good.

So, where does this leave us? What ethical compass can guide us in navigating the complex terrain of individualism in a collective world? The answer, I believe, lies in embracing a synthesis, a dynamic equilibrium between the strengths of both Western and Eastern perspectives. We must cultivate what I call "Ethical Individualism" — a framework that acknowledges the inherent worth and autonomy of the individual while grounding that individuality in a deep awareness of our interconnectedness and responsibility to others.

Ethical Individualism demands several key commitments:

- **Self-Awareness and Self-Cultivation:** Individual freedom is not a license for unchecked ego. It requires a constant process of self-reflection, a critical examination of our own biases and motivations. We must strive to understand ourselves, our strengths and weaknesses, and actively cultivate virtues like empathy, compassion, and integrity. This is the foundation upon which ethical choices are built.

- **Respect for the Dignity of Others:** Recognizing the inherent worth of the individual means respecting the dignity and rights of all individuals, regardless of their background, beliefs, or circumstances. This demands tolerance, open-mindedness, and a willingness to engage in respectful dialogue, even with those who hold opposing views.

- **Responsibility and Interdependence:** True freedom comes with responsibility. We must acknowledge that our actions have consequences, both for ourselves and for others. Recognizing our interdependence means understanding that we are all part of a larger web of life and that our well-being is inextricably linked to the well-being of others. This necessitates a commitment to social justice, environmental stewardship, and the common good.

- **Conscientious Choice and Ethical Action:** Ethical Individualism is not a passive philosophy. It demands active engagement with the world, a willingness to make difficult choices based on principles of justice, compassion, and integrity. It requires us to be mindful of the impact of our choices on others and to strive to act in ways that promote the well-being of all.

- **Continuous Learning and Growth:** The ethical landscape is constantly evolving. We must remain open to new perspectives, willing to learn from our mistakes, and committed to continuous growth and development. This requires intellectual humility and a willingness to challenge our own assumptions and beliefs.

The path of Ethical Individualism is not an easy one. It requires constant vigilance, self-reflection, and a willingness to challenge the status quo. But it is a path that leads to a more just, compassionate, and sustainable world. It is a path that allows us to embrace our individuality while recognizing our interconnectedness, to pursue our own dreams while contributing to the greater good.

Ultimately, the ethics of "me" cannot exist in isolation. It must be intertwined with the ethics of "we." By embracing Ethical Individualism, we can forge a future where individual freedom and collective responsibility are not opposing forces, but rather complementary aspects of a flourishing human existence. The journey is ongoing, the questions are complex, but the potential for a more ethical and fulfilling life, both individually and collectively, is within our reach. Let us choose, then, to walk this path with courage, compassion, and a unwavering commitment to the well-being of all. The future is not predetermined; it is a canvas upon which we, as ethical individuals, can paint a more beautiful and just world.

Forging a Future of Ethical Individualism

The journey through the labyrinth of ethics and individualism has led us to a crucial juncture. We've explored the foundational tenets of Western and Eastern philosophies, dissected the complexities of moral frameworks, and wrestled with the inherent tension between personal autonomy and collective obligation. Now, the critical question remains: what have we learned, and how can we apply this knowledge to build a future worthy of our highest aspirations?

This book has advocated for the embrace of Ethical Individualism — a philosophy that champions the inherent worth and autonomy of the individual while simultaneously recognizing the inextricable link between personal action and its impact on the world. It is not a doctrine of selfish isolation, but rather a call for a deliberate and conscious approach to navigating the ethical landscape, grounded in self-awareness and a profound respect for the dignity of others.

Western thought, with its emphasis on reason, individual rights, and the pursuit of truth, has provided us with invaluable tools for ethical analysis. From the Socratic quest for self-knowledge to Kant's categorical imperative, we inherit a legacy that prioritizes individual agency and the moral imperative to treat each person as an end in themselves, never merely as a means. The Enlightenment's focus on liberty and the development of democratic principles further reinforces the individual's right to self-determination within a framework of just laws.

Yet, Western individualism, in its extreme forms, can also be a breeding ground for unchecked egoism, a relentless pursuit of self-interest that disregards the well-being of the community and the environment. The pitfalls of unchecked capitalism, the erosion of social trust, and the growing chasm between the haves and have-nots serve as stark reminders of the potential consequences of an individualism untethered from ethical considerations.

Here, Eastern philosophies offer a vital corrective. Traditions like Buddhism, Confucianism, and Taoism emphasize interconnectedness, compassion, and the cultivation of inner harmony. The concept of interdependent origination in Buddhism reveals the profound truth that nothing exists in isolation, and that our actions ripple outwards, impacting the entire web of existence. Confucianism stresses the importance of social harmony and the responsibilities that accompany our roles within the family and the community. Taoism encourages us to align ourselves with the natural flow of the universe, recognizing the inherent wisdom in balance and moderation.

However, it is crucial to avoid romanticizing Eastern thought. Just as unchecked Western individualism can lead to destructive outcomes, an uncritical embrace of collectivism can stifle individual expression, suppress dissenting voices, and perpetuate oppressive social structures. The sacrifice of individual rights on the altar of the collective good can be as detrimental as the abandonment of social responsibility in the pursuit of individual gain.

The essence of Ethical Individualism lies in transcending this false dichotomy. It is not about choosing between the individual and the collective, but rather about recognizing that the true flourishing of one is inextricably linked to the flourishing of the other. It requires a conscious effort to cultivate self-awareness, to understand our own motivations, biases, and limitations. It demands that we critically examine the ethical implications of our choices, considering not only their immediate impact on ourselves, but also their long-term consequences for the wider world.

This is not a call to asceticism or self-denial. Ethical Individualism recognizes the validity of pursuing personal goals, achieving financial success, and experiencing the joys of life. However, it insists that these pursuits be guided by a deep-seated sense of ethical responsibility. It asks us to consider how our actions affect others, to contribute to the well-being of our communities, and to act as responsible stewards of the planet.

Embracing Ethical Individualism requires a profound shift in perspective. It necessitates moving beyond the narrow confines of self-interest and embracing a wider circle of concern. It demands empathy, compassion, and a willingness to engage in meaningful dialogue with those who hold different views. It requires courage to challenge injustice, to speak out against oppression, and to stand up for what is right, even when it is difficult or unpopular.

The path of Ethical Individualism is not always easy. It requires constant vigilance, self-reflection, and a willingness to learn from our mistakes. But it is a path that leads to a more meaningful and fulfilling life, a life lived in accordance with our deepest values and a profound sense of purpose.

By learning from the strengths and weaknesses of both Western and Eastern philosophical traditions, by embracing the principles of self-awareness, ethical responsibility, and interconnectedness, we can forge a future where individual freedom and collective responsibility are not opposing forces, but rather complementary aspects of a flourishing human existence. This is the promise of Ethical Individualism: a future where we can all thrive, not at the expense of others, but in harmony with each other and the world around us. The Ethics of Me, then, becomes the Ethics of We, a future where the individual flourishes because the collective prospers, and the collective thrives because the individual is empowered to act ethically and responsibly in the world. Let us embark on this journey together.